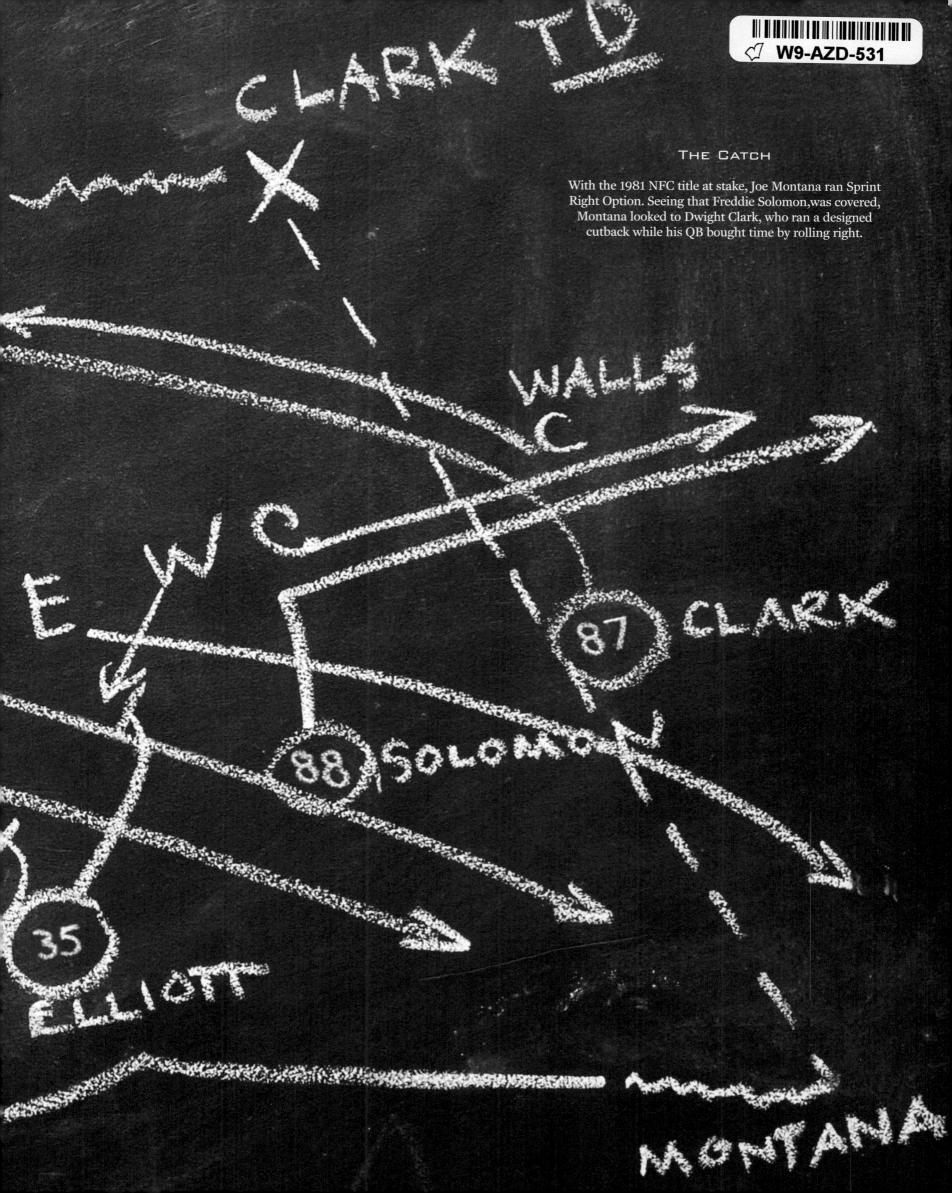

The Catch

With the 1981 NFC title at stake, Joe Montana ran Sprint Right Option. Seeing that Freddie Solomon, was covered, Montana looked to Dwight Clark, who ran a designed cutback while his QB bought time by rolling right.

THE REDSKINS' COUNTER TREY

Joe Gibbs didn't invent this play, which had been used prominently by the Nebraska Cornhuskers, but his team rode it to glory in the championship 1980s, with John Riggins running behind guard Russ Grimm.

Sports Illustrated

FOOTBALL'S GREATEST

REVISED AND UPDATED

Sports Illustrated

FOOT
GREA

BALL'S TEST

DICK BUTKUS

NO. 2

LINEBACKER

PHOTOGRAPH BY NEIL LEIFER

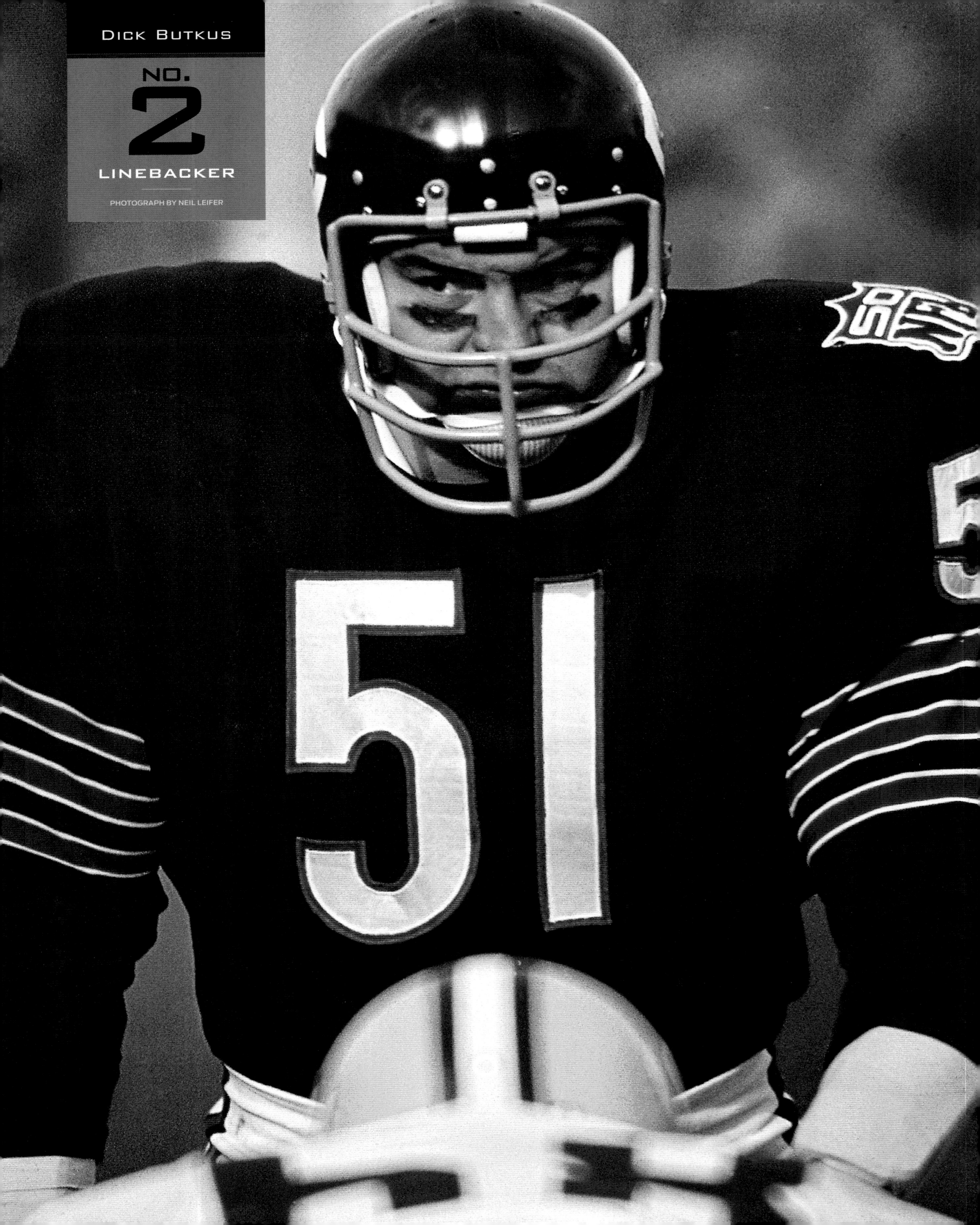

CONTENTS

BILL SYKEN *Editor* / STEPHEN SKALOCKY *Art Director*

CRISTINA SCALET *Photo Editor* / KEVIN KERR *Copy Editor* / STEFANIE KAUFMAN *Project Manager*

STEVEN HOFFMAN *Series Creative Director*

QUEST FOR THE BEST

OUR PANEL FOUND THAT CHOOSING THE TOP PLAYERS OF ALL TIME IS NO EASY TASK. HERE NFL STARS TAKE THEIR SHOT AT IT, AND THEIR PICKS SHOWED JUST HOW MUCH GREATNESS FOOTBALL HISTORY HAS TO OFFER

INTERVIEWS BY EMILY KAPLAN

EARL CAMPBELL, RB, OILERS/SAINTS, 1978–1985

Running Back: Jim Brown. "He set the standard. Everyone wanted to be as good as Jim Brown, including me. When I got to the University of Texas, I got a hold of some of his tape, and I loved the way he played. I was built kind of like him—thick legs, kind of flat-footed—but the way he ran, so powerful. That's what everyone wanted to be."

RANDALL CUNNINGHAM, QB, FOUR TEAMS, 1985–2001

Cornerback: Darrell Green. "He's a great athlete, he's not just tough but relentless, he's forever focused. You would go against him and, it's like if you mess around just a little, he'd pick you off and make you look like a fool. I remember one time at home against the Washington Redskins, I was running down the field, I was gone. I thought, *'Oh my god, I'm going to score.'* Then suddenly it turned to, *'Oh my god, Darrell Green is over there.'* I turned, saw him coming out from the corner of my eye with his little 5' 9", 180-pound self, and he caught me at the five-yard line and knocked me out-of-bounds. It was the hardest hit I had taken in a long time. How could he come from so far across the field and then get me like that?"

ISAAC BRUCE, WR, RAMS/49ERS, 1994–2009

Wide Receiver: Henry Ellard. "I won't base my picks off stats, because I believe that Henry Ellard is the greatest wide receiver of all time. His ability to get open is something that always impressed me. He saw the game really well and anticipated what a defense was trying to do better than anybody. At first he was primarily a punt returner, and he accumulated more than 13,000 receiving yards in his career. That is a remarkable accomplishment."

Single-Season Team: 2007 Patriots. "This is the team that began 18–0. The talent that they had both offensively and defensively was incredible, but even more incredible was the way they handled the pressure from the beginning of the season all the way to the end. It was an amazing accomplishment and one I'm not sure we'll ever see again."

BOOMER ESIASON, QB, THREE TEAMS, 1984–1997

Quarterback: Tom Brady. "Not only because of all he has achieved on the field—and he has achieved a lot. Think of the passing records, the championships, the incredible sustained success. To me, Brady is the greatest of all time because

"MARSHALL FAULK MADE EVERY-BODY AROUND HIM BETTER. HE ALWAYS KNEW WHAT TO DO WHEN HE HAD THE BALL. HE WAS THE ULTIMATE ALL-PURPOSE BACK AND, MOST IMPORTANTLY, THE GREATEST TEAMMATE. HIS KNOWLEDGE AND PASSION FOR THE GAME WERE SECOND TO NONE."

—Kurt Warner, QB, three teams, 1998–2009

of where he came from. He overcame tremendous adversity, from a little-thought-of sixth round draft pick to future Hall of Famer, it's a story of persistence, of excellence, and it highlights the best of football."

JONATHAN OGDEN, OL, RAVENS, 1996–2007
Offensive Lineman: Anthony Muñoz. "Because of his technique, his physical play and his smarts. Muñoz had it all. He was the most dominant player I ever watched play left tackle, and even on a very mediocre team for a lot of years he managed to stand out—and set the standard for the position."
Defensive Lineman: Reggie White. "From power, size and speed, he brought everything to the table. Reggie could rush the passer, stop the run, and he pretty much changed Green Bay's fortune single-handedly. That's dominance."

JERRY RICE, WR, THREE TEAMS, 1985–2004
Stadium: Candlestick Park. "I'm a bit biased, but I put Candlestick right up there with Lambeau Field as places to be cherished in history. I had so many great memories there, so many great games were played there—that's where Dwight Clark made The Catch! It was a difficult place to play, sometimes windy and wet, but that was all part of the package."

KENNY EASLEY, DB, SEAHAWKS, 1981–1987
Greatest Play: Immaculate Reception. "I was 13 years old at the time. Terry Bradshaw drops back, scrambles right, then back towards the middle of the field and throws down the middle of the field, but [Frenchy Fuqua] is blasted by Jack Tatum and the ball bounces backwards and up into the air and Franco Harris, who was running toward the throw catches the ball off of his shoetops and runs it in for the winning touchdown."
Quarterback: Joe Montana and John Elway. "They were both great competitors and efficient quarterbacks. They hardly ever held the ball. They knew from the time they got out of the huddle who they were going to throw the football to, and they did that. That's why they hardly ever got sacked."

MARK SCHLERETH, OL, REDSKINS/BRONCOS, 1989–2000
Tight End: Rob Gronkowski. "If he stays healthy Gronkowski could be the greatest tight end of all time. He can run-block, he can split outside the numbers, he can line up in the slot—anything you want in a modern tight end, he can

do. Most of the receiving tight ends, even though they're putting up big numbers, don't want to mix it up in the briar patch. Gronkowski is a unique talent that way. He'll do everything, and he'll do everything well."
Franchise: Packers. "They won all those championships with Vince Lombardi. However, not only have the Packers remained relevant, but also they've become consistent winners, longer than anyone. You have to respect that kind of history. As a player, one of your bucket list events is to go to Lambeau Field in December for a game. For fans too. That's on everybody's bucket list. Why? It's hallowed ground for one of the greatest franchises in all of sports."

LYNN SWANN, WR, STEELERS, 1974–1982
Defensive Lineman: Joe Greene. "He had size, power, speed, desire and football IQ—Joe had it all. Now, add leadership, and you get four Super Bowl rings."

STEVE GLEASON, SPECIAL TEAMS, SAINTS, 2000–2006
Game: Falcons-Saints, Sept. 25, 2006. "Sports give fans the opportunity to appoint their heroes, but can you recall a game where the clear and obvious heroes were the people in the stands? Well, on that day in the Superdome, that is exactly how it played out. A year prior, Hurricane Katrina destroyed New Orleans. When everyone outside the region doubted that the area should be rebuilt, these steadfast, hare-brained citizens doubled down. People say the 2006 Saints gave hope to the people of New Orleans. I see it differently. When I blocked the punt on that Monday night, with the world watching, I was buoyed by a stadium and a city full of unyielding heroes."

BRIAN URLACHER, LB, BEARS, 2000–2012
Linebacker: Ray Lewis. "His longevity is unbelievable, and his accomplishments, both from an individual and a team standpoint, speak for themselves."

WARREN MOON, QB, FOUR TEAMS, 1984–2000
Defensive Back: Deion Sanders. "I played in four decades [including six years in the Canadian Football League] and I'd say the defensive back I tried to stay away from the most was Deion Sanders. He had catlike quick reflexes so you had to be very, very accurate with the football, but accurate from away from where he was. You had to throw to your receiver open,

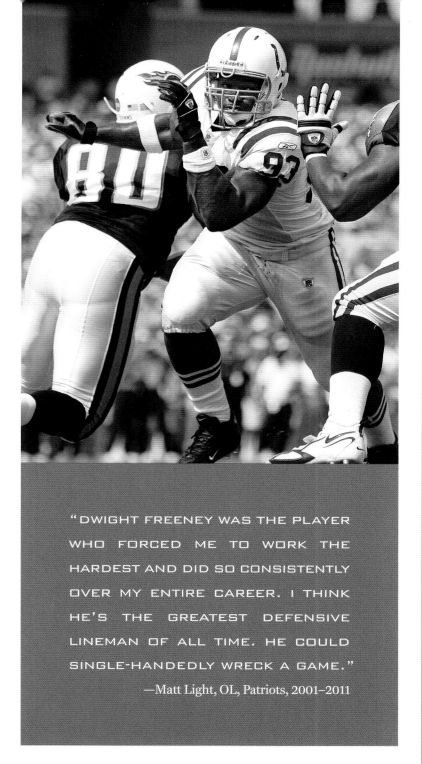

"DWIGHT FREENEY WAS THE PLAYER WHO FORCED ME TO WORK THE HARDEST AND DID SO CONSISTENTLY OVER MY ENTIRE CAREER. I THINK HE'S THE GREATEST DEFENSIVE LINEMAN OF ALL TIME. HE COULD SINGLE-HANDEDLY WRECK A GAME."

—Matt Light, OL, Patriots, 2001–2011

you couldn't just throw it to where he was, you had to throw it to where Deion wasn't. If you threw a deep ball against him, you could not overthrow it."

Stadium: The Meadowlands. "I always enjoyed playing in the Meadowlands. I think because it was New York, and I love the fans in New York, for both the Giants or the Jets, because they were going to let you know exactly how they felt. I loved the crowd, I loved being able to silence those crowds because they were so boisterous, and they usually had good football games during the Lawrence Taylor, Bill Parcells days, and the Jets had good teams too."

AHMAN GREEN, RB, THREE TEAMS, 1998–2009

Game: Super Bowl XXIV. "Joe Montana and Jerry Rice just lit it up. Montana threw for five touchdowns, Rice was incredible.

To limit John Elway's Broncos to only 10 points was remarkable as well. It wasn't just the passing game, but it was physical defensive performance too. They were hitting John Elway. If you're going to win a championship, that's how you do it."

TORRY HOLT, WR, RAMS/JAGUARS, 1999–2009

Play: Malcolm Butler's interception in Super Bowl XLIX. "The ebb and flow of the game was tremendous but to see how it ended—I was there in the stadium—I was just shaking my head. Did I really just see that? Malcolm Butler's interception? Really? That was the most dramatic, improbable ending you could script."

Defensive Back: Ronnie Lott. "He was an All-Pro as a cornerback and as a safety. His tenacity and his ability to influence a game stand out. He was one of those leaders that I looked up to."

Stadium: CenturyLink Field. "I loved playing in Seattle. The atmosphere is unlike anything else in the league. It's so impressive in terms of crowd noise. Some people I talk with don't even know it's an open air stadium. That's how loud it is."

HARRY CARSON, LB, GIANTS, 1976–1988

Coach: Bill Parcells. "There was no better teacher of fundamentals than coach Parcells, who was my defensive coordinator before he became head coach. But what sets him apart is the way he understood personalities. He understood what made players tick. Whether you were a young player or a veteran, you respected him and you wanted to play hard for him. He'd chew you out, but he'd also be fair. He asked us to play for a different standard—the Giants standard. But what Coach really wanted was to hold everyone accountable, and he sure achieved that."

JERRY KRAMER, OL, PACKERS, 1958–1968

Running Back: Jim Brown. "He was a magnificent ballplayer: a physical talent that was virtually unmatched. He was a sculpted athlete who was extremely well-conditioned with speed, power, strength and intelligence. It's a package that you'll rarely find. I saw Brown make a run one time, he got the ball around the 15-yard line, he started to go around the right end, got hit at the line of scrimmage, shuffled his feet a little bit, got rid of the guy, got hit again and again. He got hit about four or five times, and the last time he got hit, he was in the middle of spinning, he got hit from behind at the knees, lifted his knees up and went over the defensive tackler and on to the end zone."

"CRIS CARTER CONTROLLED THE OFFENSE, HE CONTROLLED THE GAME. HE WAS LIKE A QUARTERBACK ON THE FIELD. HE WOULD COME INTO A HUDDLE AND TELL ME EXACTLY WHAT WAS GOING TO HAPPEN ON A PLAY. AND HE WAS AS STRONG AS AN OFFENSIVE LINEMAN."

—Randall Cunningham, QB, four teams, 1985–2001

Coach: Vince Lombardi. "He wasn't only a coach but also a psychologist and a teacher. He was a very bright man; he read ancient Greek, he read Latin, he was religious, he was practical. Most importantly, he had a vision and found a way to make it contagious. He told us, 'I'm willing to make the sacrifice, to pay the price to put the team first. If you aren't, you can get the hell out.' He held true to that. Vince Lombardi took over a team that was 1-10-1 the year before he arrived. His first season he was 7–5. The next year the team was in the championship game, and the rest is history. The roster he inherited had 13 future Hall of Famers on it. None of them realized their potential until Lombardi arrived."

OTIS WILSON, LB, BEARS/RAIDERS, 1980–1989

Linebacker: Dick Butkus. "He was intimidating, and he could take the ball away. Obviously he was feared for his hits, and those big, violent hits were something that transcended."

Stadium: Memorial Coliseum, Los Angeles. "I always loved playing there. The crowds were lively, there was immense history there, but the field itself was great. It's California, and the grass not only grew well, but it also was manicured to perfection. It was like falling on a cushion. When I played, AstroTurf was the big trend in the East and Midwest, but I loved going to the West Coast where teams played on grass, and the Coliseum was the best of them. When you're trying to preserve your body, you think about those things."

ANDY RUSSELL, LB, STEELERS, 1963–1976

Linebacker: Jack Lambert. "He never made a mistake. His technique and ability to take away angles were both admirable, and he killed you with his precision."

NICK HARDWICK, OL, CHARGERS, 2004–2014

Offensive Lineman: Jonathan Ogden. "Never has a player coupled such an incredible level of physical size and talent with mental acumen and nastiness. Ogden consistently put himself in the right body positions to make his blocks and then finished his opponent with ill intentions. He's what every offensive lineman wishes they were."

FRANCO HARRIS, RB, STEELERS/SEAHAWKS, 1972–1984

Franchise: Steelers. "It goes beyond accomplishments. Pittsburgh simply won big games against other great teams and did it consistently. The tradition includes the defense which is the greatest trio of linebackers of all time: Jack Ham, Jack Lambert and Andy Russell. Every position was strong throughout the '70s, and the team was coached by one of the greatest [Chuck Noll], to bring it all together. The tradition set back then carries on today."

EUGENE ROBINSON, DB, FOUR TEAMS, 1985–2000
Stadium: Lambeau Field. "You'd get chills walking onto the field there, not just because it's cold, but because of the history. It's iconic. And there's something to be said about those fans. It's −5°, and there's a guy in suspenders—wearing no shirt—standing right behind our bench. His cheeks are red and he's cold as can be and he's yelling, *'Let's go, Pack! Let's go, Pack!'* like none of that matters."

Franchise: Patriots. "I'm an old-school guy, and I want to say the Steelers or the 49ers, but the New England Patriots are the greatest franchise of all time. What they've been able to do to consistently—not only get into the playoff mix every year, but win—is remarkable. I wonder if we'll ever see a stretch of dominance like this again in the free agency era."

JOE THEISMANN, QB, REDSKINS, 1974–1985
Quarterback: Tom Brady. "I have so much respect for Joe Montana, but when I look at what Brady has accomplished with the Patriots, from statistics to Super Bowls, I see this: Everything around him, especially the wide receivers, is a turnstile. The only constant on the field is Tom Brady."

WILLIE GAULT, WR, BEARS/RAIDERS 1983–1993
Coach: Bill Belichick. "What he has been able to do in the age of free agency—to keep that team on top for a decade, with five Super Bowls victories and seven Super Bowl appearances, is a truly remarkable feat."

LEONARD MARSHALL, DL, THREE TEAMS, 1983–1994
Play: Immaculate Reception. "Why? Because that play has stood the test of time. That was more than 40 years ago now, and people are still talking about it."

Franchise: 49ers. "People love to hate the 49ers. But people love to hate them because they were winners in an era that I respected because it was an era where teams were built. There was no free agency. Players came back every year. In terms of commitment and devotion, they created a culture that was the standard."

HOW WE RANKED THEM

These Top 10 lists bring together the expert opinions of seven writers and editors whose knowledge of the game runs deep

FOR THIS BOOK SI WRITERS AND EDITORS WERE polled during the 2016 season and asked to submit Top 10 lists for 14 main categories. Votes were tallied with 10 points awarded for a first-place vote, nine points for a second-place vote and so on. Voters were also asked to justify their choices, and those comments appear with each Top 10 selection. In most cases, if one panelist had a player ranked higher than his colleagues did, he was asked to speak on that player's behalf.

Panelists were not directed toward any set of nominees or limited by any preset criteria for what constituted all-time excellence. They were simply given categories and asked to select 10 names from the vast history of professional football. Panelists were also given the opportunity to create one list on their own, choosing the topic as well as the population of the Top 10. Those personal lists close out the book, along with a compendium listing everyone who received a vote in every category. Some names there go back to the NFL's beginnings, which gives a sense of how deep panelists went in their search.

DON BANKS *Former SI.com Senior Writer*
GREG A. BEDARD *Former SI Senior Writer*
GREG BISHOP *SI Senior Writer*
CHRIS BURKE *SI.com Staff Writer*
MARK GODICH *SI Senior Editor*
TIM LAYDEN *SI Senior Writer*
PETER KING *SI Senior Writer*

PHOTOGRAPH BY GREG NELSON

DOWN 3   MINUTES
YARDS TO GO 6 TO PLAY
BALL ON | 9 YD. LINE

FOOTBALL GREA

FORREST GREGG

NO.
3

OFFENSIVE
LINEMAN

PHOTOGRAPH BY JAMES DRAKE

BALL'S TEST

10

THE

BEST QUARTERBACKS

IF JOE MONTANA HAD BEEN DRAFTED BY CHICAGO, AS NEARLY HAPPENED, WOULD HE HAVE ACHIEVED AS MUCH? "WHO KNOWS, IF HE CAME HERE, THAT HE WOULD HAVE HAD THE CAREER THAT HE'S HAD IN SAN FRANCISCO?" BEARS PLAYER PERSONNEL DIRECTOR BILL TOBIN REFLECTED IN A 1990 PROFILE BY PAUL ZIMMERMAN IN SI. MONTANA'S HIGH SCHOOL COACH, CHUCK ABRAMSKI, ASKED "WHAT IF HE HAD BEEN IN A SYSTEM WHERE HE HAD TO DROP BACK SEVEN STEPS AND THROW 50 YARDS DOWNFIELD?" BUT MONTANA, OUR NO. 2 PICK AT QB, DID PLAY IN THE OFFENSE OF BILL WALSH, RANKED OUR NO. 4 COACH—AND HE ALSO HAD AS A TARGET OUR NO. 1 RECEIVER, JERRY RICE. MONTANA WAS FORTUNATE, AS WERE MANY OF OUR TOP 10 QUARTERBACKS: SIX PLAYED FOR TOP 10 COACHES AND FIVE OF THEM THREW TO TOP 10 RECEIVERS OR TIGHT ENDS.

OUR TOP QB, TOM BRADY, PLAYED FOR OUR NO. 2 COACH. BUT AS A SIXTH-ROUND PICK HE COULD HAVE LANDED ANYWHERE, LEAVING QUESTIONS AS TO WHETHER HE WOULD HAVE BEEN HISTORICALLLY SUCCESSFUL WITHOUT THE GUIDANCE OF BILL BELICHICK.

MONTANA RECOGNIZED THAT PLAYING FOR WALSH WAS THE BEST OF ALL POSSIBLE WORLDS: "THERE'S NO COACH I COULD HAVE PLAYED FOR WHO WOULD HAVE BEEN BETTER FOR MY CAREER," HE SAYS. "ABSOLUTELY NONE." AMID A SEA OF HYPOTHETICALS, WE KNOW THIS: THE PIECES CAME TOGETHER, AND THE RESULTS MADE HISTORY.

1

TOM BRADY

PATRIOTS 2000–PRESENT

" The biggest steal in NFL draft history, Brady, the sixth-round pick out of Michigan, single-handedly changed the fortunes of the New England franchise. " —DON BANKS

≥ MOST WINS, BEST WINNING PERCENTAGE OF ANY QB IN SUPER BOWL ERA
≥ MOST SUPER BOWL WINS (FIVE) AND APPEARANCES (SEVEN) OF ANY QUARTERBACK

WITH HIS voice rising as he leaned forward in his chair, Brady said that playing 10 more seasons "is a big goal of mine, a very big goal. I want to play until I'm 41. And if I get to that point and still feel good, I'll keep playing. I mean, what the hell else am I going to do? I don't like anything else." People say, 'What will you do if you don't play football?' Why would I even think of doing anything else? What would I do instead of run out in front of 80,000 people and command 52 guys and be around guys I consider brothers and be one of the real gladiators? Why would I ever want to do anything else? It's so hard to think of anything that would match what I do: Fly to the moon? Jump out of planes? Bungee-jump off cliffs? None of that s--- matters to me. I want to play this game I love, be with my family and enjoy life."

—Peter King, SI, June 1, 2009

Brady has thrown 456 TDs and only 152 interceptions

PHOTOGRAPHS BY WALTER IOOSS JR. (LEFT) AND SIMON BRUTY

2

JOE MONTANA

49ERS 1979–1992
CHIEFS 1993–1994

❝ His measurable qualities have alway[s]
been underrated: footwork, timing an[d]
accuracy. His immeasurable qualities a[re]
the best in history: leadership, calmne[ss]
under pressure and instinctive footba[ll]
intelligence. ❞ —TIM LAYDEN

≥ THREE-TIME SUPER BOWL MV[P]
≥ 39 300-YARD GAMES

HE SOMEHOW seems to breathe
slower when everyone else
breathes fast. Remember that final
drive in the 1989 Super Bowl? You
fell off your chair. Was there ever
any doubt that he simply was going
to move those Niners 92 yards
down the field in the final 3:20 to
beat the Cincinnati Bengals? Of
course not. Didn't you read what
he said at the start of the drive?
"Hey, check it out," he said to tackle
Harris Barton. "Check out what?"
Barton asked. "There, in the stands,
standing near the exit ramp,"
Joe said. "There's John Candy."
Wasn't that the greatest? Your
father remembers reading about
someone named Chip Hilton who
did the same things Joe does. Your
grandfather mentions someone
named Frank Merriwell. You don't
know any of that. Weren't those
characters from fiction?
Joe is real. A real Joe.

—Leigh Montville, SI, December 24, 1990

Montana threw for 318 career touchdowns.
PHOTOGRAPH BY JOHN IACONO

3

PEYTON MANNING

COLTS 1998–2011
BRONCOS 2012–2015

" Manning was known as The Sheriff, but a more applicable nickname would have been The Computer. He was ferocious in both his preparation and his deciphering of defenses. " —GREG A. BEDARD

≥ NFL CAREER LEADER IN PASSING YARDS AND TOUCHDOWNS

IN SEPTEMBER the only thing Manning seemed sure to lead the league in was obstacles. Wideout Marvin Harrison was allowed to leave after 11 seasons and into his starting spot had stepped a 2008 sixth-round pick from tiny Mount Union (Ohio) College, Pierre Garçon. Starting wideout Anthony Gonzalez went down with an injury in the first game, forcing Austin Collie to play much more than planned. Coach Tony Dungy had retired, ceding the job to an unknown, Jim Caldwell. Compounding the problems has been a feeble running game. But Manning has made Indianapolis slump-proof. The Colts have gone 112 games—seven full seasons—without losing three straight. Indy isn't the winningest regular-season team this decade by accident. Anytime Manning steps behind center and starts pointing, history tells us, good things are about to occur.

—*Peter King, SI, November 16, 2009*

Manning won a record five MVP awards.

PHOTOGRAPH BY JOHN W. MCDONOUGH

THE DRIVE TO GLORY

At the top of his game and coming off a Super Bowl win, Peyton Manning laid bare the inner workings of his mind as he got to talking about the game he loves

BY PETER KING

THERE IS A PEYTON MANNING Fan Club among NFL quarterbacks, a group effusive in its praise and admiration for the Colts passer. Tom Brady dines with Manning a few times every year and considers him a good friend. "Cool guy," Brady says. Carson Palmer has driven from Cincinnati to Indianapolis, incognito, to watch him play. In Kansas City's playoff loss to Indianapolis last year, Chiefs rookie Brodie Croyle kept straying from the offensive area near the bench to get closer to the field so he could watch Manning.

Usually you can find athletes in every sport to dis a great player (off the record) for some kind of perceived fault. Not with Manning. Now that he's won a Super Bowl, he's ascended to a level at which he is practically beyond criticism. SI rates him the No. 1 player in the NFL—big surprise there—and the people he goes up against have no problem with that. "It's not even close," says Broncos coach Mike Shanahan. "He's the best."

His peers see him as a guileless, innovative competitor. As he enters his 10th NFL season, how does Manning see himself? "I play because I love the game, not because it's what I'm supposed to be doing. I think as soon as I'm not excited to be driving to training camp, that's when it'll be over. You know, it's an hour-and-15-minute drive from Indy. I loaded an oldies CD [wife] Ashley just got for me for the drive, then sent out a mass text message to all my teammates whose numbers I have, which is a large majority of them. I wrote, 'Hey boys, let's go bust our asses in camp and do this thing again.' And it was exciting to see all the responses. Booger McFarland saying, 'That's what I'm talking about.' Dwight Freeney goes, 'Hell yeah.' Dungy gave me an 'Amen.' Priceless. So I was excited to be coming up here again. I can't imagine thinking the day before camp, Golly, I wish I didn't have to go.

"I always worry about the teammate that comes up and asks me for an autograph. You don't really want that. I'm like, 'Oh, this is for your brother?' And they're like, 'No, no, it's for me.' And I'm, 'Man, I need you to *block* for me. I don't need you to look up to me. You need to be my equal.'

"I'm just a football meathead. I did *Saturday Night Live* just to have fun. I'm a lot more nervous for a game. On *Saturday Night Live* the people who are nervous are trying to get Alec Baldwin to put them in his TV show. But preparing for *Saturday Night Live* was like preparing for a football game. I told them I wanted it to be funny. I went up there on a Monday. It's the same as a football week: Monday and Tuesday you put the plan in; Wednesday, Thursday and Friday you practice, although you only do each script the one time. The nervous thing is on Wednesday, you sit around with the whole crew, cast, cameras and makeup. They give you a stack of scripts and about 30 minutes to read all 40 of them on your own. Then Lorne Michaels reads the scene, and you have to do the reading. There's nothing about character or whatever, and you sound like a moron in front of these people. That's when they decide what's funny and what's not.

"I'd like to do one of those reality-TV shows on the ultimate debate—what is the toughest job in sports? You'd put a pitcher in there, a golfer, a basketball player, a tennis player, a hockey player, a football player. I wouldn't have to be the football representative. I'd probably put Brett Favre in there, but I'd write his material. And I would say you can't compare anything to quarterback. A pitcher has no time factor, no hurry. He doesn't like the call from the catcher, he steps off, doesn't waste a timeout. I haven't found one job that really compares to what the quarterback has to go through. You take all those things: time, weather, noise and then you get to dealing with the rush, dealing with the speed. And you truly have the game in your hands.

"At the Pro Bowl, Belichick and I had a beer at the pool one day. We talked for a few hours and somebody said, 'All they're doing is telling a bunch of lies to each other.' There's some truth to that. But when we were stretching for practice one morning, we were kind of waiting to see who was going to break the ice first, and he came up to me and said, 'Now, that third-and-two in the championship game when you ran the ball, were y'all going to go for it on fourth down?' And I said, 'Look, on the sideline Tony [Dungy] basically said, 'Don't make me have to decide.' So after that, it was like, 'You asked one, now I have a couple for you.'

"My first question to him? I went back to my rookie year, 1998, against the Jets. We went 3–13, and he's coaching under Parcells and they go 12–4. We beat them at home, my biggest win at the time. We stunk. We had a fourth-and-14 where they were going to blitz like crazy. Our left guard false-starts, but the ball is snapped and you see [the blitz], so we come back and go max protection, thinking they would blitz, and he drops eight [defenders into coverage]. I'm doing what my coach told me—you know, dump it down to your back. So I throw a four-yard pass to Marshall Faulk on fourth-and-19. He gets the first down, and we go on to beat them. I asked Belichick if he remembered that play. Oh, he remembered. 'Damned Mo Lewis missed the tackle.' Unbelievable. We ended up going to dinner. I had an enjoyable week just talking football with the guy.

"The most sincere voice-mail I got after the Super Bowl was from Dan Marino. He did the coin toss that day, and he said it was an honor to be on the field with me. I'll remember that for a long time.

"Once you win, you don't want to quit; you want to win another one. So you have that same hunger, for sure. At least I do. I know I do." ▪

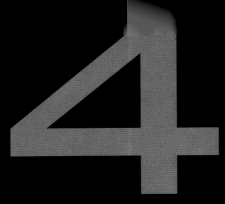

4
JOHNNY UNITAS

" He was the smartest play-caller of his day (and likely any day), the definition of an on-field commander. He led the Colts down the field to tie the 1958 NFL title game in the final minute and again to win it in overtime. " —PETER KING

≥ THREE-TIME NFL MVP
≥ 40,239 CAREER YARDS, 290 TDS

IN THOSE halcyon days, they didn't have coaches telling quarterbacks what plays to call. Quarterbacks were field generals, not field lieutenants. I never saw war, so that is still my vision of manhood: Unitas standing courageously in the pocket, down amidst the mortals. Lock and load.

—*Frank Deford, SI, September 23, 2002*

Unitas threw TD passes in 47 consecutive games.

PHOTOGRAPH BY WALTER IOOSS JR.

BALL AT BAT VISITORS H E
STRIKE OUT INN. CLEVELAND H E

5

OTTO GRAHAM

BROWNS 1946–1955

Graham was well-protected in the 1954 title game.

PHOTOGRAPH BY EVAN PESKIN

" He's the greatest winner among quarterbacks ever, and that cannot be disputed: seven championships in 10 professional seasons—and he lost in the championship game the other three years. " —PETER KING

≥ NINE-TIME ALL-PRO
≥ SIX TOUCHDOWNS IN 1954 NFL TITLE GAME

UNTIL JOHN UNITAS and Joe Montana arrived no one was as accurate as Graham. One story was about how one of his teammates bent a wire coat hanger into a diamond shape one day and challenged Graham to throw a football through it from 15 feet away. He went 10 for 10.

—*Paul Zimmerman, SI, December 29, 2003*

6

JOHN ELWAY

BRONCOS 1983-1998

" It's fitting that a player who directed so many clutch drives saved his best for last, guiding the Broncos to victory in the Super Bowl at the end of the 1997 and '98 seasons. " —MARK GODICH

≥ RETIRED SECOND ALL-TIME IN PASSING YARDS AND COMPLETIONS
≥ FIVE SUPER BOWL APPEARANCES

WHEN YOU order up the statue, make sure you get the sock right. It has to be pulled all the way down, preferably with a defensive end's fingernail still in it. Give the right shoe a flat tire, and show the jersey yanked off one shoulder pad, the work of a blitzing linebacker who thought he had himself an appearance on the next NFL's Greatest Hits video but instead got only a fleeting handful of orange-and-blue nylon. While you're at it, see if the sculptor can put in a hint of the bulges of tape and a knee brace underneath the legs of the pants, and of the limp that made Elway walk like John Wayne in high heels yet vanished when he took off sprinting, needing six yards and somehow always getting six yards and an inch. Try to show the power of that right arm, the one that shredded receivers' gloves and knocked the wind out of strong men.

—Rick Reilly, SI, December 30, 1996

Elway led 47 fourth-quarter drives to win or tie games.

PHOTOGRAPH BY PETER READ MILLER

A LEAP INTO HISTORY

After suffering three losses on the game's biggest stage, John Elway flipped the narrative with a late-game hurdle that earned him a Super Bowl victory at last

BY MICHAEL SILVER

E SPENT 15 YEARS PUSHING the physical limits of football, making jaws drop and decorating highlight clips with bursts of brilliance. Then, with one fearless thrust of his 37-year-old body late in the third quarter of Super Bowl XXXII, John Elway finally lifted himself and the Denver Broncos to the top. In the greatest Super Bowl ever, the pivotal moment, fittingly, belonged to one of the NFL's all-time greats.

For all the importance of coach Mike Shanahan's dazzling game plan, of running back Terrell Davis's MVP performance and of the game-ending stand by Denver's oft-slighted defense, it was Elway, with his self-described "three-inch vertical leap," who elevated himself into immortality and his franchise into the realm of champions with the Broncos' 31–24 upset of the Green Bay Packers on Sunday.

The play said everything about the defiant Broncos and their unlikely march to the title. With the game tied at 17 and Denver facing third-and-six at the Green Bay 12, Elway dropped back to pass, found no open receivers and took off down the middle of the field. He darted right and was met near the first-down marker by Packers strong safety LeRoy Butler, who ducked his head and prepared to unload on the quarterback. Elway took to the air, and Butler's hit spun him around so that he came down feet-forward as he was absorbing another shot from defensive back Mike Prior.

When Elway hit the ground at the four, an adrenaline rush surged through the Broncos. Denver scored two plays later, and though the Packers came back to tie the score again, Green Bay was a depleted team fighting a losing battle against an opponent that had been recharged. When the Broncos launched their game-winning drive from the Packers' 49 with 3:27 remaining, it was like watching a battle of the bands between Pearl Jam and the Kingston Trio. "When Elway, instead of running out-of-bounds, turned it up and got spun around like a helicopter, it energized us beyond belief," Denver defensive lineman Mike Lodish said after the game. Added tight end Shannon Sharpe, "When I saw him do that and then get up pumping his fist, I said, 'It's on.' That's when I was sure we were going to win."

Though only an infinitesimal slice of the earth's football-viewing population believed Denver would dethrone Green Bay, the Broncos carried a confidence into this game that belied their station as a double-digit underdog. Shanahan and Elway could barely contain their excitement the evening before the Super Bowl as they reviewed the game plan in Elway's hotel room.

Green Bay manufactured some incentive for the game, most of it derived from the media's focusing on Elway's quest to win a Super Bowl after three washouts. "We've heard all about poor John Elway," defensive tackle Santana Dotson scoffed three days before the game. "We're all very touched. But, hey, that's the classic pregame story. As long as we're the focus of the postgame story, that's cool."

Sorry, Santana. History will show that this was Elway's week of glory. Sure, his stats were wimpy. He threw for only 123 yards, didn't complete a pass to a wideout until Ed McCaffrey's 36-yard catch-and-run midway through the third quarter and blew a chance to build on a seven-point lead by throwing an end zone interception to free safety Eugene Robinson with 11 seconds left in the third quarter. But Elway carried the day with his poise. "That was the ultimate win, there's no question," he said. "There have been a lot of things that go along with losing three Super Bowls and playing for 14 years and being labeled as a guy who has never been on a winning Super Bowl team."

On his biggest pass of the game, Elway made a perfect delivery, throwing a quick toss to fullback Howard Griffith that went for 23 yards and gave Denver a first-and-goal at the eight with two minutes remaining. That set up Davis's winning one-yard touchdown run, which the Pack conceded on a second-down play with 1:45 left in a futile attempt to get the ball back with enough time to win. (Mistakenly thinking it was first down, Green Bay coach Mike Holmgren, with only two timeouts left, feared the Broncos might run down the clock and kick a field goal in the closing seconds.) "John makes mistakes; he is human after all," Broncos receiver Rod Smith would say later. "But you never see fear in his eyes. He's like a linebacker with a good arm."

On the first two nights after the Broncos arrived in San Diego, Elway and his backups, Jeff Lewis and Bubby Brister, commandeered a limousine to take them around town. At several bars Elway elected to remain in the limo, alone with his thoughts. "One time I stayed in the car with him," Lewis said, "and he was so focused, it was amazing. He said, 'I can't wait for this game. Before the other Super Bowls, I really didn't grasp how big they were. But I've never been this ready for a game in my life.'"

Later Shanahan celebrated with owner Pat Bowlen in the limo while his 18-year-old son, Kyle, discussed how relaxed his father had been in the hours before the game. "He got one of my friends a field pass, and he gave another one money to buy a ticket," Kyle said. "He was ultramellow. We were sitting in his hotel room watching *White Men Can't Jump*, and he was laughing his head off."

Funny how things work out. White men can't jump? Don't try telling that to the Packers—not after Elway's leap into history. ∎

7

DAN MARINO

DOLPHINS 1983–1999

" The most prolific passer in league history, only the lack of a Super Bowl title mars Marino's record-setting 17-year career in Miami. " —DON BANKS

≥ SET CAREER PASSING MARKS IN YARDS, COMPLETIONS AND TDS
≥ SET SINGLE-SEASON MARKS IN YARDS AND TDS

WHEN DON SHULA drafted Marino in May 1983, he was advised by Pittsburgh sportswriter Pat Livingston that in "Danny" he would have a quarterback with "the touch of a Sammy Baugh, the release of a Norm Van Brocklin, the arm of a Terry Bradshaw, the . . . " etc., etc. No reluctant dragon, Pat. Reckless praise doesn't pour so freely from Shula. He got through the 1983 season without conceding much more than how "amazing" it was that "Danny" (ahem) got sacked only 10 times and threw just six interceptions in 306 pass plays, and despite his inexperience was "never indecisive," even in the face of man-eating red-dogs and the best secondary schemes and ploys money could buy. But when Shula was asked what Marino would have to do to improve in 1984, he practically bristled. "Maintain, you mean," he said. It was the Shula equivalent of a standing ovation.

—*John Underwood, SI, September 5, 1984*

Marino was the first to break the 5,000-yard barrier.

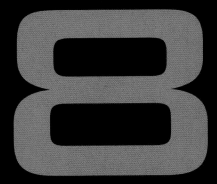

8

BRETT FAVRE

FALCONS 1991
PACKERS 1992–2007
JETS 2008
VIKINGS 2009–2010

" Favre started every game for almost two decades, broke nearly every meaningful NFL passing mark and retired as one of the game's great characters. " —GREG BISHOP

≥ NFL'S ALL-TIME LEADER IN PASSING ATTEMPTS AND COMPLETIONS
≥ 297 CONSECUTIVE STARTS

IN THIS age of corporate quarterbacking Favre remains a "gunslinger." No Green Bay offensive series of more than four or five plays can be broadcast without that word. In fact the nature and number of clichés Favre attracts would make for a potent drinking game. And since he himself has long since sworn off, hoist a few in his honor. Drink a shot of redeye when you hear *gunslinger*. A dram of rum for *swashbuckler*. A glass of wine whenever the phrase *vintage Favre* is used. Drink a mug of Ovaltine when you hear *He looks like a kid out there*. Chug whenever you hear *He's just trying to make something happen*. And if you're a Packers fan, drink a double shot and turn off the TV when you hear *He tried to force that one in there*.

—*Jeff MacGregor, SI, December 4, 2006*

Favre was named NFL MVP on three occasions.

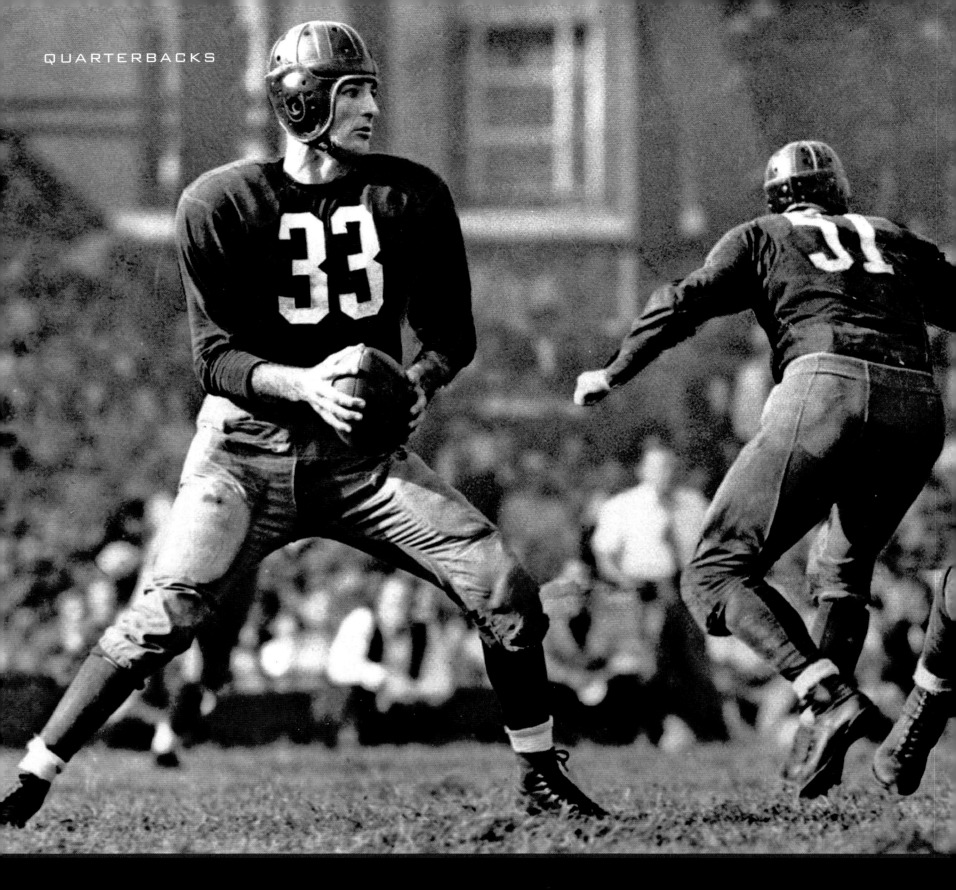

QUARTERBACKS

33

9

REDSKINS 1937–1952

Quarterbacking was only one of Baugh's skills.

PHOTOGRAPH BY AP

❝ The best all-around player ever. In 1943 Baugh led the league in punting (45.9-yard average) and completion percentage (55.6 percent) and was second with 23 touchdown passes in 10 games. Plus, as a safety he led the league with 11 interceptions. ❞ —PETER KING

≥ SIX-TIME NFL PASSING LEADER
≥ SEVEN-TIME ALL-PRO

THE PROS were pushovers for Sammy Baugh, fresh out of TCU. He became an All-Pro in his rookie year while taking the Redskins to the NFL championship. Until Baugh, pro football in Texas was a one-paragraph story on the third page of the Monday sports section.

—*Dan Jenkins, SI, August 31, 1981*

SAMMY BAUGH

10

BART
STARR

PACKERS 1956–1971

"Starr is a two-time Super Bowl MVP and an icon for an historic franchise. Not too shabby for a 17th-round draft pick." —CHRIS BURKE

≥ FIVE-TIME NFL CHAMPION
≥ 9–1 POSTSEASON RECORD

WHEN STARR came to the Packers he was not imbued with the cocky self-confidence that is part of the makeup of most pro quarterbacks. At Alabama he had just finished a shattering senior year sitting on the bench. J. B. (Ears) Whitworth had taken over the Alabama team and decided that he would live or die with his sophomores. This meant that Starr had to spend his senior year out of the action. "If I hadn't got married my junior year, I wouldn't have been able to stand it. My wife was a wonderful help." He was drafted, he says, because, "Johnny Dee, the Alabama basketball coach, was a good friend of the late Jack Vainisi, the Green Bay scout, and he talked him into taking a chance." In early summer before he reported to the Green Bay camp, Starr worked to improve himself. He and Cherry, his wife, spent the summer at her parents' home. "I built an A-frame in their front yard," Starr recalls. "I hung a tire on it and practiced throwing the ball through the tire from different angles for hours every day. Cherry fielded the ball for me."

—Tex Maule, SI, October 31, 1966

Starr was a precise passer and an expert game-caller.

PHOTOGRAPH BY NEIL LEIFER

10 THE

BEST RUNNING BACKS

WHEN IT COMES TO CARS, THE '57 CHEVY REMAINS AN ICON OF EXCELLENCE, NO MATTER HOW MUCH MORE POWERFUL OR EFFICIENT THE NEWER MODELS ARE. SO IT IS WITH RUNNING BACKS. THE CURRENT CROP IS SWIFT AND SLEEK AND VERSATILE, BUT OUR PANELISTS COULD NOT HELP BUT LOOK BACK TO THE PAST.

AND IT WENT BEYOND A FONDNESS FOR JIM BROWN—A ROOKIE IN 1957, INCIDENTALLY—WHO WAS THE NEAR CONSENSUS CHOICE AT NO. 1. THE TOP EIGHT IN THIS CATEGORY IS COMPRISED ENTIRELY OF PLAYERS WHO HAVEN'T SEEN THE FIELD IN AT LEAST A DECADE, AND USUALLY MUCH LONGER THAN THAT. TWO MORE MODERN BACKS, LADAINIAN TOMLINSON AND ADRIAN PETERSON, DID FIND THEIR WAY ONTO THE BOTTOM OF THE LIST, AT POSITIONS NINE AND 10.

ONE CULPRIT FOR THE SENSE OF FADING GREATNESS AT THE POSITION: THE SPLIT BACKFIELD. MANY COACHES NOW DIVIDE CARRIES BETWEEN TWO OR THREE BACKS, KEEPING EVERYONE FRESH BUT THEIR RUSHING TOTALS LOWER. THEN THERE'S THE SHIFT TO THE PASSING ATTACK. BEFORE RULE CHANGES BEGINNING IN 1978, RUSHING ATTEMPTS ALWAYS OUTNUMBERED PASSES, BUT SINCE THEN THE BALANCES HAVE FLIPPED. IT'S A LITTLE LIKE THE AUTOMOBILE, WHICH HAS LOST SOME OF ITS MAGIC IN THE AGE OF FREQUENT FLYING. WHEN IT COMES TO ACCUMULATING POINTS THESE DAYS, WE'RE ALL UP IN THE AIR.

1

JIM BROWN

BROWNS 1957–1965

" A gliding, powerful force of nature who was just too big, fast and strong for his era. At 6' 2", 232 pounds, he played only nine seasons and led the league in rushing eight times. " —TIM LAYDEN

≥ FOUR-TIME NFL MVP
≥ RETIRED AS NFL'S CAREER RUSHING LEADER WITH 12,312 YARDS

GLENN HOLTZMAN, a very good 250-pound defensive tackle for the Los Angeles Rams, recently explained what it is like to face Brown from the wrong side of the line: "He's just the best back in the league . . . fast as the fastest, hard as the hardest. He gets off to the quickest start of any big man I've ever seen. An arm tackle is no soap; he runs right through you. The only way I've found to stop him is hit him right at the ankles with your shoulder . . . otherwise, it's like tackling a locomotive." Brown has tremendous lateral speed and balance; he can be hit, knocked sideways and land on his feet running in another direction, picking up full speed again in a few steps. One league coach made Brown's importance clear after his team had dropped a thriller to the Browns: "If they ever lose Jim Brown, then they'll be even with the rest of us."

—Tex Maule, SI, November 10, 1958

Brown averaged a record 104.3 yards per game.

PHOTOGRAPH BY NEIL LEIFER

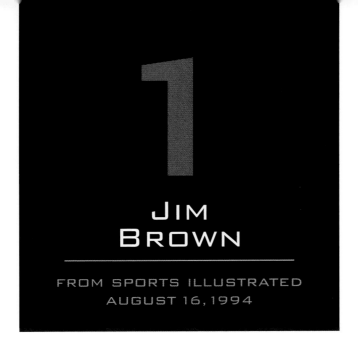

THE LONG HARD RUN

Long after Brown left the NFL for Hollywood, he still showed the toughness—and the elusiveness—that made him a legend

BY STEVE RUSHIN

OT A PENCIL?" JIM BROWN asks when you call to arrange a visit. "Here's what you do. Call 310-652-7***. Ask for Rockhead Johnson. He has my calendar. You two work out the date."

"I'm sorry," you respond. "What was the first name?"

"Rockhead."

"*Rockhead?*"

"Rockhead. Rockhead Johnson."

So you dutifully dial the number and wait for Rockhead to answer, but instead you get a receptionist at Amer-I-Can, Brown's public-service organization. Summoning the most businesslike voice that circumstances will allow, you ask, "May I please speak to Rockhead? Rockhead Johnson?" A long and awkward pause follows, after which you're told that *Rock* is out of the office. *Rock* will be back in an hour. Can *Rock* return your call?

"This is Rock," Rock says when he phones back later. "Rock Johnson."

By now the full horror has hit you: You've been had—suckered, as Brown likes to say. The man's name isn't Rockhead at all. Only one person calls him that, and only one person gets away with it. You've just been juked by Jim Brown.

HE IS STILL A FAMILIAR PRESENCE ON TELEVISION, AN imposing bust on the small screen. At 58 he remains an enormous Rock 'em Sock 'em Robot of a man. His arms are crisscrossed with scars, his fingers veer off at each joint in unexpected directions, rem-

nants of the cartoon-violent NFL of the 1950s and '60s. But that vision of a massive, muddied Brown begins to evaporate in your head while you drive, high above Sunset Boulevard, on a serpentine street that runs like a stream through the Hollywood Hills, Benzes and BMWs docked bargelike on both curbs. You turn off and plunge down into Jim Brown's driveway, where a young, besuited chauffeur, who has been dispatched by a local television studio, takes it upon himself to try to shoo you and your sorry blue Pontiac from the premises.

Moments later you are rescued, and Brown is amused. "I live in a *bool*shit world," he says of Hollywood. "But that's cool. When I go out, it's like, 'Put on your suit, baby, you're going down into the *circus*.' You go to Roxbury's, you know what you're going for: To see the stars and the girls and the *bool*shit—'Hey, what's goin' on, babe?' 'Aaaaay, Big Jim, what's happenin', man?' There's a time and place for that, as long as you don't buy into it. My way to cut through the *bool*shit is with simplicity. And when I stay here, everything is simple."

Jim Brown tolerates no *bool*shit. It is practically his credo. Ask him why he so unabashedly admires Muhammad Ali, and Brown tells you straight up: "He has the heart and courage to stand up for beliefs that are unpopular." Bill Russell? "Exceptionally smart, exceptionally principled, no boolshit." Conversely, in his autobiography Brown calls O.J. Simpson a "phony" and adds: "The Juice likes to pretend he's modest, but that's just the Juice *being* the Juice. O.J. is extremely smart, man knows how to make a buck, and his 'aw shucks' image is his meal ticket. He's not about to jeopardize it by being honest." The book was published five years ago.

Today, just down the hill, lies the circus, Los Angeles, a scary riot of Simpson hearings and Menendez shootings and King beatings—an apocalyptic place of fire, earthquake, mudslide and pestilence that only four decades ago was an Eden to Walter O'Malley. But up here at the Brown residence, all appears to be placid and predictable simplicity. He has lived in the same house, driven the same car, had the same telephone number since 1968.

That was the spring when the Reverend Dr. Martin Luther King Jr. was assassinated in Memphis. A framed portrait of King hangs in Brown's foyer. But nowhere on display in the house is a single personal memento of Brown's own varied careers—as a football superstar, as a film actor, as an activist in what he calls "the movement for dignity, equality and justice."

Toward that end Brown has opened his immaculate home through the years to an astonishing cross section of humanity. Recently, Brown says, former Secretary of Housing and Urban Development Jack Kemp and the head of the Nation of Islam shared the couch on which we now sit. "I can have Louis Farrakhan here, you, 15 Jews," he says. "It don't make no damn difference."

Never has. As a child he was thrown in with all races and generations, almost from the time his father, Swinton (Sweet Sue) Brown, a fighter and a gambler, abandoned him at birth. Jim Brown was raised by his great-grandmother, whom he called Mama, on St. Simons Island, off the coast of Georgia. He went to school in a segregated, two-room shack, went to the toilet in the backyard. When he was eight, Mama gave him a box lunch, buttoned him up and put him on a train for Manhasset, N.Y., where his mother worked as a domestic. In that white and wealthy community Jim Brown became an athletic prodigy. At Manhasset High he was a kind of ward of a group of white professional men, doctors and lawyers and teachers, who demanded that he study and run for student government.

"Without Manhasset, without Dr. Collins and Ken Molloy and Mr. Dawson and Ed Walsh, it would've been impossible," Brown says of his remarkable existence. "These people actually saved my life, man. I would never, ever have been anything without them. And it was so pure. If kids can see honesty and interest from people of that age, that's what builds, man. So you can't fool me with all of the other *bool*shit, 'cause I've got an example for the rest of my life. You wanna see what goodness is? I look at those people. I know what love is. I know what patience is. I know what consistency is. I know what *honesty* is."

Ken Molloy was a Manhasset lawyer and a former Syracuse lacrosse player who insisted that Brown select Syracuse over the dozens of schools that were recruiting him for football, basketball and baseball. It was only after Brown arrived on campus, housed in a different dorm from the rest of the football team, eating on a different meal plan, that he first fully encountered discrimination. It made him miserable in that freshman year of 1953–54.

You have asked Jim Brown to look at his remarkable life. You are seated in his living room, which overlooks the pool, which overlooks the yard, which overlooks Los Angeles. You have come to take in the view: of race, celebrity, the real world and the star athlete's obligations therein these last four decades. Brown has seemingly lived every issue

in sport and society since he left home for Syracuse so long ago. He continues to work in places like South Central and San Quentin. You ask Jim Brown to assess this public life he entered 40 years ago, and he says, "I am oh, so tired."

"I CAME UP AT THE CROSSROADS OF SEGREGATION," SAYS BROWN. "There were still colleges where black players couldn't play. There were teams that would go south and black players had to stay in private homes. These were very difficult times. It was a blessing on the one hand because there were opportunities, but it was demeaning because you were still looked on as inferior. It was almost as if you'd been given a *favor*. And you always felt you had to perform much, much better."

And so Jimmy Brown, the only black on the freshman football team at Syracuse, went from fifth-string halfback to the best player in the nation in his four years of playing for a coaching staff that—save for an assistant named Roy Simmons—initially begrudged his presence there.

Jim Brown scored 38 points a game as a high school basketball player. He was drafted by the Syracuse Nationals of the NBA in 1957 even though he had stopped playing basketball after his junior season in college. He received a letter of inquiry from the great Stengel of the Yankees—even though, by Brown's own admission, "I wasn't that good."

On his final day as an athlete at Syracuse, Brown won the discus and shot put in a varsity track meet, returned to the dressing room to change for a lacrosse match and was called back to the track by a student manager. *Could he throw the javelin?* Brown threw the javelin 162 feet on one attempt. Syracuse won the meet.

The man belonged to a higher species. Jim Brown was built like a martini glass, with a 46-inch chest and a 32-inch waist; he was an exceptionally fast man who looked slow in motion on the football field: gracefully slow, a man running in a swimming pool.

Pulling out of his stance and bursting through the line, he accumulated would-be tacklers, men hopping a moving train, until he slowed and finally collapsed eight or 10 or 12 yards upfield, buried beneath violent giants. One didn't really try to tackle Brown; one tried only to catch him, as one catches the 8:05. "All you can do is grab hold, hang on and wait for help" is how Hall of Fame linebacker Sam Huff put it.

Brown rose slowly from the scrum after every carry and hobbled back to the huddle in apparent pain. This was the earliest hint of Brown's acting aspirations, for he wasn't really hurt, or at least not hampered. No, in his entire nine-year professional career, he never missed a game. He played all of the 1962 season with a severely sprained wrist just this side of broken. He did not wear hip pads, ever. And so it finally became apparent to opposing defenses that Brown wasn't ever going to be hurt by conventional malevolence.

He was simply that rarest kind of competitor, who made men and women gape, whose performances each Sunday displayed the pure athlete in his prime. Jim Brown is why we love sports in the first place, the reason we tolerate the big dough, the crybabies, the *bool*shit. ∎

The rugged Brown never missed a game in nine seasons.

2

WALTER PAYTON

BEARS 1975–1987

❝ No back before or since has run the ball quite like Payton did, with those exaggerated, almost upright strides, the way he palmed the football, and, of course, the power. "Sweetness" was a nickname earned. ❞ —CHRIS BURKE

≥ HELD RECORDS FOR CAREER RUSHING TOUCHDOWNS (110) AND YARDS IN A GAME (275)
≥ TWO-TIME NFL MVP

"IN THEIR Super Bowl year [1985], we played them at Lambeau," says former Green Bay Packers linebacker Brian Noble. "It was my rookie season, and we were having a great game, up 10–9 late in the fourth quarter. They had the ball at about our 30. I weighed 265 pounds, and Walter came right at me with the ball. I teed up, and there was a huge collision. I hit that man as hard as I hit anybody in my career. I knocked him back about four yards, but he stayed up and just kept going. Touchdown. I was devastated; I cost us the game. Sitting in the locker room afterward, I was ready to quit. But my teammate [linebacker] John Anderson put his arm around me and said, 'Believe me, that's not the first time and it won't be the last time that Walter Payton breaks a tackle like that.' "

—Peter King, SI, November 8, 1999

Payton had 77 games of 100 or more yards rushing.

3

BARRY SANDERS

" Sanders walked away early, at age 30, having never rushed for fewer than 1,304 yards when he played a 16-game season. No back better combined power between the tackles with breathtaking open-field elusiveness. " —TIM LAYDEN

≥ 15,269 CAREER YARDS RUSHING
≥ 2,053 YARDS IN 1997

SANDERS IS what people in the NFL call a "freak runner." His style follows no predictable pattern. It's all improvisation, genius, eyes that see more than other people's do, legs that seem to operate as disjointed entities, intuition, awareness of where the danger is—all performed in a churning, thrashing heartbeat.

—Paul Zimmerman, SI, December 8, 1997

Sanders led the league in rushing four times.

PHOTOGRAPH BY JOHN BIEVER

Smith starred on three Super Bowl–winning teams.

PHOTOGRAPH BY DAVID E. KLUTHO

4

EMMITT SMITH

COWBOYS 1990–2002
CARDINALS 2003–2004

"A key cog in the Cowboys' dynasty, Smith is still the only back to win a Super Bowl and a rushing crown as well as MVP awards for the regular season and Super Bowl in the same season." —GREG BISHOP

≥ NFL'S ALL-TIME LEADING RUSHER WITH 18,355 YARDS
≥ 176 CAREER TOUCHDOWNS

WITHOUT HIM the Dallas attack wilts. "If Troy Aikman is out, his replacement can just hand Emmitt the ball and watch the options open up," says Giants linebacker Corey Miller. "But if Emmitt is out, defenses can pin their ears back and go after the quarterback. There is no one to replace Emmitt."

—Rick Telander, SI, February 9, 1995

5

O.J. SIMPSON

BILLS 1969–1977
49ERS 1978–1979

"Our job is not to be judge and jury of whatever he did later in life, off the field. It's to judge him as a player—and there aren't three backs in NFL history who combined the electric moves and power of Simpson." —PETER KING

≥ FOUR NFL RUSHING TITLES
≥ FIRST BACK TO RUSH FOR 2,000 YARDS IN A SEASON

IN THE season's opener O.J. set a league record for a single game when he rushed for 250 yards against New England. The Hall of Fame urgently requested his jersey. Twice in the first four weeks he was named AP Offensive Player of the Week. Two weeks ago, against Baltimore, he set another league record with his seventh consecutive 100-yard game. The media began to document his every move. When he left the field briefly in the Philadelphia game the press box was solemnly informed. "Simpson suffered a broken shoelace." . . . The person who seems the least ruffled by all the excitement is Simpson himself. He is not a 26-year-old suddenly encountering fame but a man settling comfortably into a familiar role, O.J. Simpson, superstar. "Being the best is something I've lived with," he says, "and I like living with it."

—Joe Marshall, SI, October 29, 1973

Simpson set a record with 23 TDs in 1975.

PHOTOGRAPH BY HEINZ KLUETMEIER

6

ERIC DICKERSON

1983–1987 RAMS
1987–1991 COLTS
1992 RAIDERS
1993 FALCONS

" He was a football supernova. The start to Dickerson's career was unlike anything the NFL had ever seen—he rushed for a record 9,915 yards over his first six seasons. " —CHRIS BURKE

≥ RECORD 2,105 YARDS
RUSHING IN 1984
≥ LED NFL IN RUSHING
FOUR TIMES

WHEN HE showed up at that first minicamp with the Rams, head coach John Robinson and running backs coach Bruce Snyder were expecting this hoss. And that was why, when they discovered what they really had, Dickerson so awed them. "He made no noise when he ran," Robinson says. "You couldn't hear anything," Snyder agrees. "You can usually hear a runner's pads; they'll flop around a little bit. And you'll hear feet on the ground. With a big man, you'll get more sound vocally, a kind of breathing and grunting." There was none of that with Dickerson. "If you were blind, he could run right by you," Robinson said. "I don't think you'd know he was there unless you felt the wind. He is an extremely powerful runner, but he's so graceful it's really deceiving. He's the smoothest runner I've ever seen."

—William Nack, SI, September 4, 1985

The 6'3" Dickerson rushed for 13,259 career yards.

7

GALE SAYERS

BEARS 1965–1971

" His brilliance was relatively brief due to an injury-shortened career, but no one delivered more highlight-reel moves and wow factor than Sayers did in his prime. " —DON BANKS

≥ RECORD 22 TDS AS A ROOKIE
≥ TWO NFL RUSHING TITLES

HIS CAREER has passed into the realm of grainy film mythology, and within that mythology certain assumptions have taken root. Such as this one: He was uniquely great. That assumption is true. "There really has never been anybody else like him, even to this day," says Steelers defensive coordinator Dick LeBeau, who as a defensive back for the Lions played against Sayers 10 times and has been a coach in the NFL for 37 seasons. "He was the best runner with a football under his arm I've ever seen," says Mike Ditka, who played with Sayers and, notably, coached Walter Payton. Here's another assumption: The injuries that blunted Sayers's career left him unfulfilled. That assumption is false. His battered knees ended his football career and started a rich second life, and he offers up two statements, spoken countless times since 1972, to describe this transition, *"As I prepared to play, I prepared to quit. I walked away, and I never looked back."*

—Tim Layden, SI, August 23, 2010

Sayers sped through the hole in 1968.

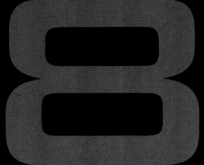

EARL CAMPBELL

OILERS 1978–1984
SAINTS 1984–1985

Campbell was lightning and thunder all in one.
PHOTOGRAPH BY RICHARD MACKSON

" One of the most powerful backs in NFL history thanks to his thick 5' 11" frame, Campbell lasted just eight pro seasons because of the brute physicality of his running style. But he also had surprising agility. " —GREG A. BEDARD

≥ 1979 NFL MVP
≥ 1,934 YARDS RUSHING IN 1980

"HE CAN inflict more damage on a team than any back I know of," says Pittsburgh's Mean Joe Greene. "O.J. did it with speed, Campbell does it with power. He's a punishing runner. He hurts you. There are very few tacklers in the league who will bring Earl Campbell down one-on-one."

—Bruce Newman, SI, September 3, 1979

9

❝ He single-handedly turned the dark helmet visor into a must-have NFL accessory. He also broke the NFL's record for most touchdowns in a season, and ranks among history's best pass-catching backs. ❞ —GREG BISHOP

"WE SEE the sense of urgency LT has on each and every play," says right tackle Shane Olivea. "Then we look at film, and he's blocking a defensive back 20 yards downfield, after the play is over. People don't realize how many little things he does and don't understand how great he is."

—*Michael Silver, SI, December 25, 2006*

LaDainian Tomlinson

≥ 145 CAREER RUSHING TDS
≥ 2006 NFL MVP

Tomlinson ranks fifth in career rushing yards.

PHOTOGRAPH BY JOHN W. MCDONOUGH

10

ADRIAN PETERSON

VIKINGS 2007–2016
SAINTS 2017

" All Day is a three-time rushing champ, and in 2012 he gained 2,097 yards, eight yards short of Eric Dickerson's NFL single-season mark. " —MARK GODICH

≥ 2012 NFL MVP
≥ RAN FOR NFL RECORD 296 YARDS IN A GAME IN 2007

PETERSON GOT his 25th and final carry against the Browns with a little more than six minutes left and Minnesota leading by two touchdowns. Starting eight yards behind the line of scrimmage at the Vikings' 36, Peterson took a handoff from Brett Favre and shot the left-side gap between tackle and guard. He shook off Browns free safety Brodney Pool with a head-and-shoulder fake and glided to the left. Then, in a blink, his feet stopped near the sideline at the Browns' 41 as he tossed cornerback Eric Wright out-of-bounds with the heel of his gloved right hand. Cornerback Brandon McDonald had two shots to bring Peterson down as his legs started churning again, but Peterson separated himself with a stiff arm at the 36. From there he streaked into the end zone. "He didn't want to run by someone, he wanted to feel them," says tight end Visanthe Shiancoe. "I guess they felt him."

—*Damon Hack, SI, September 21, 2009*

Peterson has a record 13 TD runs of 60 yards or more.

10 THE

BEST WIDE RECEIVERS

THERE'S SOMETHING TO BE SAID FOR FINISHING STRONG, WHICH IS EXACTLY WHAT LARRY FITZGERALD HAS BEEN DOING THESE LAST COUPLE OF YEARS. THE CARDINALS' RECEIVER, WHO ENTERED THE NFL IN 2004 AND HAS BEEN NAMED TO 10 PRO BOWLS, HAD HIS TWO HIGHEST RECEPTION TOTALS FOR A SEASON IN 2015 AND 2016. THOUGH HE ISN'T AS POTENT A DEEP THREAT AS HE USED TO BE, HIS ABILITY TO EXCEL AS MORE OF A SHORT-TO-INTERMEDIATE RECEIVER HELPS MAKE HIS CASE AS AN ALL-TIME GREAT.

STANDING OUT IS DIFFICULT FOR MODERN-DAY RECEIVERS, WITH SO MANY OUTSTANDING ONES VYING FOR ATTENTION. WHILE FITZGERALD MADE OUR TOP 10, RELATIVELY RECENT STARS SUCH AS MICHAEL IRVIN, TIM BROWN, CRIS CARTER AND CALVIN JOHNSON JUST MISSED OUT. STEVE SMITH, WHO RETIRED AFTER THE 2016 SEASON, PULLED IN A VOTE TOO.

AS PANELIST AND HALL OF FAME VOTER PETER KING HAS OFTEN NOTED ON THEMMQB.COM, THE WIDE RECEIVER POSITION IS A TOUGH ONE TO JUDGE, BECAUSE OF THE WAY RECEIVING STATS HAVE BEEN INFLATED WITH THE GROWTH OF THE PASSING GAME. OF OUR SEVEN PANELISTS, SIX PLACED FITZGERALD IN THEIR TOP 10, WHICH BODES WELL FOR HIS PROSPECTS OF CATCHING ON IN CANTON.

1

JERRY RICE

49ERS 1985–2000
RAIDERS 2001–2004
SEAHAWKS 2004

" Considered by many the single greatest player of all time, regardless of position, Rice and the 49ers' dynamic West Coast offense didn't just dominate football. They changed it. Rice was before his time, a modern wideout in a running back world. Always open. " —GREG BISHOP

≥ NFL RECORD 208 CAREER TDS
≥ NFL RECORD 22,895 CAREER RECEIVING YARDS

"PEOPLE COME up to me and say, 'I'd love to be in your shoes,'" he says with a sigh. "I say, 'No, you wouldn't.' They don't know what it's like. The pressure. Before games I can't sleep. Before Super Bowl XXIII I woke up at 4 a.m. and just paced. I can't relax. I should be able to enjoy it, but I can't. The table can turn." Someday Rice will probably score his 200th touchdown, which will be 74 more than his closest competitor, Jim Brown, who has been retired for almost 30 years. It's a figure so high, it's crazy. But it may not be enough for this most graceful and obsessive of men. "It's a lot of wear and tear on me," he says needlessly of his intensity down the stretch. "I might not survive," he grimaces. Constant vigilance is required. The table must not move.

—Rick Telander, SI, December 26, 1994

PACKERS 1935–1945

Hutson invented many standard pass routes.

2

DON HUTSON

"With all respect to Jerry Rice, I've valued Hutson as the best receiver ever because of his game-changing speed, and because he set the bar for receiving records so high that many lasted for two or three generations." —PETER KING

≥ RETIRED WITH 18 MAJOR NFL RECORDS

≥ TWO-TIME NFL MVP

WITH HIS momentum carrying him the other way, Hutson reached back, past the defender,—his arms seemed five feet long— made the catch, kept his balance and scored. I ran the play back, frame by frame. It was an impossible catch. I've only seen one other like it: Lynn Swann's against the Cowboys in the '76 Super Bowl.

—Paul Zimmerman, SI, September 11, 1989

Moss was particularly potent as a deep threat.

PHOTOGRAPH BY DAMIAN STROHMEYER

3

RANDY MOSS

VIKINGS 1998–2004
RAIDERS 2005–2006
PATRIOTS 2007–2010
VIKINGS, TITANS 2010

❝ Blessed with a freakish ability to go up and get the ball, Moss's touchdown total speaks to his unrivaled playmaking ability. ❞ —DON BANKS

≥ 14,858 CAREER RECEIVING YARDS
≥ SECOND IN CAREER RECEIVING TOUCHDOWNS (156)

"HE JUST doesn't know," says Vikings quarterback Randall Cunningham. "He doesn't understand that when we're playing Kansas City, he's up against the best [secondary]. It hasn't hit him. There's no fright, just this kind of innocence. He's like all of us when we're young, before we do fail. A very few of us never do."

—Richard Hoffer, SI, September 7, 1998

4

LANCE ALWORTH

CHARGERS 1962-1970
COWBOYS 1971-1972

"Alworth was deservedly the first AFL player named to the Hall of Fame, and he dominated that pass-happy league with seven consecutive 1,000-yard seasons. He's still considered one of the most graceful receivers who ever ran a route." —DON BANKS

≥ 18.9 YARDS PER CATCH
≥ 85 CAREER RECEIVING TDS

"I DON'T believe the NFL is the best," Alworth says. "Their defenses are not as complex and advanced as ours have become in the AFL. And their cornerbacks are just people. Our top four teams and the NFL's top seven are not far apart. I hope we get to play against them someday and shut them up."

—*Edwin Shrake, SI, December 13, 1965*

Tne brown-eyed Alworth was nicknamed Bambi.

5

RAYMOND BERRY

COLTS 1955–1967

❝ Berry was the first real technician in the modern passing game. ❞ —TIM LAYDEN

≥ RETIRED WITH MOST CAREER CATCHES, RECEIVING YARDS
≥ 12 RECEPTIONS, 178 YARDS IN 1958 TITLE GAME

WHEN I was a skinny kid just out of high school in an east Texas town called Paris, I went to see a movie named *Crazylegs* five times. It was about Elroy Hirsch, who played end for the Los Angeles Rams, and I decided then that the thing I wanted to do most in the world was to catch passes for a professional football team the way Hirsch did. I guess I haven't reached that goal completely. I play end for the Colts, but I don't catch passes the way Elroy did. I've spent hours a day studying game movies of Hirsch and other great offensive ends. But there are things you can't do—I should say I can't do—because I don't have the physical equipment. Some of the moves they make I can copy to a T—all the fakes and feints—but I'm not as fast as some of these guys and not as big or as tall as others, and there's nothing I can do about that. You can't grow and you can't run faster than your physical equipment lets you. All you can do is squeeze the very most out of what you have.

—Raymond Berry and Tex Maule, SI, October 5, 1959

Berry was an unheralded 20th-round pick from SMU.

PHOTOGRAPH BY WALTER IOOSS JR.

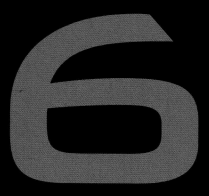

6

LARRY FITZGERALD

CARDINALS 2004-PRESENT

" Fitzgerald is a complete receiver who can run away from defenders, come down with contested catches and block defenders on the edge or down the field. His hand strength and body control make impossible catches seem routine. " —GREG A. BEDARD

≥ THIRD ALL-TIME IN CAREER RECEPTIONS (1,125)
≥ EIGHT 1,000-YARD SEASONS

FITZGERALD HAD the greatest postseason ever by a wideout, setting playoff marks for catches (30), yards (546) and touchdowns (seven). As Arizona went deeper into the playoffs, he dug deeper into the record book to know what marks were within reach. Fitzgerald studies the greats who preceded him—he can recite Jerry Rice's stats as if they were his own—and uses their numbers and stories as motivation. One day after concluding a training session with 14 straight 110-yard sprints—each to be completed in 16 seconds or less, with 45 seconds rest in between—Fitzgerald plopped onto a metal bench and asked a visitor if he'd ever seen an NFL player work harder. When the visitor told him he hadn't, Fitzgerald said, "Good. Because if you had said someone was working harder than me, I would've had to get up and run two more."

—Jim Trotter, SI, September 7, 2009

Fitzgerald is both a deep threat and a chain-mover.

PHOTOGRAPHS BY JOHN W. MCDONOUGH (LEFT) AND PETER READ MILLER

7

TERRELL OWENS

49ERS 1996–2003
EAGLES 2004–2005
COWBOYS 2006–2008
BILLS 2009
BENGALS 2010

" Terrell Owens was one of the most dominant wideouts ever. Just ask him, he'll tell you. He was a receiving threat whose talent was as outsized as his personality. " —CHRIS BURKE

≥ THIRD IN CAREER RECEIVING TOUCHDOWNS (153)
≥ 1,078 CAREER RECEPTIONS

FEW ATHLETES are as motivated by anger as Owens. He was so incensed after dropping four passes in a 30–26 loss to St. Louis that he scored six times over the next three games. He had 20 receptions and four touchdowns in the two weeks following his return from last season's suspension [for celebrating a touchdown on Dallas's midfield star]. . . . Owens is sincere, honest and loyal to those who back him. He's also a distrustful loner who doubts that a leadership role would fit him easily. "Jerry [Rice] always told me that when you're in the spotlight, you have to be a politician," Owens says. "That's one thing that I never agreed with. I know I can't change the way people feel about me, but that's fine. Because they will never change the way I play."

—*Jeffri Chadiha, SI, November 26, 2001*

Talented but difficult, Owens inspired strong reactions.

PHOTOGRAPH BY BOB ROSATO

HAVE 'TUDE, WILL TRAVEL

If the talented, tempestuous wideout and a counterpart from the NBA ever conversed, would they come to appreciate the reasons why their careers came to such unceremonious ends?

BY PHIL TAYLOR

LAST WEEK WAS QUITE A COMEDOWN for a pair of job-hunting former stars, Terrell Owens and Allen Iverson. Owens held a workout at a Los Angeles–area high school, but no NFL teams took him up on his invitation to attend. (T.O. also had to deal with a report that he had tried to commit suicide with an overdose of pills in early October, which he denied through his publicist.) After a year out of the NBA, Iverson, who once said he felt disrespected when asked to come off the bench, told Yahoo! Sports that he's now willing "to help any squad in any capacity." If the temperamental twosome had commiserated with each other, I know just how the conversation would have gone. O.K., actually I don't. But don't you suspect it would have sounded something like this?

T.O.: You get any phone calls yet?

A.I.: Nope. I haven't even heard a rumor. You?

T.O.: Nothing.

A.I.: This is crazy. We're A.I. and T.O.—there's a reason you can't have an alphabet without us. I mean, you have six Pro Bowls in your back pocket, T.O. There's no club that could use a receiver with the second-most yards in NFL history? I know you're 37 and you had ACL surgery in April, but you're healthy now. Teams should be chasing you the way I used to chase my next jump shot.

T.O.: Trust me, you don't have to remind me how fantastic I am. I'm obviously in great shape—that's why I take my shirt off every 20 minutes. But what about you, A.I.? You're an 11-time All-Star guard with four scoring titles, a former MVP. You might be 36, but you could go out there right now and score 20 in your robe and slippers. A future Hall of Famer like you shouldn't have to send out word that he'd do anything for a roster spot. I never thought I'd hear the great A.I. sound so hum . . . so hum . . . .

A.I.: *Humble?* I know, I have a hard time saying it too. I guess you'll have to get used to it, considering the way the whole NFL ignored your workout last week.

T.O.: You should have stopped by. I could have used the company.

A.I.: No, that's not for me, man. A workout sounds too much like practice, and you know how I feel about practice. I mean, *practice?* We're talking 'bout *practice ?* Not a game. *Practice.* We're talking 'bout *prac* . . . .

T.O.: Yeah, sorry. I forgot. Didn't mean to get you going on that. I can't figure it out, though. The only team that's shown interest in me so far is from the Arena league, and I'm pretty sure they were just looking for some attention. I hate when people do that.

A.I.: All this free time has given me a chance to think, T.O. What if the only reason teams put up with us all those years was that we were so talented they had no choice? What if nobody seems interested in us now because we're not good enough to be worth the trouble anymore? People always did say that we weren't team players, that we were too wrapped up in ourselves. T.O.? You listening to me?

T.O.: What? Oh, sorry. I was staring at my abs.

A.I.: O.K., turn away from the mirror for a second. Think about it. Guys like us, superstars who happen to be a little high maintenance, don't get to go out on our own terms once we start to slip a bit. Look at Randy Moss. No one signed him because he's moody and demanding and can't give you a 1,200-yard season anymore. Same with Barry Bonds. He didn't want to retire after his Giants career ended, but no one wanted to take on all his baggage. Maybe if we had been easier to handle in our prime . . . .

T.O.: You could be right. It's a shame, though, because there's so much we could teach young players. We're a dying breed, A.I. Where are the prima donnas of tomorrow going to come from? Look at Larry Fitzgerald in Arizona. He hasn't had a quarterback who could get him the ball in two years, but he has to be so classy about it. He should be whining like a preschooler at nap time, the way I used to. I'm pretty sure Donovan McNabb has only 80 percent hearing in his right ear from all my yapping.

A.I.: Yeah, you were the master at that.

T.O.: Same with Calvin Johnson of the Detroit Lions. He made two touchdown catches in Dallas a few weeks ago, and did he once run to the star at midfield and do a look-at-me pose? No. Does he even *own* a Sharpie he can pull out of his sock to autograph the ball after he scores? I mean, how do these guys expect to get their own reality shows if they don't call attention to themselves? They're all about team, team, team.

A.I.: You don't have to tell me. Check out the NBA. You know what's amazing about Derrick Rose of the Bulls? It's not that he's the MVP at age 22; it's that he shows up at every practice. On time. That's wild. All the young stars today, like Kevin Durant in Oklahoma City and the Clippers' Blake Griffin, pretty much play with halos over their heads. It's as if nobody ever informed them that when you're that good, you can get away with doing—or not doing—whatever you want. Maybe they're lucky no one ever told them that.

T.O.: So you're saying that we're the ones who should take a lesson from them? Hmm. Could be. As soon as I get back in the league, I'll be a better teammate. I'll be different. It's never too late to learn.

A.I.: I don't know, T.O. Maybe sometimes it is. ∎

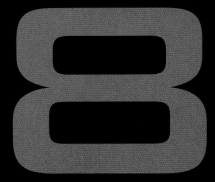

8

MARVIN HARRISON

COLTS 1996–2008

" Marvin Harrison and Peyton Manning were on the same page for longer than any receiver and quarterback pairing in NFL history. " —DON BANKS

≥ NFL RECORD 143 SINGLE-SEASON CATCHES
≥ 1,102 CAREER RECEPTIONS

IN AN era in which every touchdown seems to require a dance, Harrison is a stoic. "The big end zone demonstrators, they can't carry his sweatshirt," says Bills general manager Marv Levy. "Marvin Harrison makes fewer mistakes. He comes to play. He doesn't come to talk." An insatiable desire for the ball is one trait Harrison shares with his flamboyant contemporaries. When few passes are thrown his way, teammates know to keep away from him. His hunger extends to practices, where he still performs with the zeal of an undrafted rookie. ("We see a lot of Wow! catches," Colts coach Tony Dungy says.) When receivers coach Clyde Christensen suggested during training camp that Harrison decrease his reps—standard procedure for veterans—the receiver declined. "He works the cones in Week 14 just like he did in training camp of his fifth year in the league," says Christensen. "I get paid to practice," says Harrison. "I play the games for free."

—Nunyo Demasio, SI, January 8, 2007

STEVE LARGENT

SEAHAWKS 1976–1989

❝The future congressman was not especially tall (5' 11"), thick (187 pounds) or fast. But Largent excelled at getting open, turning route running into a science, his precision evident in each step.❞ —GREG BISHOP

≥ RETIRED AS CAREER RECORD HOLDER FOR RECEPTIONS (819)
≥ 100 CAREER RECEIVING TDS

"HE'S THE most deceptive receiver in football," says Raiders All-Pro cornerback Michael Haynes. "What makes him so special is that he'll change patterns to fit the situation. That's very unusual. It's almost as if the quarterback says to him in the huddle, 'Do whatever you want. Just get yourself open, and I'll throw to you.' " One time he ran downfield with Lester Hayes, the Raiders' All-Pro cornerback, in hot pursuit. Largent stopped, spun completely around and then took off across the middle to catch the ball. Then there's his signature move, the one where he leans so far in one direction that he looks as if he's going to topple over. But he doesn't. Without warning, he zips off in the other direction. "Steve is the master of tomfoolery," Hayes says. "He has run pass routes on me that I've never ever seen or dreamed about."

—*Jill Lieber, SI, October 20, 1986*

Largent missed only four games in his first 13 seasons.

10

PAUL WARFIELD

BROWNS 1964–1969
DOLPHINS 1970–1974
BROWNS 1976–1977

"One of the game's most fluid receivers, Warfield was a first-round pick of the Browns and later played in three Super Bowls for the Dolphins. He averaged 20.1 yards per reception for his career." —MARK GODICH

≥ EIGHT-TIME PRO BOWL
SELECTION
≥ PLAYED ON THREE
CHAMPIONSHIP TEAMS

PAUL WARFIELD is the one who never touches the ground, who dances around out there and, eventually, looks to heaven and pulls down a Bob Griese touchdown pass behind those poor fools on the other team who think they can cover him forever. On the Dolphins' second possession [in the AFC title game], second-and-five on the Miami 25, Griese faked a handoff, then quickly set himself to throw. His play-action froze Baltimore's Rick Volk, the safety on that side. Warfield took off, was bumped in a delaying tactic by cornerback Rex Kern and then fled past him. Kern tried to recover. Too late. Volk tried to recover. Too late. Griese's spiral arched over the head of the leaping Kern at midfield, and Volk on a motorcycle couldn't have caught Warfield.

—John Underwood, SI, January 10, 1972

Warfield got by his man in 1968.

10 THE

BEST TIGHT ENDS

NOT THAT OTHER POSITIONS HAVEN'T EXPERIENCED THEIR OWN EVOLUTIONS, BUT TIGHT ENDS HAVE HAD A PARTICULARLY PAINED CRAWL FROM THE PRIMORDIAL OOZE. IT'S NOT JUST THE AWKWARD PULL BETWEEN THE NOT-OBVIOUSLY-COMPATIBLE TASKS OF BLOCKING AND RECEIVING. AT TIMES THE POSITION'S VERY EXISTENCE HAS BEEN THREATENED. IN A 1992 SI STORY EXCERPTED ON THE PAGE DEVOTED TO NO. 7 TIGHT END OZZIE NEWSOME, ONE EXECUTIVE ACTUALLY PREDICTED THE EXTINCTION OF THE POSITION.

THAT EXECUTIVE'S PREDICTION WAS OFF—WAY OFF. IN THE PAST 25 YEARS THE POSITION HAS GROWN MORE PROMINENT IN THE MODERN OFFENSE. THREE TIGHT ENDS WHO WERE ACTIVE DURING THE 2016 SEASON WERE VOTED ONTO THE ALL-TIME LIST, WHICH IS THE HIGHEST NUMBER OF ACTIVE PLAYERS IN ANY CATEGORY. THIS IS THEIR TIME.

BUT THE TIGHT END'S MUDDLED HISTORY IS ONE REASON WHY, IN THIS CATEGORY, THERE'S A NOTABLE DISCONNECT BETWEEN RANK AND STATISTICAL PRODUCTION. JOHN MACKEY NEVER HAD MORE THAN 55 CATCHES IN A SEASON, A TOTAL THAT WOULD HAVE RANKED 14TH AMONG TIGHT ENDS IN 2016. BUT KEEP IN MIND WHEN YOU VIEW THEIR STATS THAT THE OLD-TIME TIGHT ENDS MADE THEIR MARK NOT JUST WITH CATCH TOTALS, BUT ALSO BY CHANGING THE WAY THE POSITION ITSELF WAS VIEWED.

1

TONY GONZALEZ

CHIEFS 1997–2008
FALCONS 2009–2013

" Among the first in a wave of tight ends who played basketball in college (his: Cal), Gonzalez revolutionized his position. " —GREG BISHOP

≥ HOLDS NFL CAREER RECORDS FOR RECEPTIONS, YARDS, TDS AT THE POSITION

GONZALEZ SAYS he was one of the worst players on one of the worst Pop Warner teams in Orange County, Calif. The league rules said that every kid whose parents paid the $180 entry fee had to play six downs in every game. That's how many Gonzalez played: six. Off the field his life was even worse. In eighth grade he was stalked by a pair of bullies. At the end of eighth grade, a couple of things changed. First, he stopped worrying about the bullies. Second, he found basketball. He scored 18 points in the first game he ever played, in a rec league in Huntington Beach. Basketball gave him confidence. "The next year, I went out for football at the high school because my brother was playing," he says. "The first day of practice, Eric Escobedo, a friend of mine, looked up and said, 'Gonzalez? What are you doing back out here?' Well, he didn't know I was different. After basketball, well, I got it. I figured it out. I could play football too."

—*Leigh Montville, SI, December 27, 1999*

Gonzalez is second only to Jerry Rice in career receptions.

2

JOHN MACKEY

COLTS 1963–1971
CHARGERS 1972

" Mackey had the hands and route-running abilities of a receiver, but he was more like a fullback after the catch. He couldn't be covered or tackled by one person. He was a revolutionary weapon at tight end. " —GREG A. BEDARD

≥ SIX TDS OF 50 OR MORE YARDS IN 1966
≥ INFLUENTIAL PLAYERS ASSOCIATION PRESIDENT

CENTER BILL CURRY, now the Colts' player rep, vividly recalls the first time Mackey ever opened up at a team meeting. "John has always been a great inspiration on the field," says Curry. "Late in a tough game most of us will be dragging ourselves around, working hard to give 98 percent. Then we'll see Mackey grabbing the ball and knocking guys down even though he is beat too, and so we all start giving 120 percent just the way he is. But he never used to say anything, just do it. Then once at a team meeting before an important game Johnny Unitas called on Mackey to say something and this time he did. 'Men,' he said, 'these guys really need their butts kicked, and we're going to go out and do just that.' It was simple and yet somehow electrifying and we did just that."

—Gwilym S. Brown, SI, August 30, 1971

Mackey was a rare deep threat for a tight end.

Winslow had three seasons with 88-plus catches.

PHOTOGRAPH BY ANDY HAYT

CHARGERS 1979–1987

3

"In the '80s, there were two tight ends who were as dangerous as wide receivers, and Winslow was just slightly more dynamic than Ozzie Newsome." —TIM LAYDEN

≥ FOUR-TIME ALL-PRO
≥ 13 CATCHES, BLOCKED FG IN 1982 PLAYOFF GAME AGAINST MIAMI

KELLEN
WINSLOW

WINSLOW IS a specimen—not only big, but also amazingly talented. "I've never seen anybody with his athletic ability," says Dan Fouts. "He may be the best player in the game, at any position. And I'm not saying that to cause controversy, just as a description. He can throw a football 80 or 100 yards."

—Rick Telander, SI, September 1, 1982

4

SHANNON SHARPE

BRONCOS 1990–1999, 2002–2003
RAVENS 2000–2001

" With the skills of a wide receiver, Sharpe retired as the game's most prolific tight end at the time, with 815 catches, 10,060 yards and 62 touchdowns. " —DON BANKS

≥ NAMED TO NFL ALL-DECADE TEAM FOR 1990S
≥ THREE 1,000-YARD SEASONS

"MY LISP didn't make me loud," Sharpe says. "That's just who I am. I was little and skinny as a kid. They called me Pee Wee. So I had to be loud. People say, 'Since you got rich and famous, you've become insufferable.' I say, "That's not true. I've always been insufferable."

—*Rick Reilly, SI, February 1, 1999*

Sharpe led his teams in receptions seven times.

5
MIKE DITKA

BEARS 1961–1966
EAGLES 1967–1968
COWBOYS 1969–1972

" Before there was Rob Gronkowski, an astoundingly precocious tight end early in his career who blocked well and caught touchdowns, there was Ditka. Check out Ditka's 14-game rookie-year numbers for Da Bears: 56 catches, 1,026 yards and 12 touchdowns. " —PETER KING

≥ 1961 NFL ROOKIE OF THE YEAR
≥ FIRST TE IN HALL OF FAME

DITKA WAS a Bear even at Aliquippa (Pa.) High when, as a scrawny 135-pound sophomore, he got kicked off the practice field for his own protection. Immediately Ditka was cleaning the locker room latrines and pounding out push-ups with such effort at home "you could hear the house rock," remembers his father, Mike Sr. The family was originally from the Ukraine, the grandfather's name was Dyzcko. Two uncles changed it to Disco, but Mike's dad went with the tougher-sounding Ditka. "I wasn't always the best, but nobody worked harder," says Ditka. "One-on-one. You and me. Let's see who's tougher. I lived for competition. Every game was a personal affront. Everything in my life was based on beating the other guy."

—Curry Kirkpatrick, SI, December 16, 1985

Ditka was named to five Pro Bowls, all with the Bears.

The three-time All-Pro plays with an obvious joy.

PHOTOGRAPH BY BRIAN SNYDER/REUTERS

6

ROB GRONKOWSKI

PATRIOTS 2010-PRESENT

" Gronkowski scored 38 touchdowns over the first three seasons of his career, and in the process helped to complete the shift of how tight ends are utilized. He is as tough a matchup as any Hall of Fame receiver. " —CHRIS BURKE

≥ 68 TDS IN 88 CAREER GAMES
≥ CAREER AVERAGE OF 15.0 YARDS PER CATCH

"PEOPLE SAY, 'He's doing too many things,' but [I do them] because I got nothing to do," Gronkowski said, sitting on what he calls his "chill couch" with his arms behind his head. "That's why I hit up every charity event and party I'm invited to. If I'm sitting at home, that's not productive. That's boring."

—*Chris Ballard, SI, September 3, 2012*

GRONK THE MASTERMIND

He's better known to the public as a fun-loving party machine, but talk to him about the Patriots offense and you'll see that Rob Gronkowski has conquered the complexities of football

BY ANDY BENOIT

LET'S START WITH A DISCLAIMER. This is a story about Rob Gronkowski: Tight End, not to be confused with the celebrity known as Gronk. There will not be a single scene set inside a club, at a beach or on a pool deck. No Instagram photos whatsoever. We're not here because Gronkowski is the NFL's best tight end. (He is.) We're here because he just might be the smartest.

Skeptical? Then consider Patriots coach Bill Belichick's take: "Tight end is, probably after quarterback, the hardest position to play in our offense. That's the guy who does all the *formationing*. The running back is usually in the backfield. The receivers are receivers. But the tight ends could be in their tight end location, they could be in the backfield, they could be flexed. They could be in the wide position. To formation the defense, those are the guys you're going to move. It's moving the tight ends that changes the defensive deployment."

And with that, we introduce you to a player you've seen but never truly known: Rob Gronkowski, Football Mastermind.

Gronkowski has seen significant playing time at four positions for the Patriots: traditional tight end, slot receiver, wide receiver and X-iso receiver (where he's split out alone on the weak side). This flexibility is what Belichick means by "formationing." As Belichick explains, "If you're always in the same spot, you're probably going to see only a few different looks. When you're in a lot of different spots, the look changes. Different assignments. Different techniques. A different picture on the defense. And as those multiples go together, it just becomes exponential. Three different plays become *15* plays."

A player is asked to do a litany of things only if he can do them well. Coaches and teammates marvel at Gronkowski's attention to detail. In particular, getting open has become a science for him.

"When I first got into the league, I just used to run," Gronkowski says. "Just run the route. Really no technique to it. I really couldn't separate myself from the defender." That, of course, was not good enough for the future Hall of Famer throwing him the ball.

"Tom [Brady] is a teacher," Gronkowski says. "At first he just tells you what to do. If you don't get it right after that, he'll come at you hard." One particularly brutal practice from his rookie season still sticks with Gronkowski. "Tom wanted me to get outside leverage on this flag route, and I just couldn't. I just kept going inside. And he just flipped out on me about it. He said, 'All right, the ball's not going to you then.' "

Brady stopped hounding the young tight end after he learned that route running is "all about little techniques," Gronkowski says. "Having defenders think you're going somewhere else. And always remembering to run what looks like the same route as before, but boom: At the top you stick it off one way or you stick it off the other."

Perhaps the biggest factor behind his success has been "learning how to read the safeties. There are a lot of routes, about five or six in the playbook, where if it's split-high [translation: two safeties deep], I have to run one route, and if it's single-high [one safety deep], I have another. My rookie year I always got it wrong. But eventually you know it in a second."

Here's where Gronkowski sets himself apart from other great pass-catching tight ends—and maybe solidifies his place in history. Offenses can't treat him as simply a receiver because, as Bills coordinator Greg Roman explains, "He can block like an offensive tackle. Nobody can run-block like him." People inside the Patriots' organization also say that Gronkowski, on his own volition, learns not only his own run-blocking assignments, but also those of players on the other side of the formation. That way he's prepared in case Brady flips the direction of a running play.

Keith Butler was an esteemed linebackers coach with the Steelers before being elevated to defensive coordinator last year. His debut was Week 1 in Foxborough. "I learned a lot from that game," Butler says. In it, Gronkowski caught three touchdowns from three positions. If you remove Gronkowski from the Patriots, Butler says, "their passing game would take a big blow. Big blow." Indeed. Last season, when Gronkowski was on the field, New England averaged 7.27 yards per pass play. When he was off, that number plummeted to 5.24.

Given that defensive play-callers often game-plan around Gronkowski, his effectiveness is even more impressive. After all, defenses apply more double-team concepts to him than any other tight end. Here, Gronkowski's impact is enormous. You could argue it's the reason New England doesn't have to invest in expensive wide receivers or pass-catching backs.

In conversation there's nothing Gronkowski can't elaborate on. He's asked about his mental process for reading the coverage on, say, second-and-10 near midfield.

Well, first off, "if it's a 10-yard route on second down and you accidentally do a nine-yard route but you get wide-open, that's fine. Totally fine, 100%," he says. But before that, "you have to figure out if it's man or zone defense. Throughout the week you go over the opponent's second-down scenarios. So when you put your hand down, it's like you're already watching the filming. Knowing something like, if this defender points to the safety, he's going to be in man. Or if he's way backed up, it's going to be zone."

O.K. But what happens if your opponent on film does one specific thing, but then you line up out there and see something totally different?

Gronkowski brightens: "That's the game of football, right there." ■

7

OZZIE NEWSOME

BROWNS 1978–1990

"In a game against the Bengals on Oct. 21, 1979, Newsome caught five passes for 90 yards. He would make a reception in his each of his next 149 games." —CHRIS BURKE

≥ RETIRED AS NFL'S FOURTH-LEADING RECEIVER ALL-TIME
≥ 7,980 CAREER YARDS, 47 TDS

THE NFL tight end has gone from being a multipurpose weapon of the 1960s, '70s and '80s—a real star—to being treated like a third tackle, the stepchild of the offensive line, in the '90s. Offensive coordinators have gone so far as to diagram tight ends right out of game plans. "At the peak of my career, I was a threat on every down," says Ozzie Newsome, who retired with more catches than any other tight end in NFL history. "But later on a tight end was lucky to be in for 60% of the snaps in a game." Today the all-around tight end is virtually obsolete. It's going to be up to newcomers like Derek Brown and Johnny Mitchell, this year's first-round draft picks of the Giants and Jets, to prove there's still a place in the game for the classic tight end. A dubious NFL watches. "I don't think there will ever be a classic tight end again," says San Diego player personnel director Billy Devaney. "The position really is extinct."

—Peter King, SI, September 7, 1992

Newsome's 662 career receptions were a tight end record.

PHOTOGRAPH BY ANTHONY NESTE

8

ANTONIO GATES

CHARGERS 2003–PRESENT

" Gates is a pass-catching machine. He has five seasons of at least 900 yards receiving and four with 10 or more touchdown catches. " —DON BANKS

≥ 111 CAREER RECEIVING TOUCHDOWNS, SIXTH-BEST AMONG ALL RECEIVERS
≥ FRANCHISE LEADER IN CATCHES, RECEIVING YARDS AND TOUCHDOWNS

Gates was named to the NFL's 2000s All-Decade team.

PHOTOGRAPH BY JOHN W. MCDONOUGH

"THE FIRST touchdown he ever caught was a corner route," says Doug Flutie, the quarterback who threw it. "Because he was so athletic, he could keep people's hands off him and get that inside release down by the goal line. I just put it up in the corner and he got it. By halftime I realized, This guy's a weapon."

—Damon Hack, SI, October 25, 2010

9

DAVE CASPER

RAIDERS, 1974–1980, 1984
OILERS 1980–1983
VIKINGS 1983

" The Ghost was acclaimed as both a pass catcher and a blocker. His 52 TDs rank ninth all-time among tight ends. " —MARK GODICH

≥ FOUR-TIME ALL-PRO
≥ MADE RENOWNED "GHOST TO THE POST" AND "HOLY ROLLER" PLAYS

Casper slipped by the Colts' coverage in 1977.
PHOTOGRAPH BY WALTER IOOSS JR.

KEN STABLER lofted the ball not at the left post but rather towards the right corner of the end zone. "I picked up the ball when it was halfway to me," Casper said. "When I looked up, it was going to the corner, not the post, so I just ducked the old head, turned and ran. When I looked up, it was there."

—Ron Reid, SI, January 2, 1978

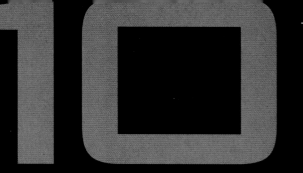

10

JASON WITTEN

" Mr. Consistent. Whatever the Cowboys have needed, Witten has done well. Terrific run blocker, precise route runner who lived in the seams, and his hands are among the softest at the position. " —GREG A. BEDARD

≥ 10-TIME PRO BOWL SELECTION
≥ 1,089 CAREER RECEPTIONS, SEVENTH ALL-TIME

BILL PARCELLS has never been fond of playing guys right out of college. So the most telling stat about Witten, a 2003 third-round pick out of Tennessee who excels as a blocker and a receiver, isn't that he averaged 63 catches over his first three pro seasons, but rather that he has 38 starts and just turned 24.

—*Sports Illustrated, September 4, 2006*

Witten has four of Dallas's top five receiving seasons.

PHOTOGRAPH BY DAMIAN STROHMEYER

THE 10

BEST OFFENSIVE LINEMEN

IN A POST-*MONEYBALL* WORLD, TALENT EVALUATORS TAKE PRIDE IN BACKING UP THEIR OPINIONS WITH STATISTICAL EVIDENCE. BUT WHEN YOU'RE TALKING ABOUT OFFENSIVE LINEMAN, IT'S MORE ABOUT THE BONE-CRUNCHING THAN NUMBER-CRUNCHING. THERE ARE NO STATS HERE. IF YOU ARE DESPERATE TO QUANTIFY GREATNESS MAYBE YOU CAN TALLY PRO BOWL SELECTIONS, BUT THAT IS REALLY NOTHING MORE THAN A CODIFICATION OF EYEBALL ANALYSIS.

IT'S NO SURPRISE THEN, THAT WHEN OUR PANELISTS SOUGHT TO JUSTIFY THEIR CHOICES FOR TOP LINEMEN, THEY INVOKED, MORE THAN THEY HAD WITH OTHER POSITIONS, THE TESTIMONY OF COACHES—VINCE LOMBARDI SAID THIS, JOHN MADDEN SAID THAT. BECAUSE IF THEY DON'T KNOW, THEN WHO DOES?

IN 1981 PAUL ZIMMERMAN WROTE A COVER STORY, EXCERPTED IN THIS SECTION, THAT BORE THE HEADLINE "THE GREATEST OFFENSIVE LINEMAN OF ALL TIME." IN IT DR. Z ASKED LEAGUE VETERANS TO NAME THE BEST-EVER, AND HE CAME UP WITH A NO.1 AND A NO.2. THOSE SAME PLAYERS WERE SLOTTED BY THIS PANEL NO. 2 AND NO. 8. SOME OF THE DISCREPANCY IS OWED TO THE PASSAGE OF TIME—THE NEW NO.1 PLAYER WAS JUST A PUP BACK THEN— BUT IT ALSO UNDERLINES THE SUBJECTIVITY OF OFFENSIVE LINE EVALUATION. THIS IS A BOOK OF OPINIONS, BUT NO PLACE MORE SO THAN HERE.

1

ANTHONY MUÑOZ

BENGALS 1980–1992

" Legendary offensive line coach Jim McNally once said: 'There has never been a lineman as great as Anthony Muñoz, and I doubt whether we will see his equal again.' " —DON BANKS

≥ 11-TIME ALL-PRO
≥ THREE-TIME NFL OFFENSIVE LINEMAN OF THE YEAR

WHEN THE helmet of a Texas Tech player struck Muñoz's left knee in the opening game of his senior season, he required major reconstructive surgery. Desperate to fulfill every Trojan's dream— participating in at least one Rose Bowl—Muñoz made it back for the game. He threw the key block that sprung tailback Charles White for the winning touchdown against Ohio State. At the game were Paul Brown, founder and general manager of the Bengals, and his sons, Mike, the assistant G.M., and Pete, the player personnel director, who were facing a decision: Whatever Muñoz's potential, could they risk using a first-round draft pick on a player with a questionable knee? Muñoz spent the day blowing away Buckeyes and the Brown family's fears. "The three of us sat there and laughed out loud," says Mike. "The guy was so big and so good it was a joke."

—*Jay Greenberg, SI, September 10, 1990*

The agile Muñoz caught four touchdown passes.

2

JOHN HANNAH

PATRIOTS 1973–1985

"The fourth overall pick in the 1973 NFL draft, Hannah was named All-Pro for 10 consecutive seasons, from 1976 to '85." —MARK GODICH

≥ NAMED TO NFL ALL-DECADE TEAMS FOR 1970S AND '80S
≥ MISSED ONLY FIVE GAMES DUE TO INJURY

ONE-BY-ONE, the Patriots' five starting offensive linemen lumbered into the locker room and gathered around a couch. The Pats had just beaten the Bills and the linemen were swapping tales—some a little taller than others—when Patriots offensive line coach Jim Ringo approached with a bottle of Johnny Walker Red in his hand. New England, in the penultimate game of the 1978 regular season, had broken the NFL's single-season team rushing record of 3,088 yards that had been set by the Bills in '73. Ringo poured congratulatory shots for his players, and for more than an hour they sat there together, drinking in their triumph and their whisky. "That season, that day, was as good as it got for me in pro football," says John Hannah, the guard who was elected to the Pro Football Hall of Fame in '91. "Our mark [of 3,165 yards] still stands. It was a total team effort."

—*Lars Anderson, SI, February 14, 2000*

Hannah cleared a path for Sam Cunningham.

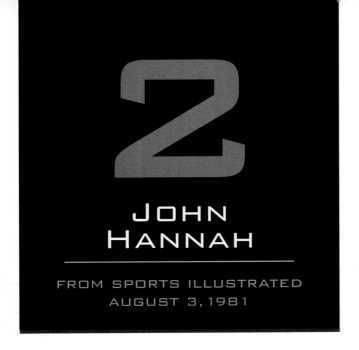

2

JOHN HANNAH

FROM SPORTS ILLUSTRATED
AUGUST 3, 1981

HANNAH DOESN'T FIDDLE AROUND

When Dr. Z evaluated offensive linemen three decades ago,
he concluded that the powerful Patriot was the best ever

BY PAUL ZIMMERMAN

SEE NOW, IT'S STARTING. AH, what a parade. Simply magnificent. All the great linemen in NFL history, the offensive linemen, those quiet, dignified toilers in anonymity. Here they come now, Look who's leading the way. Jim Parker. So big, so graceful. God was certainly generous when He created him. And see that little one snorting and pawing the ground, the one with the blood on his jersey? That's Abe Gibron. And there's the Boomer, Bob Brown. Look at those forearms. He once shattered a goalpost with one of them. And that giant blotting out the sun, that's Bob St. Clair, all 6' 9" of him. And there's Mike McCormack, tall, humble, brainy. Yes indeed, this is a parade.

What's that you say? You want to know who's the best of them? The very best? Now how can someone pick something like that? The mere act of it would be an insult to so many players who were so great in their eras. You say I must? O.K., fasten your seat belt. The greatest offensive lineman in history is playing right now and probably hasn't even reached his peak. He is John Hannah, the left guard for the New England Patriots, out of Alabama. He stands 6' 2½" and his weight fluctuates between 260 and 270. (No lineman can honestly claim only one weight.) He is 30 years old and is in his ninth year and is coming off the best season he ever had. He is a pure guard; he's never been anything but a left guard since he started playing in the NFL. He hasn't bounced around between guard and tackle as Parker did, or Forrest Gregg or Bob Kuechenberg; never had to go the offense-defense route like McCormack and Gibron and Chuck Bednarik.

Is it sacrilege to pick a current performer as the greatest who ever lived, in anything? Greatest actor, chef, rodeo rider? Should we wait until he's retired and enshrined and halfway forgotten? Weeb Ewbank, the former coach of the Baltimore Colts and New York Jets, thinks so. "Back off a little, give it some historical perspective," he says. "Let John make the Hall of Fame first."

Weeb's man is Parker, whom he coached for six years in Baltimore. Parker is also the choice of most of the coaches and personnel men who have been around the NFL for a few decades. McCormack generates surprising support, particularly from the Cleveland Browns' faction. Gibron is a dark horse. Hannah's line coach, Jim Ringo, favors a troika of Hannah, Parker and his old Green Bay teammate, Jerry Kramer, but some people feel that although Kramer and right tackle Forrest Gregg were legitimate superstars, they fell under the category of a perfect mesh in a perfect offensive line. The big-name centers of the past—Mel Hein, Frank Gatski, Bulldog Turner, Bednarik, Ringo—receive little support. The opinion is that guards and tackles work in a less protected environment. Only George Halas might remember Cal Hubbard, the legendary giant of the 1920s, and Halas isn't returning phone calls.

But Hannah has his following. Former Denver coach Red Miller says he's the man. So does John Madden, who coached against Hannah when he was with the Raiders. New England general manager Bucko Kilroy, one of the pioneers of modern scouting, who has been rating and evaluating players ever since he lined up against Bronko Nagurski in 1943, says Hannah and McCormack are the only offensive linemen to whom he'd award a perfect "9."

It starts with the firepower, with Hannah's legs, incredibly massive chunks of concrete. "Once we measured John's thighs, and they were

98

33 inches," says Hannah's wife, Page, a slim ash blonde. "I said, 'I can't bear it. They're bigger than my bust.'"

The ability to explode into an opponent and drive him five yards back was what first attracted the college recruiters to Albertville, Ala., where Hannah grew up and played his final year of high school ball. Hannah says he always had that ability, but it was his first coach at Baylor School for Boys in Chattanooga, a tough, wiry, prematurely gray World War II veteran named Major Luke Worsham, who taught him how to zero in on a target, to aim for the numbers with his helmet, to keep his eyes open and his tail low. Next came the quick feet. Forget about pass blocking if you can't dance. Worsham helped there too.

"Oddly enough," Hannah says, "he helped me develop agility and reactions by putting me on defense in a four-on-one drill. You'd work against a whole side of an offensive line. It was the most terrible thing in the world. If the guard blocked down you knew you'd better close the gap and lower your shoulder. If the end came down and the guard came out, buddy, you grabbed dirt because you knew a trap was coming."

"For all his size and explosiveness and straight-ahead speed," Kilroy says, "John has something none of the others ever had, and that's phenomenal, repeat, *phenomenal* lateral agility and balance, the same as defensive backs. You'll watch his man stunt around the opposite end, and John will just stay with him. He'll slide along like a toe dancer, a tippy-toe. And that's a 270-pound man doing that, a guy capable of positively annihilating an opponent playing him straight up."

Jim Parker said the only lineman he enjoyed watching was Hannah.

Parker, 47 years old now and the owner of a successful liquor store in Baltimore, says he's only gone to three games since he retired in 1967. "I get so flustered watching football nowadays," he says, "so carried away by watching guys making $100,000 a year and making so many mistakes in technique. I get so upset that I wake up with a headache the next morning from banging my head all night in my sleep. But I like to watch Hannah play. He's the only one out there who can do it all—every aspect. If you want me to rate myself, compared to him, I'll say that I sure would have enjoyed playing alongside him.

"I see some things in him that remind me of myself, the way he teases 'em on plays going the opposite way, the way he changes his style on aggressive pass blocking. One time he'll fire out, the next time he'll sit back, lazy, and make 'em think it's a regular pass and then—pow! He'll pop 'em. And on the running plays he's big enough to beat the hell out of them. I've seen him beat them right down into the ground. That's the joy of it, the joy I got out of it."

The joy of being even bigger in a big man's game. And quicker. The joy of being a superior athlete. Parker and Hannah were both gifted in other sports. They were both wrestlers. Parker was a mid-America champion. Hannah won the National Prep Championship and was unbeaten as a freshman at Alabama, before he quit wrestling because it was cutting into spring football. Hannah was also a three-year letterman in the shot and discus at Alabama and his 61' 5" toss in the shotput was a school record at the time. "He didn't even work at track,"

says his brother Charles, an offensive tackle for the Tampa Bay Buccaneers. "He'd just show up for the meets. At that time he might have been the greatest large athlete in the world."

The scouts were noting his numbers carefully. In the spring of Hannah's junior year, Bear Bryant, in an unaccustomed moment of generosity, let a combine scout onto the campus to time him in the 40 at the end of a track workout. Hannah weighed 305 pounds. He finished the last five yards falling on his face. "I apologized to the scout for being fat and out of shape," he says. "The guy said, 'Don't apologize. You just ran a 4.85.'"

It is 8:30 p.m. in Crossville, Ala. Hannah's 253-acre cattle and chicken farm is here, 15 miles northeast of Albertville, on a plateau in the Sand Mountain range. It's bedtime for the little Hannahs, nine-month-old Mary Beth and 2½-year-old Seth, except that Seth has no such plans. He's giving a graphic demonstration of what is known as bloodlines.

Seth is running wind sprints—through an obstacle course of chairs and toys. He weighs 37 pounds, not extraordinarily big, but sturdy enough, very solid through the shoulders and chest, big in the legs, like his daddy. He is running at top speed, all-out, but under complete control, with absolutely perfect balance. There's not a trace of a wobble. Every now and then he stops and throws back his head and lets out a loud roar. The Hannahs watch him, waiting for the motor to run down. It shows no signs of it. He turns his head to look at his daddy, and then runs smack into a high chair, bop, forehead first. He blinks, shakes his head and starts running again. "An offensive guard for sure," Page Hannah says.

Like the giant Antaeus, Hannah gets his strength from the earth—those 253 acres of it, 75 planted in feed crops, the rest devoted to livestock. He raises chickens, 43,000 at a time, in two houses. He has a bull and three cows of his own, and a herd of 134 Holstein cattle that he's raising for a breeder in Tampa. Someday he'll have his own herd of Santa Gertrudis, a Shorthorn-Brahman crossbreed developed in Texas. It is a Saturday afternoon in June, and the temperature is in the 90s. Hannah has just finished inspecting his chickens and trimming weeds around half a mile of electric fencing. His shirt is black with sweat, and he sits on the ground, his back against a wooden fence, watching his 2,200-pound Santa Gertrudis bull.

The bull is walking slowly to the water trough, the rich red-brown of his hide gleaming in the afternoon sun, his hindquarters swaying gently, the huge muscles of his shoulders bunching and relaxing. A gentle, magnificent animal. The three heifers at the trough slide sideways to let him through, and then stare at him as he drinks. Hannah laughs and shakes his head.

"Goes anywhere he wants, does anything he wants," he says. "Who's gonna argue with him? People come from all over just to see him. He's still a baby, only four years old. He'll be 2,800 pounds, at least, when he's full-grown. I like to come down here and sit against this fence and just look at him.

"Ain't he something?"

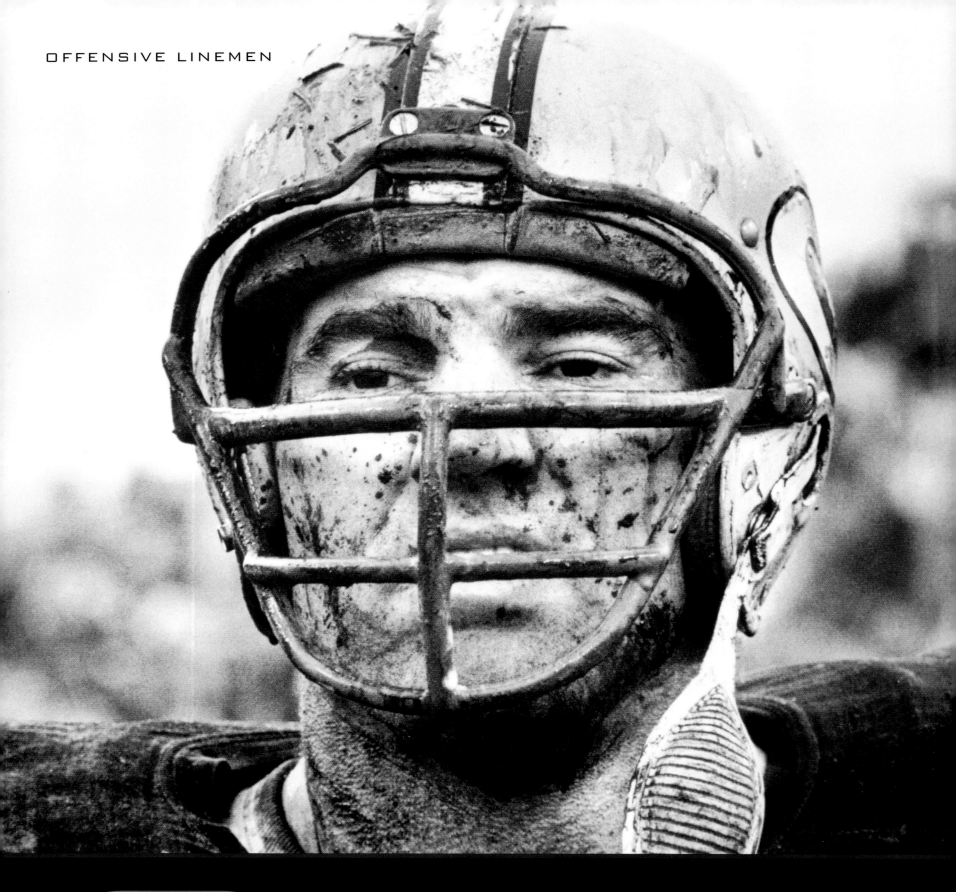

3

FORREST GREGG

PACKERS 1956, 1958–1970
COWBOYS 1971

"Vince Lombardi declared the right tackle the finest player he ever coached. Gregg's technique was flawless, and his ability to drive-block and finish opponents on the move opened up the Packers' run game." —GREG A. BEDARD

≥ EIGHT-TIME ALL-PRO
≥ PLAYED ON SIX CHAMPIONSHIP TEAMS

Undersized for tackle, Gregg relied on his smarts.

PHOTOGRAPH BY VERNON BIEVER/AP

AT 35, Forrest Gregg is one of the oldest players on the team. His assignment was blocking Deacon Jones. Most teams block Jones with two and sometimes three men but for the most part Gregg took on Jones alone. Gregg plays his position with more finesse than any other player in the league.

—Tex Maule, SI, October 28, 1968

4

BRUCE MATTHEWS

OILERS/TITANS 1983–2001

"One of the most durable and versatile big uglies of all time, Matthews played 296 games over 19 seasons and started at least one game at every position on the offensive line." —TIM LAYDEN

≥ RECORD-TYING 14 CONSECUTIVE PRO BOWL SELECTIONS
≥ ALL-PRO AT BOTH CENTER AND GUARD

WHEN CLAY and Bruce Matthews get together for a little brotherly competition, it's best to have an ambulance on standby. Boxing matches can turn into knock-down-drag-out fistfights; in Bruce's wedding pictures, you can see a scratch on his forehead that came from roughhousing with his brother. A simple game of one-on-one basketball on Clay's backyard court usually turns into a shouting match, or escalates into so much banging and shoving that one of them gets a black eye, bloody nose or cut lip. "We find losing so disgusting that we refuse, by sheer effort, to lose," Clay says. "With time, effort and the will to win, we prove ourselves in the long run," Bruce says. "No matter what the sport is, if we play long enough, we will beat you."

—*Jill Lieber, SI, September 10, 1990*

Matthews excelled at multiple positions.

Allen made the Pro Bowl at three positions.

COWBOYS 1994–2005
49ERS 2006–2007

"He was everything a coach could ask for in a guard—or in a tackle. Allen, with his elite combination of power and quickness, excelled from both spots over his storied career." —CHRIS BURKE

≥ SEVEN-TIME ALL-PRO
≥ NAMED TO NFL ALL-DECADE TEAMS FOR 1990S AND 2000S

LARRY ALLEN

IT'S BEEN a happy time at the Cowboys' summer camp. On timing and measuring day Larry Allen bench-pressed a team-record 600 pounds. Then he ran a five-flat 40, at 320 pounds. "I was embarrassed by the season I had last year," Allen said. "I don't even know why I was picked All-Pro."

—Paul Zimmerman, SI, August 17, 1998

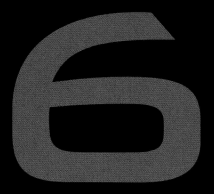

6

MIKE WEBSTER

STEELERS 1974–1988
CHIEFS 1989–1990

"His life was divided into two acts. The first is what happened during his career: four Super Bowls, nine Pro Bowls, five nods as a first-team All-Pro. Then, after: dementia, depression, months spent living out of his truck. Webster impacted football even in death, as he was among the first retired players to be diagnosed with CTE." —GREG BISHOP

≥ NAMED TO NFL ALL-DECADE TEAMS FOR 1980S AND '90S
≥ MISSED ONLY FOUR GAMES IN HIS FIRST 16 SEASONS AND PLAYED IN MORE GAMES (220) THAN ANY STEELER

IT WAS a locker room filled with huge personalities—Mean Joe Greene, Lynn Swann, Terry Bradshaw and Jack Lambert, who'd take out his teeth and growl, just to keep you loose. But if I wanted to know what really happened on the field, if I had technical questions, I went to Mike Webster. I talked to Webster in that locker room many times, and he never lied or sugar-coated. And after I'd interview him, he'd thank me, then smile and point to the crowded section of the locker room and say, "Better go talk to the superstars." In his mind he was just a workingman who played center. Many people feel no one ever played it better.

—Paul Zimmerman, SI, October 7, 2002

Webster was a Steelers captain.

PHOTOGRAPH BY TONY TOMSIC

7

JIM PARKER

" No offensive lineman accomplished what Parker did—making All-Pro four times at tackle and four times at guard. Anthony Muñoz may well have been a better pure tackle, but Parker and Bruce Matthews would probably duel for the best all-around blocker ever. " —PETER KING

≥ EIGHT CONSECUTIVE PRO BOWL SELECTIONS
≥ UNITAS'S KEY PROTECTOR

AN OFTEN overlooked sidelight to the famous Giants-Colts championship game in 1958 was the job that Parker did on defensive end Andy Robustelli. His domination of Robustelli was something different, a performance so smooth, so complete, that it was used as a textbook case for many years.

—*Paul Zimmerman, SI, September 5, 1994*

Parker battled fellow alltime great Bob Lilly in 1966.
PHOTOGRAPH BY ART SHAY

RAVENS 1996–2007

Ogden dwarfed rushers like Seattle's Okeafor.

PHOTOGRAPH BY SIMON BRUTY

8

JONATHAN OGDEN

" The first draft pick in Baltimore
Ravens history could block
out the sun with his 6' 9",
340-pound frame. What chance
did mere mortals have lining up
against him? " —DON BANKS

≥ 11 CONSECUTIVE PRO BOWL
SELECTIONS
≥ NINE-TIME ALL-PRO

AS OGDEN slides out he begins pushing
Chike Okeafor, who is futilely slapping
Ogden's long arms. "It's not only [about]
having great hands and strength but also
balance," says Ogden. "I have to engage
this guy while he's sprinting toward me
and I'm moving back. Without balance I'll
fall, and he'll be past me."

—*Peter King, SI, December 8, 2003*

GIANTS 1931–1945

Hein played linebacker as well as center.

PHOTOGRAPH BY AP

" It's a pretty big honor to be a charter member of the Pro Football Hall of Fame, particularly when men like Otto Graham and Sid Luckman weren't. And though the post-Depression years in NFL history are sketchy, eyewitnesses say he was a block of granite at center. " —PETER KING

≥ 1938 NFL MVP
≥ NEVER MISSED A GAME

HEIN PLAYED in 172 consecutive games. "And I never lost a tooth," he said with pride. An All-Pro eight years in a row, in 1938 he helped the Giants win the NFL title. "He should be barred from football," said Green Bay coach Curly Lambeau. "He's too good."

—*Sports Illustrated, February 10, 1992*

9

MEL HEIN

10

DWIGHT STEPHENSON

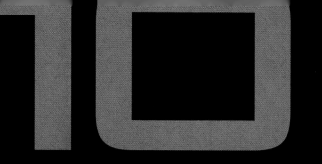

" Though he played only eight seasons and didn't start until late in his second year, Stephenson was considered the best center in the game. He anchored a line that allowed the fewest sacks in six consecutive seasons. " —MARK GODICH

≥ FOUR-TIME ALL-PRO
≥ NAMED TO NFL ALL-DECADE
TEAM FOR 1980S

THE MIAMI line has given up just 14 sacks since 1983, fewer than any other team, and Stephenson is the major reason. "We use an unusual blocking system because of him, because he can always go one-on-one," says quarterback Dan Marino. "And that system is why teams can't blitz us."

—*Rick Telander, SI, September 30, 1985*

Stephenson brought athleticism to the center position.

PHOTOGRAPH BY JOHN IACONO

10 THE

BEST DEFENSIVE LINEMEN

OFFENSIVE PLAYERS MAY ENJOY A DISPROPORTIONATE SHARE OF GRIDIRON GLORY, BUT SAY THIS FOR THE DEFENSE— THEY GET THE BETTER NICKNAMES, AT LEAST AS FAR AS UNITS ARE CONCERNED. JUST IN THIS SECTION ON DEFENSIVE LINEMEN, WE HAVE REPRESENTATIVES OF THE STEEL CURTAIN, THE PURPLE PEOPLE EATERS AND THE FEARSOME FOURSOME. IF ONLY PLAYERS FROM THE NEW YORK SACK EXCHANGE OR THE ORANGE CRUSH HAD MADE IT, THIS SECTION COULD DOUBLE FOR A LIST OF THE BEST UNIT NICKNAMES EVER.

THE CREATIVITY WANES ON THE INDIVIDUAL LEVEL—AMONG THE TOP 10 WE HAVE BOTH A "MINISTER OF DEFENSE" AND A "SECRETARY OF DEFENSE," FOR EXAMPLE. ONE OF THE COWBOYS REPRESENTED HERE WAS KNOWN AS "MR. COWBOY." THE MOST MEMORABLE PLAYER NICKNAME HERE IS THE SIMPLEST: MEAN.

WITHIN THE DEFENSIVE LINE THE DIVISION OF LABOR TENDS TO SHINE MORE ATTENTION ON THE ENDS. THEY ARE THE ONES MORE LIKELY TO SACK THE QUARTERBACK—AND THEN DANCE OR POSE IF THE MOOD STRIKES THEM—WHILE THE HUSKIER TACKLES TAKE ON BLOCKERS INSIDE. IN CHOOSING THE TOP 10 LINEMAN THOUGH, THE PANEL, THROUGH NO PLAN OR DESIGN, HONORED TACKLES AND ENDS IN EQUAL NUMBER, WHICH IS A HAPPY COINCIDENCE. ON THIS SIDE OF THE BALL, IT'S ALL ABOUT PUTTING TOGETHER A GOOD UNIT.

1

REGGIE WHITE

EAGLES 1985–1992
PACKERS 1993–1998
PANTHERS 2000

" The Rev. White, an ordained minister (dubbed "The Minister of Defense" during his career) was a force from his rookie year with the Eagles. In his second, third and fourth seasons, he averaged 19 sacks. " —TIM LAYDEN

≥ TWO-TIME NFL DEFENSIVE
PLAYER OF THE YEAR
≥ SECOND ALL-TIME IN
CAREER SACKS WITH 198

WHITE IS the locker room sage to whom the younger Packers turn for inspiration or advice. Older teammates kid him about everything from his habit of calling team meetings—"He calls more meetings than Congress," says safety LeRoy Butler—to his staunch refusal to listen to practically anything but gospel music during his and Butler's shared rides to practice. White's teammates know that his preaching about putting the team first isn't just talk. Despite the meat-grinder nature of the position he plays, until last season he had never missed a nonstrike NFL game. He came into the NFL saying that he wanted to be the best defensive lineman ever, and more than a decade later, he's still rolling toward quarterbacks like a wave of lava, burying whatever is in his path.

—Johnette Howard, SI, September 2, 1996

White was an eight-time All-Pro.

PHOTOGRAPH BY PATRICK FERRON/GREEN BAY PRESS-GAZETTE/AP

DEACON JONES

RAMS 1961–1971
CHARGERS 1972–1973
REDSKINS 1974

" Thank the Lord for pro football researchers. Studying play-by-play sheets from the era before official sack stats were kept, they found these numbing numbers: In a 14-game season, Jones, from 1963 to 1969, put up 20, 22, 19, 18, 26, 24 and 15 sacks in those seasons. No wonder his old coach George Allen called him the greatest defensive end of all time. " —PETER KING

≥ TWO-TIME NFL DEFENSIVE PLAYER OF THE YEAR
≥ EIGHT-TIME PRO BOWL SELECTION

IT SHOULD come as no surprise that when asked about his patented head slap, Jones is only too happy to demonstrate it in slow motion, bringing his left palm flush up against a reporter's right ear, producing a ringing sensation that lingers long after. "You think that rings?" Jones says. "I had a metal plate cut to fit in the palm of my hand." To this day his grin is distilled evil, an offensive tackle's nightmare. "I used to wrap that mother with a wet cast, then let the cast dry. That's what you got upside your head, every 30 seconds."

"I've seen the films," says the Giants' Michael Strahan. "This guy was the best ever. He made defensive end a glamour position."

—*Sports Illustrated*, August 30, 1999

Jones was credited with inventing the term "sack."

PHOTOGRAPH BY NEIL LEIFER

3

JOE GREENE

STEELERS 1969–1981

"The cornerstone around which Pittsburgh's famed Steel Curtain was built, Greene could terrorize the quarterback and discourage the running game equally well from his tackle position." —DON BANKS

≥ TWO-TIME NFL DEFENSIVE PLAYER OF THE YEAR
≥ 10-TIME PRO BOWL SELECTION

PROFESSOR STUDIES SUPER BOWL, SAYS HAS MYTH QUALITY read the headline in the (New Orleans) *Times-Picayune* on Thursday morning before the game. Andy Russell was reading the story aloud at breakfast. "Sociologically speaking," said the lead, "the Super Bowl is a 'propaganda vehicle' which strengthens the American social structure." "I can't stand that stuff!" Joe Greene shouted. "'More than a game, it is a spectacle of mythical proportions which becomes a 'ritualized mass activity,' says Michael R. Real, assistant professor of communications at the University of California at . . . ." "----!" Greene cried. He seized the paper and tore it to shreds. "I'd like to run into that guy," he said. The Steelers have a number of stars and leaders of various kinds, but Greene is their sun. The main strength of the team is the defense, of the defense the front four, of the front four, Greene.

—Roy Blount Jr., SI, February 17, 1975

Greene was a master at finding angles of attack.

HE JUST DOES WHAT HE WANTS

He had the skills and he had the size, but it was his outrageous temperament that intimidated opponents, amazed teammates and made Joe Greene a gridiron terror

BY ROY BLOUNT JR.

JOE GREENE'S NICKNAME DERIVES from that of his college team, the Mean Green (thought up, incidentally, by a lady named Sidney Sue), but in the pros Greene has done a number of things to deserve it. In his rookie year he was ejected from two games. Once he threw his helmet so hard at a goalpost that pieces of helmet went flying. Another time, after an opposing guard had hit him a good clean block, he seized the offender with one hand on each shoulder pad and kicked him flush between the legs. One day he was glaringly outplaying a good Cincinnati guard named Pat Matson, a 245-pound ball of muscle, until at last Matson developed a bad leg and began limping off the field. Greene ran over and grabbed him before he reached the sideline and tried to coax him back into play, crying, "Come on, I want you out here." "I'll never forget the look on Matson's face," says Steelers defensive captain Andy Russell. There is even a story that once after being thrown out of a game Greene returned to the bench in such a rage that he opened up the equipment manager's tool chest and pulled out a screwdriver. Whatever he intended doing, he had second thoughts and threw it down.

Then there was the time he spit on Dick Butkus. The Bears were humiliating the Steelers. Butkus was blitzing at will, taking long running starts and smashing into the Steeler center just as he snapped the ball, and Greene couldn't stand it any longer. The Steeler offense was on the field. Greene had no business out there, but when Butkus passed within 10 feet of the Steeler bench, Greene bolted out at him, yelling challenges, and drew back and spit full in Butkus's face.

"Butkus didn't look intimidated," says Russell, "but there was Greene obviously wanting to fight him, and fully capable of it, and you could see Butkus thinking, 'This wouldn't be the intelligent thing to do.'" So Butkus turned and walked back into the security of the carnage on the field. When Russell ran into Butkus in the off-season and asked him how he could let a guy spit in his face without retaliating, Butkus said, "I was too busy making All-Pro." Greene—who was himself named All-Pro for the fourth time, and NFL Defensive Player of the Year for the second time, last season—is perhaps the only man alive who could make Butkus come off sounding rather prim.

"Joe's first year," says Russell, "I didn't see how all that emotionalism could be real. It looked like showboating. But I realize now that he's that way. When I get beat I just think, well, I was out of position, I made a mistake, I'll do this to correct it. With Joe, it's in his psyche. It's like it's war, and the other side is winning because they're more violent. And he's the only guy I know, he can be playing a great game himself but if the team's losing he gets into a terrible depression. It could be an exhibition game!"

This season Greene looks different. His upper body is more conventionally muscular, his distinctive spare tire is gone. He has a championship to defend. Does all this mean he will be even better?

"When I dream at night," he says, "I visualize techniques. Some of 'em are just ungodly. It's just cat quickness; run over a guy, hurdle him, jump six feet, put three or four moves on him so he freezes. No flaws in those moves. Perfect push and pull on the guard, jump over the center. Another blocker, slap him aside. Block the ball when the quarterback throws it, catch it and run 99 yards. 'Cause I don't want it to be over quick! The only thing that ever matched the dreams I had was the Super Bowl."

Greene and team founder and owner Art Rooney seemed to enjoy the Super Bowl more than anybody. Rooney, the Chief, was in camp one afternoon this summer, standing beside the practice field. "I knew we were going all the way last year before the playoff game with Oakland when Joe came up to me. He grabbed my hand and said, 'We're gonna get 'em.' That was an emotional moment. I never had a moment like that."

Greene comes over and greets the Chief. They chat for a moment and then Greene moves away, saying, "Enjoy yourself now." It seems an odd thing, but a friendly thing, to say to one's owner.

"That Joe Greene," says the Chief. "He takes you. I've never seen a player lift a team like he does. I just hope he plays out his full years. He's the type of player who wouldn't want to be associated with a team that didn't play all-out."

There was a time when Rooney voiced doubts about Joe Greene. That was when the Steelers had drafted him No. 1 and he was holding out. "Who is he anyway?" the Chief grumbled. "I don't know that he's so good."

A few years later, Art Jr. would gesture at the photographs of old Steeler greats—Ernie Stautner, Whizzer White, Bullet Bill Dudley—covering the walls of his father's office and say, "Someday you'll have to take all these down and throw them away and put up one of Joe Greene."

But he didn't say that when the Chief questioned how good Greene might be. "Joe Greene is as good," is what Art Jr. told his father, "as you can imagine."

And if things stay close enough to being as good as Greene can imagine, pro football may be able to hold on to him—oops, that's the wrong term—may be able to keep him around a while longer. Meanwhile Mean Joe is nervous, and waiting, and doing, one way or another, what he wants to out there.

■

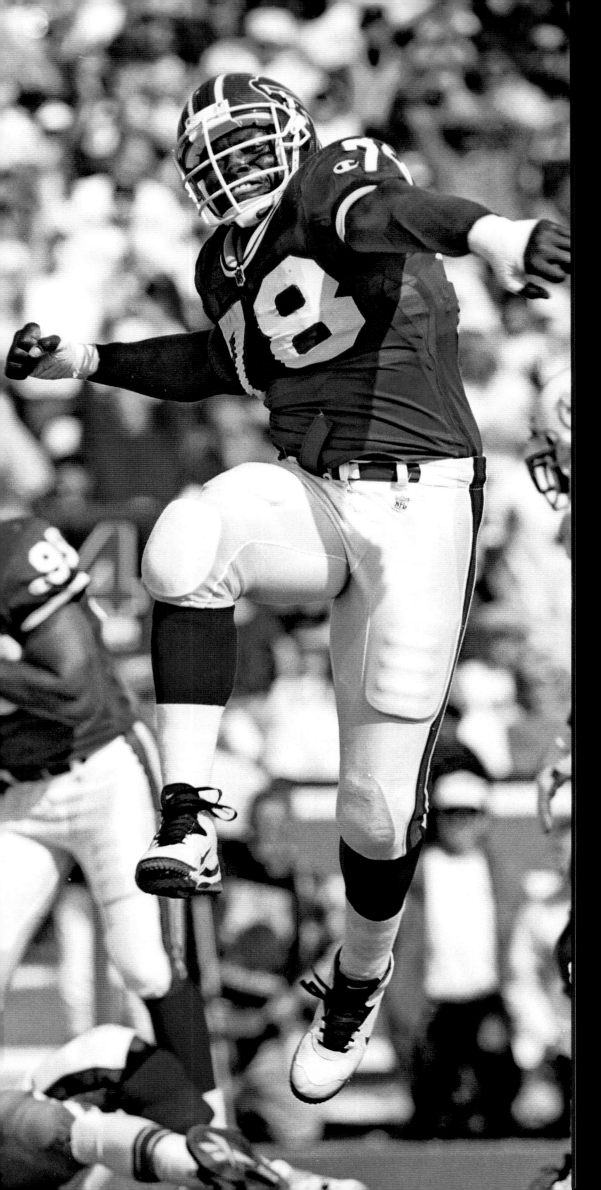

4

BRUCE SMITH

BILLS 1985–1999
REDSKINS 2000–2003

“Is Bruce Smith's spin move the greatest pass-rushing move of all time? It has to be close. But he could dominate with speed to the outside or power inside too. His sacks record could stand for decades.” —CHRIS BURKE

≥ ALL-TIME NFL SACKS LEADER WITH 200
≥ NAMED TO NFL ALL-DECADE TEAMS FOR 1980S AND '90S

"I THINK he's double-jointed," says Bills center Kent Hull. "He'll line up over me, and I'll try to hit him, and there's nothing there—he's going back and coming forward at the same time. There's no way a human being should do what he does." "Sometimes I've been in pass coverage and just laughed," says linebacker Darryl Talley. "The other team will have a tackle and a guard and a back blocking him, and if he beats them, the center comes over to help. It's just funny to see. It's like they're bees and Bruce has got sugar on him, like he's dipped in honey. But the most amazing thing to watch is his rush. Cornelius [Bennett, another Buffalo linebacker] and I can't figure it out—it's like a speedskater coming around the corner, he's so low to the ground, almost flat, with offensive linemen literally chasing him."

—Rick Telander, SI, September 2, 1991

Smith had 13 seasons with double-digit sacks.

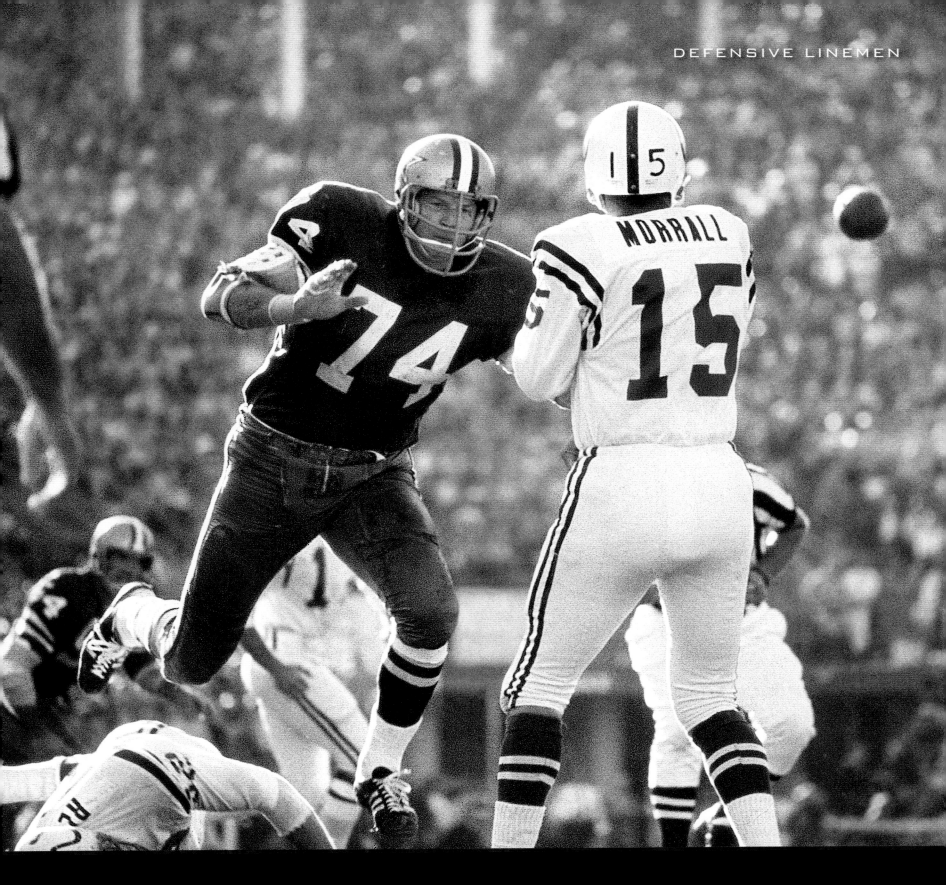

COWBOYS 1961–1974

Lilly was known as Mr. Cowboy.

PHOTOGRAPH BY NEIL LEIFER

5

BOB LILLY

" The best defensive tackle in NFL history, Lilly was the interior powerhouse in coach Tom Landry's flex defense. To move the ball on the Cowboys in the '60s and '70s, you had to block Lilly. " —TIM LAYDEN

≥ EIGHT-TIME ALL-PRO, 11-TIME PRO BOWL SELECTION
≥ MISSED JUST ONE GAME IN 14 SEASONS

BOB LILLY IS is one of the very few men who, merely by his personal contribution, can establish the whole character of a game. . . . He is a big, rock-hard man with a face that conceivably could make him a fortune in Western movies when John Wayne retires.

—*Tex Maule, SI, December 18, 1972*

6

ALAN PAGE

VIKINGS 1967–1978
BEARS 1978–1981

" A ferocious competitor for Minnesota's Purple People Eaters, Page's blend of quickness off the ball and strength made him one of the best interior pass rushers in league history. " —GREG A. BEDARD

≥ FIRST DEFENSIVE PLAYER VOTED LEAGUE MVP
≥ 173 SACKS, 28 BLOCKED KICKS

THE TURNING point was Alan Page. Until he arrived, the Vikings had good outside pressure but were weak at tackle. Page came as an end, a position he had played at Notre Dame, was quickly switched to tackle and went from mediocrity to greatness, and so did the Vikings. "I didn't want to change," Page says, "but now it's the only place I want to play. I was restricted at end. Inside I can do more things, go in more directions." "Carl Eller is probably the premier pass rusher today," says Bob Hollway, the Vikings' defensive coach. "He has strength, quickness and great leverage. Jim Marshall is probably the finest athlete on the defensive team. He has extraordinary balance and quickness. And Page is the most relentless player I've ever seen. He drains himself totally every game, and nobody gets off the ball quicker than he does."

—Pat Putnam, SI, December 14, 1970

Page's Vikings played in four Super Bowls.

THANKS, YOUR HONOR

The author met his childhood hero, who had graduated from being a football star to become a Minnesota Supreme Court justice, and found himself once again flooded with wonder

BY STEVE RUSHIN

T HE NATIONAL FOOTBALL LEAGUE was born in an automobile showroom in Canton, Ohio, on Sept. 17, 1920. Alan Page was born in that city nearly 25 years later—on Aug. 7, 1945, in the 72 hours between the bombings of Hiroshima and Nagasaki.

"Born between the bombs," affirms Page, the former Minnesota Vikings and Chicago Bears defensive tackle and 1971's NFL Most Valuable Player, now seated in his office in St. Paul, contemplating the era of his birth. "It's interesting, isn't it, given the significance of those bombs? It's funny you ask, because I *have* thought on occasion about what it all means. I haven't yet come to any conclusions."

Page has the disarming habit of saying "I don't know" when he doesn't know the answer to a question. It's a quality rare among star athletes and unheard of in elected officials. For most of his adult life Page has been one or the other: a gridiron luminary enshrined in 1988 in the Pro Football Hall of Fame—which was under construction in Canton when Page attended Central Catholic High there—and an off-the-field overachiever elected in November 1992 to the Supreme Court of Minnesota, on which he still sits.

"There's a danger for judges to assume they have all the answers," says Page, who seldom submits to interviews, explaining his reluctance to pontificate. "There's a saying one of my former colleagues used quite a bit in talking about this court: 'We're not last because we're right. We're only right because we're last.' I think that's something that you have to keep remembering."

I haven't yet told Page that he was my childhood hero, or that we have met before, nearly 26 years earlier, but I have come here to do just that—to St. Paul, hometown of F. Scott Fitzgerald, who wrote, "Show me a hero and I'll write you a tragedy."

"I've never understood the phenomenon of athlete worship, of how we get our athletic heroes," says Page, 54, when Fitzgerald's line is recited to him. "I can remember from the beginning, by which I mean my sophomore or junior year in high school, being looked on as a good football player, yes, but it went beyond my ability as a football player." People who had never met Page nonetheless began to admire him, and he found this profoundly disquieting. "I like to think that I was a good human being," he continues, "but people couldn't know that from watching me play football. So I kind of rejected the whole hero notion early on.

"There were times," he adds, a trifle unnecessarily, "when I didn't sign autographs."

You couldn't buy a number 88 Vikings jersey in Minnesota in 1974.

You could buy the 10 of Fran Tarkenton or the 44 of Chuck Foreman, but if you wanted the 88 of Alan Page your parents had to find a blank purple football shirt and have the numbers ironed on. As far as I know, my parents were the only ones who ever did. The jersey became my security blanket—what psychologists call a "transition object," the item that sustains a child in moments away from his mother. I wore the shirt until it simply disintegrated in the wash.

I grew up in the town in which the Vikings played their home games. Yet even in Bloomington, Minn., in the 1970s, I was alone among my schoolmates in worshipping Page. I knew only that he was genuinely great and that his Afro sometimes resembled Mickey Mouse ears when he removed his helmet. I at once loved Alan Page and knew nothing about him.

Then one unfathomable day in September '74, the month in which I turned eight, a second-grade classmate named Troy Chaika invited me to a Saturday night sleepover at the Airport Holiday Inn, which his father managed and where the Vikings bivouacked on the night before each home game. I could meet the players when they checked in and, if I asked politely, get their autographs.

After an eternity, Saturday came. My mom—God bless her, for it must have pained her beyond words—allowed me to leave the house in my 88 jersey, now literally in tatters.

I took my place in the Holiday Inn lobby—Bic pen in one damp hand, spiral notebook in the other—and recited my mantra rapid-fire to myself, like Hail Marys on a rosary: *"Please Mr.PagemayIhaveyour autograph?PleaseMr.PagemayIhaveyour autograph?PleaseMr.Page. . . . "*

Moments before the Vikings' 8 p.m. arrival, my friend's father, the innkeeper, cheerily reminded me to be polite and that the players would in turn oblige me. "Except Page," he added offhandedly, in the oblivious way of adults. "Don't ask him. He doesn't sign autographs."

Which is how I came to be blinking back tears when the Vikings walked into the Holiday Inn.

Page strode purposefully toward the stairwell. I choked as he breezed past; I was unable to speak. Still, I had never seen Page outside a television set and couldn't quite believe he was incarnate, so—my chicken chest heaving, hyperventilation setting in—I continued to watch as he paused at the stairs, turned and looked back at the lobby, evidently having forgotten to pick up his room key.

But he hadn't forgotten any such thing. No, Page walked directly toward me, took the Bic from my trembling hand and signed his name, *Alan Page*, in one grand flourish. He smiled and put his hand on top of my head, as if palming a grapefruit. Then he disappeared into the stairwell, leaving me to stand there in the lobby, slack-jawed, forming a small puddle of admiration and urine. ∎

7

MERLIN OLSEN

RAMS 1962–1976

" Olsen was a dominating defensive tackle whose superb technique and tenacity earned him a record 14 consecutive Pro Bowl selections. " —DON BANKS

≥ PLAYED IN 198 STRAIGHT GAMES
≥ LINCHPIN OF THE "FEARSOME FOURSOME"

AFTER A 15-year career, Olsen went into acting, playing a genial farmer on *Little House on the Prairie*, then an 1870s frontiersman do-gooder in *Father Murphy*. "That's who he was in real life," former Rams teammate Jack Youngblood says. Throughout his career, all in L.A., he took it upon himself to teach new players how to play the right way. A 1982 Hall of Fame inductee, he returned to Canton often to work with Hall of Fame Enterprises, which raises money for indigent former players. "He looked at the game and said, 'Darn it, this is wrong,' " Youngblood says. " 'We've got to treat retired players better.' " As one of the players in the Rams' famed Fearsome Foursome, Olsen's bullish presence helped the men to his left—Deacon Jones and later Youngblood—earn busts in Canton. The mark of a good teammate is to make those around you better, and Olsen did that during, and after, his life in football.

—*Peter King, SI, March 22, 2010*

Olsen dominated through smarts as well as size.

PHOTOGRAPH BY JOHN G. ZIMMERMAN

8

GINO MARCHETTI

TEXANS 1952
COLTS 1953–1964, 1966

Marchetti was named to 11 Pro Bowls.

PHOTOGRAPH BY WALTER IOOSS JR.

" Lauded as the NFL's best defensive end of its first 50 years, Marchetti was best known for his tenacious pass rush. He broke his leg in the epic 1958 NFL title game, but not before his key stop gave the Colts the chance to win. " —MARK GODICH

MARCHETTI DEVELOPED a new pass rush technique—grabbing and throwing—and relied on quick moves and footwork. "I've heard defensive players say, 'Hell, I didn't even get my uniform dirty playing against Marchetti,' " said Weeb Ewbank, Marchetti's coach with the Colts. "Well, he dirtied a lot of quarterbacks' uniforms."

—Paul Zimmerman, SI, August 28, 2000

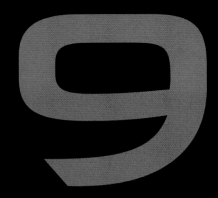

9

MICHAEL STRAHAN

GIANTS 1993-2007

" The gap-toothed sackmaster was long and lean and plowed into quarterbacks with his patented bull rush. He also set the single-season sack record with 22½ in 2001, and in Super Bowl XLII he led the Giants' upset of the undefeated Patriots. " —GREG BISHOP

≥ 141 ½ CAREER SACKS
≥ 2001 NFL DEFENSIVE PLAYER OF THE YEAR

"ON THIS play I'm in a rush to get to Kurt [Warner] because I'm close, he's still got the ball and I see it, and this may be my last chance in the game to make something big happen. Even though [Rams tackle Ryan] Tucker's holding me, I see Kurt"—now the tape is rolling in super slo-mo— "and I know I got him. Just another second . . . There it is! Right there. I got him, I got him, I got him, I got him." Warner cocks his arm, but before he can pull the trigger, Strahan, with Tucker still hanging on, plows into the quarterback. The ball pops loose, and the Giants recover. "The double whammy!" Strahan says. "You know what my favorite part of the sack is, most times? I look over at our bench, and our coaches are jumping up and down. After the game Kurt came up to me and said 'Michael, I'm going to feel this the next few weeks.' I liked that."

—Peter King, SI, December 17, 2001

Strahan's two Super Bowl appearances were both wins.

COWBOYS 1975–1988

White was called The Manster—half man, half monster.

PHOTOGRAPH BY PHIL HUBER

10

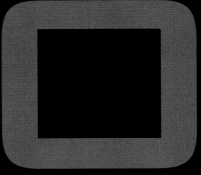

RANDY WHITE

❝ A DT as Super Bowl MVP? Almost unthinkable, but White pulled it off, splitting the award with teammate Harvey Martin at Super Bowl XII. An intimidating defender who physically wore down linemen. ❞ —CHRIS BURKE

≥ NINE-TIME ALL-PRO
≥ MISSED ONLY ONE GAME FOR INJURY IN 14 SEASONS

TO MESS with White is to reveal a flaw in your education. Hollywood Henderson said a little too much after practice, and added a slap to White's face. White put Henderson on the floor. "Thomas," he said, "let's just let this drop right now." But Henderson didn't let it drop. White then stuffed him in a locker.

—*John Underwood, SI, October 22, 1984*

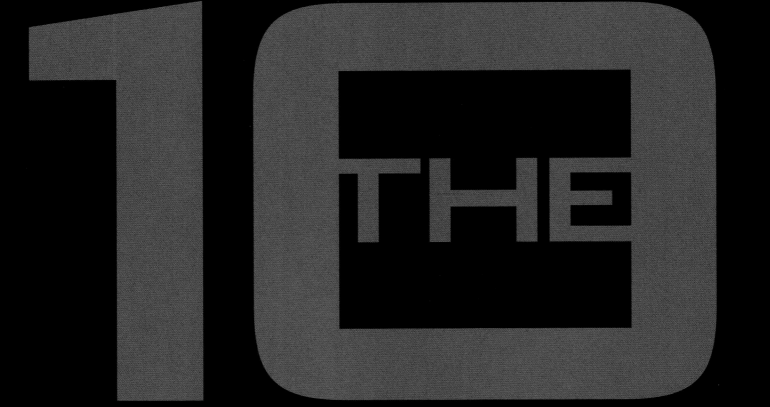

10 THE

BEST LINEBACKERS

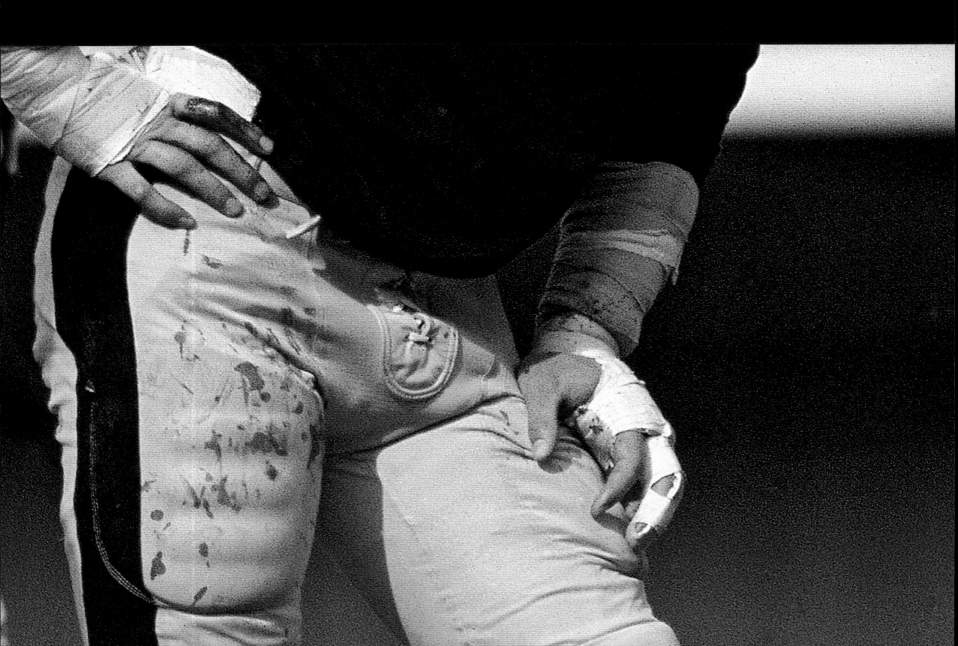

IN MOST OF OUR PLAYER CATEGORIES YOU SEE STYLISTIC DIFFERENCES AMONG THE MEN WHO MAKE UP THE TOP RANKS. AMONGST LINEBACKERS, NOT SO MUCH. HERE IT'S ONE THUNDERSTORM ROLLING IN AFTER ANOTHER. TRUE, AS OUR PANELISTS NOTED, THESE WERE THUNDERSTORMS WHO STUDIED FILM AND WHO IN MANY CASES FUNCTIONED AS THE CEREBRAL QUARTERBACKS OF THEIR DEFENSES. BUT STILL, EVERY PLAYER ON THIS LIST COULD MAKE OPPONENTS RUN FOR COVER.

THE TOP FOUR LINEBACKERS MADE A PARTICULAR IMPRESSION, ATTRACTING VOTES WITH A DEEPER UNANIMITY THAN FOUND IN OUR OTHER CATEGORIES. OUR NO. 1 MAN, LAWRENCE TAYLOR, WAS RANKED FIRST ON SIX OF THE SEVEN BALLOTS, WHICH TIED HIM WITH WIDE RECEIVER JERRY RICE FOR THE BEST OVERALL TALLY AMONG INDIVIDUALS. OUR NEXT TWO LINEBACKERS, DICK BUTKUS AND RAY LEWIS, SCORED MOSTLY 2S AND 3S. OUR FOURTH MAN, JACK LAMBERT, WAS NUMBER 4 ON MORE THAN HALF THE BALLOTS.

YOU MIGHT SAY THAT A GROUP OF LINEBACKERS FOR A DREAM 3-4 DEFENSE HAD BEEN CLEARLY IDENTIFIED, IF NOT FOR THE AWKWARDNESS OF HAVING THREE MIDDLE LINEBACKERS TAKING THE FIELD. WHO WOULD HAVE BEEN IN CHARGE—LEWIS, BUTKUS OR LAMBERT? IT'S HARD TO IMAGINE ANYONE IN THAT GROUP STANDING DOWN—WHICH IS WHY THEY ARE ALL SO HIGH ON THE LIST.

1

LAWRENCE TAYLOR

GIANTS 1981–1993

" The most feared pass rusher of his day, and likely ever. And it didn't matter the importance of the game—he was all-in. I'll never forget one game in 1987 during the players' strike, and Taylor crossed the picket line. He played his guts out, even lining up at tight end on offense, in an ugly loss to Buffalo. Afterward Giants owner Wellington Mara told him he'd never forget what he did and how he played. " —PETER KING

≥ THREE-TIME NFL DEFENSIVE
PLAYER OF THE YEAR
≥ 1986 NFL MVP

"WHAT MAKES LT so great, what makes him so aggressive, is his total disregard for his body," says Bill Belichick, the Giants' defensive coordinator. Taylor seems to get a morbid, masochistic delight out of his ferocious tackles. When Taylor is not delivering the hits, he enjoys watching them. "In defensive meetings, while we're studying film, all of a sudden Lawrence will say, 'Ah, Bill. Run that play back again,'" Belichick says. "And I'll realize he's looking at some guy 20 yards away from the ball—a wide receiver who was knocked off the screen by a defensive back. I've even seen him get his thrills watching one of our own guys get dusted."

—Jill Lieber, SI, January 26, 1987

Taylor had 132 ½ career sacks.

2

DICK BUTKUS

BEARS 1965–1973

" His name is synonymous with his position and brutal, old school football. Lost in the very real memory of Butkus's violence is his remarkable athleticism. He played the entire width of the field and also intercepted 22 passes in a career blunted to nine years by knee injuries. " —TIM LAYDEN

≥ SEVEN-TIME ALL-PRO
≥ 27 CAREER FUMBLE RECOVERIES

BEARS FANS still think of him as the ultimate in ursine violence. Take the folks at a bar called Chances R on a recent afternoon. The barkeep is a mountainous Irishman named Larry Mahoney, equally adept at bouncing a drunken housepainter or trilling a ballad in his fine tenor. "Hey, let's play a word game," Mahoney chirps to his assembled parishioners on this particular day. "What do you think of when I say 'Dick Butkus'?"

"Killer," say a young long-haired couple named Bill and Dee, whose motorcycle had just been blown over by a line squall. "Bull," says another patron. Others chime in: "Wild boar." "King Kong." "Mayor Daley." "Mean and nasty." "Elizabeth Taylor." Elizabeth Taylor? "I can see it," says Mahoney. "Butkus has the same kind of ego, the same self-dedication or cruelty or something."

—*Robert F. Jones, SI, September 21, 1970*

Butkus was defined by an unquantifiable ferocity.

RAVENS 1996–2012

Lewis delivered both tackles and leadership.

PHOTOGRAPH BY BOB ROSATO

3

RAY LEWIS

" One of the most vicious, most physical and most cerebral middle linebackers ever, Lewis was the heart and soul of a Ravens defensive unit that was among the most dominating in NFL history. " —GREG A. BEDARD

≥ TWO-TIME NFL DEFENSIVE PLAYER OF THE YEAR
≥ 13-TIME PRO BOWL SELECTION

WHEN MIKE SINGLETARY took over as Ravens linebackers coach in 2003, Lewis was playing at a level few had ever seen. But Lewis begged for instruction. Whatever Singletary said, Lewis soaked up; once he suggested Lewis play more on the balls of his feet, and in the next practice Lewis collapsed because his calves were cramping.

—S.L. Price, SI, November 13, 2006

4

JACK LAMBERT

STEELERS 1974-1984

" Menacing in demeanor, able to play
the run or the pass with equal skill,
Lambert was the heart and soul of
Pittsburgh's great Steel Curtain defense
of the '70s." —DON BANKS

≥ 1976 NFL DEFENSIVE
PLAYER OF THE YEAR
≥ NINE CONSECUTIVE
PRO BOWL SELECTIONS

ONE PITTSBURGH sportswriter
has called Lambert "the Nureyev
of linebackers," a clear reference
to his ability and balance in
the middle of muddle. "Who's
Nureyev?" Lambert asks, deadpan.
The ballet dancer is defined for
him. "I don't know if that's a
compliment or an insult," he says,
after pondering the information.
"But I guess those guys are
pretty good athletes. I'll take it
as a compliment." Other oldtime
Steelers fans liken Lambert to
the tough players of the team's
early, losing years—men like Ernie
Stautner and Bobby Layne, who
hurt you when they played you,
win or lose. "I like that comparison
better," Lambert says. "That's what
I'd really have liked, to play back in
those days even though the money
was hardly there. They played for
the game—and to hit. Cripes, 50
bucks a game, but they loved it."

—Robert F. Jones, SI, July 12, 1976

Lambert was Pittsburgh's defensive captain.

BEARS 1981–1992

" Singletary is another iconic figure in NFL history, exhaling freezing breath into the Soldier Field air. More importantly, he was the on-field brains in Buddy Ryan's "46" defense and one of the best tacklers ever. " —TIM LAYDEN

≥ TWO-TIME NFL DEFENSIVE PLAYER OF THE YEAR
≥ EIGHT-TIME ALL-PRO

"I DON'T feel pain from a hit like that," Singletary says of a punishing shot on running back Eric Dickerson. "What I feel is joy. Joy for the tackle. Joy for myself. Joy for the other man. You understand me; I understand you. It's football, it's middle linebacking. It's just . . . good for everybody.'"

—Rick Telander, SI, January 27, 1986

MIKE SINGLETARY

6

DERRICK THOMAS

" With a thirst for the ball at standup outside linebacker, Thomas nearly perfected the art of the strip-sack, causing 41 fumbles during a career that was tragically cut short by a car crash. " —GREG A. BEDARD

≥ NINE-TIME PRO BOWL SELECTION
≥ SEVEN SEASONS WITH DOUBLE-DIGIT SACKS

"HE RUSHES the passer just like a great dribbler in basketball," says Sylvester Croom, who coached Thomas in college. Croom says Thomas's best move is like a crossover dribble: He forces the blocker to commit himself to an outside stance, then blows past him to the inside.

—*Michael Silver, SI, August 1, 1996*

Thomas had a record seven sacks against Seattle in 1990

PHOTOGRAPH BY JOHN BIEVER

7
CHUCK
BEDNARIK

EAGLES 1949–1962

" Perhaps the last great two-way player, Bednarik was a crushing tackler who laid out Giants halfback Frank Gifford in 1960 in one of the league's most devastating hits ever. " —DON BANKS

≥ ALSO PLAYED CENTER
≥ NINE-TIME ALL-PRO

A TITILLATING sidelight to this game was the possibility that Bednarik, the Eagles linebacker and offensive center, might be left for dead by one or another of the Giant team in revenge for Bednarik's chilling tackle of Frank Gifford two weeks ago. Bednarik, hitting Gifford with a blindside tackle late in the game, left the Giant halfback cold as snow. The Philadelphian danced a happy, heathen victory jig after Gifford's fumble had been recovered by the Eagles, thus ensuring their victory. His histrionics were misconstrued in some quarters as unseemly joy. "I got lots of letters," Bednarik said. "All good except for one from a lady in Texas. Then I got lots of telephone calls including one at 2:30 in the morning from some woman hollering at me. I disconnected the phone. I sent Gifford some fruit in the hospital, and I wrote him a three-page letter. It was a good tackle."

—Tex Maule, SI, December 5, 1960

Bednarik rejoiced over the fallen Gifford.

PHOTOGRAPH BY JOHN G. ZIMMERMAN

CONCRETE CHARLIE

As players have become increasingly specialized in their tasks, it only serves to highlight the remarkable achievements of Chuck Bednarik on both sides of the ball

BY JOHN SCHULIAN

E WENT DOWN HARD, LEFT in a heap by a crackback block as naked as it was vicious. Pro football was like that in 1960, a gang fight in shoulder pads, its violence devoid of the high-tech veneer it has today. The crackback was legal, and all the Philadelphia Eagles could do about it that Sunday in Cleveland was carry a linebacker named Bob Pellegrini off on his shield.

Buck Shaw, a gentleman coach in this ruffian's pastime, watched for as long as he could, then he started searching the Eagle sideline for someone to throw into the breach. His first choice was already banged up, and after that the standard 38-man NFL roster felt as tight as a hangman's noose. Looking back, you realize that Shaw had only one choice all along.

"Chuck," he said, "get in there."

And Charles Philip Bednarik, who already had a full-time job as Philadelphia's offensive center and a part-time job selling concrete after practice, headed onto the field without a word. Just the way his father had marched off to the open-hearth furnaces at Bethlehem Steel on so many heartless mornings. Just the way Bednarik himself had climbed behind the machine gun in a B-24 for 30 missions as a teenager fighting in World War II. It was a family tradition: Duty called, you answered.

Chuck Bednarik was 35 years old, still imposing at 6' 3" and 235 pounds, but also the father of one daughter too many to be what he really had in mind—retired. Jackie's birth the previous February gave him five children, all girls, and more bills than he thought he could handle without football. So here he was in his 12th NFL season, telling himself he was taking it easy on his creaky legs by playing center after all those years as an All-Pro linebacker. The only time he intended to move back to defense was in practice, when he wanted to work up a little extra sweat.

And now, five games into the season, this: Jim Brown over there in the Cleveland huddle, waiting to trample some fresh meat, and Bednarik trying to decipher the defensive terminology the Eagles had installed in the two years since he was their middle linebacker. Chuck Weber had his old job now, and Bednarik found himself asking what the left outside linebacker was supposed to do on passing plays. "Take the second man out of the backfield," Weber said. That was as fancy as it would get. Everything else would be about putting the wood to Jim Brown.

Bednarik nodded and turned to face a destiny that went far beyond emergency duty at linebacker. He was taking his first step toward a place in NFL history as the kind of player they don't make anymore.

He really was the last of a breed. For 58½ minutes in the NFL's 1960 championship game, he held his ground in the middle of Philly's Franklin Field, a force of nature determined to postpone the christening of the Green Bay Packers' dynasty. "I didn't run down on kickoffs, that's all," Bednarik says. The rest of that frosty Dec. 26, on both offense and defense, he played with the passion that crested when he wrestled Packers fullback Jim Taylor to the ground one last time and held him there until the final gun punctuated the Eagles' 17–13 victory.

Philadelphia hasn't ruled pro football in the 33 years since then, and pro football hasn't produced a player with the combination of talent, hunger and opportunity to duplicate what Bednarik did. It is a far different game now, of course, its complexities seeming to increase exponentially every year, but the athletes playing it are so much bigger and faster than Bednarik and his contemporaries that surely someone with the ability to go both ways must dwell among them. And don't try to make a case for Deion Sanders by bringing up the turn he took at wide receiver last season. Bednarik has heard that kind of noise before. "This writer in St. Louis calls me a few years back and starts talking about some guy out there, some wide receiver," he says, making no attempt to hide his disdain for both the position and the player. "Yeah, Roy Green, that was his name. This writer's talking about how the guy would catch passes and then go in on the Cardinals' umbrella defense, and I tell him, 'Don't give me that b.s. You've got to play every down.' Had Green come along 30 years earlier, he might have been turned loose to meet Bednarik's high standards. It is just as easy to imagine Walter Payton having shifted from running back to safety, or Lawrence Taylor moving from linebacker to tight end. But that day is long past, for the NFL of the '90s is a monument to specialization.

"No way in hell any of them can go both ways," Bednarik insists. "They don't want to. They're afraid they'll get hurt. And the money's too big, that's another thing. They'd just say, 'Forget it, I'm already making enough.'"

He nurtures the resentment he is sure every star of his era shares, feeding it with the dollar figures he sees in the sports pages every day, priming it with the memory that his fattest contract with the Eagles paid him $25,000, in 1962, his farewell season.

"People laugh when they hear what I made," he says. "I tell them, 'Hey, don't laugh at me. I could do everything but eat a football.'" Even when he was in his 50s, brought back by then coach Dick Vermeil to show the struggling Eagles what a champion looked like, Bednarik was something to behold. He walked into training camp, bent over the first ball he saw and whistled a strike back through his legs to a punter unused to such service from the team's long snappers. "And you know the amazing thing?" Vermeil says. "Chuck didn't look." ∎

8

JUNIOR SEAU

CHARGERS 1990–2002
DOLPHINS 2003–2005
PATRIOTS 2006–2009

" Seau was ahead of his time due to his versatility and his ability to drop in coverage, but his life ended too soon in a suicide that may have been CTE-related. " —CHRIS BURKE

≥ 1992 NFL DEFENSIVE PLAYER OF THE YEAR
≥ SIX-TIME ALL-PRO

THERE ARE times when Seau puts so much pressure on himself that it becomes overwhelming. Late in a game against the Chiefs, with the Chargers ahead 14–13, a short dump pass over the outstretched arms of Seau went for a 25-yard gain. Four plays later Nick Lowery kicked a 36-yard game-winner. When [wife] Gina greeted Seau at the airport, she says, "he was really quiet and close to tears." Up all night, Seau replayed the game in his head. "He kept saying, 'I should have done this.' 'If only I had done that,' " Gina says. The next afternoon Seau asked to address the team, and just as he started to apologize for letting everybody down, he was overcome with emotion and began sobbing. Says linebacker Gary Plummer, "He's the last person anybody would blame for a loss. Junior expects perfection out of everybody, but especially himself."

—*Jill Lieber, SI, September 6, 1993*

Seau had 18 career interceptions and 56½ sacks.

PHOTOGRAPHS BY ROBERT BECK (LEFT) AND JOHN W. MCDONOUGH

9

JACK HAM

STEELERS 1971–1982

"An embodiment of the grittiness of his era, Ham was perhaps best known for his instincts, and his penchant for big plays. His 53 takeaways (32 interceptions, 21 fumble recoveries) are the most-ever for a front-seven player." —GREG BISHOP

≥ NAMED TO NFL'S ALL-DECADE TEAM FOR THE 1970S
≥ EIGHT CONSECUTIVE PRO BOWL SELECTIONS

Ham brought down O.J. Simpson in 1974.

PHOTOGRAPH BY HEINZ KLUETMEIER

JACK LAMBERT took up tennis at Jack Ham's urging. "It's good for the legs, for changing direction fast and for keeping your eye on the ball," Lambert says. Ham plays a cruel, taunting game, trying to psych Lambert into errors, a mind game calculated to test things that can become quite serious when translated to football.

—Robert F. Jones, SI, July 12, 1976

10

WILLIE LANIER

CHIEFS 1967–1977

" Lanier starred in Super Bowl IV, finishing with seven tackles and an interception in Kansas City's upset victory over Minnesota. " —MARK GODICH

≥ EIGHT-TIME PRO BOWL OR AFL ALL-STAR GAME SELECTION
≥ 28 CAREER INTERCEPTIONS, 17 FUMBLE RECOVERIES

IN THE '67 draft the Chiefs took Notre Dame linebacker Jim Lynch (who was white) with the 47th pick and Lanier three spots later. In camp that summer coach Hank Stram told the two that the best player would win the starting job. "I wondered if there was going to be an open competition," says Lanier, "but from the start, it was refreshing to see there was a purity about the competition." That season Lanier become pro football's first black starting middle linebacker. "Imagine if there had been no AFL and no Kansas City Chiefs," says Lanier. "Maybe I have to wait five years for my chance [to play in the NFL], for the chance to play middle linebacker. And five years in football is an eternity." Before he died in 2006, owner Lamar Hunt said that the Chiefs "never pretended we made a conscious effort to open things up [racially]. We made a conscious effort to go out and find the best players anywhere that we could."

—Peter King, SI, July 13, 2009

Lanier's hitting complemented his great agility.

10 THE

BEST DEFENSIVE BACKS

DEFENSIVE BACK PLAY ISN'T WHAT IT USED TO BE. FOR EVIDENCE, LOOK AT OUR PHOTO OF THE NO. 4 PLAYER ON OUR LIST, DICK (NIGHT TRAIN) LANE, AND WHAT HE IS DOING TO THAT POOR RECEIVER. IF A DB CLOTHESLINED SOMEONE LIKE THAT TODAY, HE WOULD BE SUSPENDED, FINED AND POSSIBLY BANNED. HECK, THE LEAGUE MIGHT JUST START THE SEASON OVER.

BUT RECEIVER-PROTECTING RULE CHANGES WHICH BEGAN IN THE 1970S—AND WERE INSPIRED BY THE PHYSICAL PLAY OF OUR NO. 5 DB, MEL BLOUNT—CHANGED THE POSITION. PHYSICALITY STILL HAD ITS PLACE, BUT SPEED BECAME PARAMOUNT. THE EPITOME OF THE MODERN DB IS OUR NO. 2 PICK, DEION SANDERS, WHO WAS LIGHTNING-QUICK AND A MASTER TACTICIAN, BUT WAS NEVER KNOWN AS A GREAT OR EVEN ESPECIALLY WILLING TACKLER.

MANY OF THESE SPEEDSTERS BECAME GREAT ASSETS IN THE KICK RETURN GAME AND EVEN ON OFFENSE, WHERE SANDERS STARRED AND CHAMP BAILEY AGITATED FOR TOUCHES. THIS MADE FOR A CHALLENGE IN PHOTO SELECTION FOR THIS BOOK, BECAUSE WE WANTED TO BE SURE THAT WHEN A PLAYER ON THIS LIST WAS SHOWN WITH THE BALL IN HIS HANDS, HE WAS RETURNING AN INTERCEPTION AND NOT PERFORMING IN ANOTHER ROLE. BUT WHENEVER THEY WERE ON THE FIELD, THESE MODERN GREATS HAD THE TALENT TO TAKE OVER GAMES.

1

RONNIE LOTT

49ERS 1981-1990
RAIDERS 1991-1992
JETS 1993-1994

" An All-Pro at three distinct secondary positions—cornerback, free safety, strong safety—Lott was capable of playing man-to-man defense on the best receivers or getting the best running backs to the ground. He deserves to be in the argument for best alltime player, regardless of position. " —TIM LAYDEN

≥ 63 CAREER INTERCEPTIONS
≥ NAMED TO NFL ALL-DECADE TEAMS FOR 1980S AND '90S

LOTT LAUGHS when asked about his hardest hit, a head-on-collision with Falcons running back William Andrews in 1982. "I ran 10 yards straight at him, as hard as I could," he recalls. "He didn't see me. The whole time I was saying to myself, This is it! Then, boom. I slid off of him like butter. I hit the ground, and he didn't go down. I was thinking, 'What?' People are always asking where I'll be 10 years from now, if I'll be able to walk," continues Lott. "I'm just thankful to be here today. It's not important to be known as someone who hits hard. It's important to be thought of as a guy who gives his all. Sure, I'm taking a risk of getting injured or being burned. But one thing you don't do is sell out on your heart."

—Jill Lieber, SI, January 23, 1989

Lott twice led the NFL in interceptions.

PHOTOGRAPH BY MICKEY PFLEGER

2
DEION SANDERS

FALCONS 1989–1993
49ERS 1994
COWBOYS 1995–1999
REDSKINS 2000
RAVENS 2004–2005

❝ "Neon Deion" did baseball, fashion, and even music videos, but was best known for his gridiron prowess. Even there, he did it all: locking down receivers, returning kicks, dabbling on offense, high-stepping into the end zone and making the bandanna fashionable again. ❞ —GREG BISHOP

≥ NAMED TO NFL ALL-DECADE TEAM FOR 1990S AS BOTH CORNERBACK AND PUNT RETURNER
≥ 1994 NFL DEFENSIVE PLAYER OF THE YEAR

ISAAC BRUCE, the Rams' rookie receiver, looked at Sanders across the line, and what he saw was something altogether different from what he had been expecting. Standing there as mute as a scarecrow in a deep winter field, Sanders was smiling. "That's all he did," Bruce says. "Smiled. Then later I'm running my routes, and instead of giving me a hard time, he's kind of coaching me. He's saying, 'Look, you need to stay low when coming out of your cuts, so I won't be able to tell where you're going.'" Bruce took Sanders's advice, but alas, he finished without any catches while Sanders was covering him.

—John Ed Bradley, SI, October 9, 1995

Sanders personified the shutdown corner.

PHOTOGRAPHS BY GLENN JAMES (LEFT) AND DAMIAN STROHMEYER

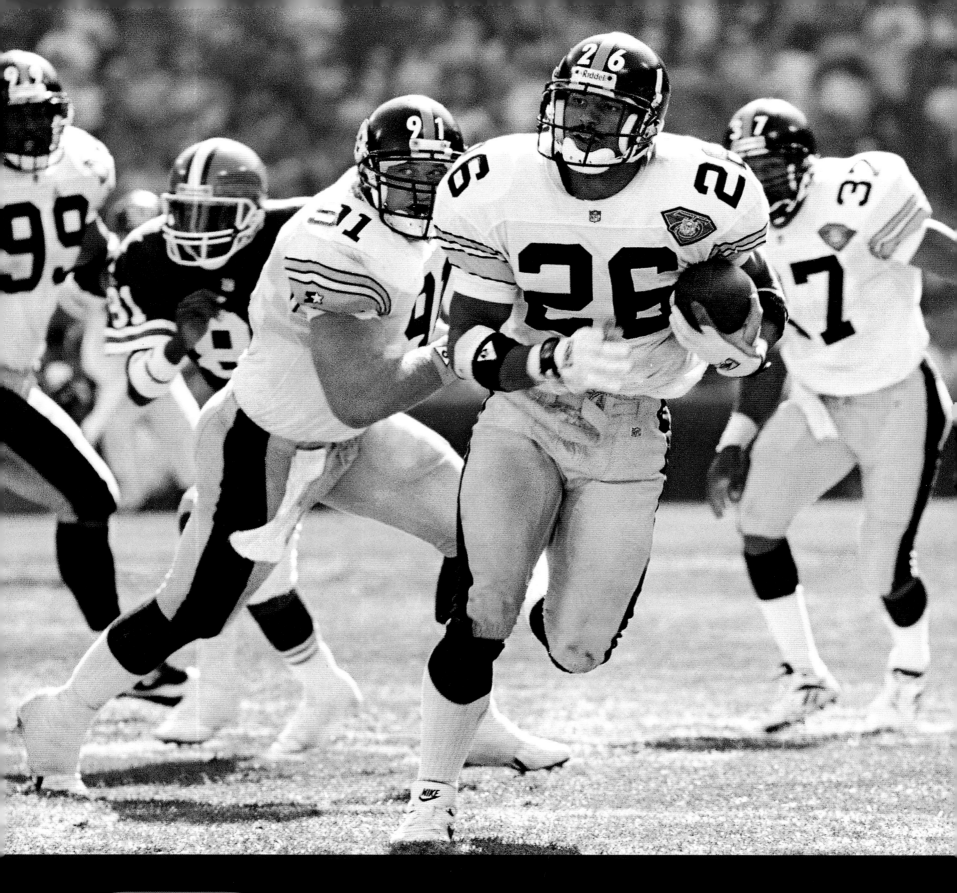

Woodson was the 1993 NFL Defensive Player of the Year.

STEELERS 1987–1996
49ERS 1997
RAVENS 1998–2001
RAIDERS 2002–2003

" In his 17-year career as a corner and safety the versatile Woodson had 71 interceptions, ranking third all-time; he returned an NFL-record 12 of those picks for scores. " —MARK GODICH

≥ CAREER LEADER IN INTERCEPTION RETURN YARDS

WOODSON WAS magnificent, returning two interceptions for a total of 73 yards, deflecting three other passes and making seven tackles. Playing left corner, Woodson looked like a combination blitzing outside linebacker, sticky-coverage corner and punishing strong safety.

—Peter King, SI, September 14, 1992

ROD WOODSON

4

DICK LANE

RAMS 1952–1953
CARDINALS 1954–1959
LIONS 1960–1965

" He set an early standard for NFL defensive backs with his record 14 interceptions in the 12-game season of 1952, and his blend of height and athleticism made him one of the game's most spectacular playmakers. " —DON BANKS

≥ SEVEN-TIME PRO BOWL SELECTION
≥ 68 CAREER INTERCEPTIONS

HE CAME up in an era when corners were still called defensive halfbacks. He played a style of football that was born of poverty and desperation. Years later Night Train Lane's technique would acquire the catchy name bump and run, but when he came into the NFL, in 1952, his approach was as elemental as the game itself. Lock on a receiver, rough him up down the field, try to knock him off his pattern, and if he still caught the ball, take his head off. Lane was the most feared corner in the game. A big guy at 6' 2" and more than 200 pounds, he was known for the Night Train Necktie, a neck-high tackle that the league eventually banned. "I've never seen anyone hit like him," Packers Hall of Famer Herb Adderley once said. "I mean, take them down, whether it be Jim Brown or Jim Taylor."

—Paul Zimmerman, SI, February 11, 2002

Night Train was a devastating tackler.

PHOTOGRAPH BY BETTMANN / GETTY IMAGES

5

MEL BLOUNT

STEELERS 1970–1983

> " What Joe Greene meant to the Steel Curtain defensive front, what nasty Jack Lambert meant to the Steeler linebacking corps, Blount meant to the Pittsburgh secondary. A ferocious hitter, Blount's downfield muggings of wide receivers forced quarterbacks to throw away from him. In his third season he allowed zero touchdown passes. " —PETER KING

≥ 1975 NFL DEFENSIVE
PLAYER OF THE YEAR
≥ 57 CAREER INTERCEPTIONS,
13 FUMBLE RECOVERIES

THE MOST Olympian sports body I've ever seen belongs to Wilt Chamberlain, who, beginning at gracefully slim ankles, broadens in unhurried geometrical progression to shoulders the size of an ox yoke. Mel has the same body only scaled down from 7' 1" to 6' 3". At the top of Blount's exquisite physique is his calmly erect, completely shaven head, which looks like a highly polished, bearded, semiprecious stone. At age 35 he weighs 205 pounds, about the same as he did at the end of his college career at Southern University. I asked him once whether he ever worried about his weight. "I don't worry about anything, man," he said. "It's not part of my makeup."

—*Roy Blount Jr., SI, July 25, 1983*

Blount's dominance led to more receiver-friendly rules.

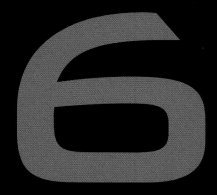

DARRELL GREEN

REDSKINS 1983–2002

" A wonder of nature who played 20 seasons with same franchise. Green paved the way for Deion Sanders to become famous as a pass defender. " —TIM LAYDEN

≥ NAMED TO NFL ALL-DECADE TEAM FOR 1990S
≥ NFL-RECORD 19 CONSECUTIVE SEASONS WITH AN INTERCEPTION

TWO VETERANS of past wars met near midfield at Foxboro Stadium. During a midweek interview, Patriots coach Bill Parcells, 55, had given the needle to his old NFC East nemesis, 36-year-old Redskins cornerback Darrell Green. "He's older than I am," said Parcells. So here came Green on Sunday, feigning anger. "Hey, Coach!" he said. "You know you're six months older than me!" Late in the third quarter Green made a play for the ages. Patriots back Curtis Martin broke into the clear near midfield, and Green, despite getting knocked down early in the play, was in hot pursuit. "I looked behind me, and I had about five yards on him," Martin said. "I was in the open field, so I started to put it in another gear. By the time I got in gear, Darrell was on my back." Green is a physical marvel. As a rookie, in 1983, he ran the 40 in 4.33 seconds. Last year he ran it in 4.28.

—Peter King, SI, October 21, 1996

Green was only 5'8" and 176 pounds.

PHOTOGRAPH BY DOUG PENSINGER/GETTY IMAGES

7
ED
REED

RAVENS 2002–2012
JETS, TEXANS 2013

"An elite ball hawk, Reed scored 12 career touchdowns and is the only player in league history to reach the end zone via an interception, fumble recovery, punt block and punt return." —DON BANKS

≥ 2004 NFL DEFENSIVE
PLAYER OF THE YEAR
≥ 57 CAREER INTERCEPTIONS

REED IS no less than "a unique, once-in-a-lifetime football player," according to Ravens defensive coordinator Greg Mattison, and his career statistics bear out that claim. His 61 combined regular-season and postseason interceptions rank him 12th alltime. He has played three fewer seasons than anyone else in the top 18. More important, says Mattison, is how Reed's experience rubs off on his teammates—how he explains to them the way an offense works; how he can create all those turnovers without gambling outside the structure of the defense. In 2010 his importance to the Ravens has been as evident as ever. In the six games Reed missed while recovering from his hip surgery, Baltimore, with a patchwork secondary, produced just three interceptions. In the 10 games Reed played, the Ravens picked off 16 passes.

—Ben Reiter, SI, January 17, 2011

Reed returned interceptions 106 and 107 yards.

PHOTOGRAPH BY SIMON BRUTY

LOOK AT ME NOW

A difficult decision to leave his parents' home as a teenager and move in with a high school secretary set Ed Reed on the path to becoming to one of the best safeties in NFL history

BY JEFFRI CHADIHA

UTSIDE A MOVIE THEATER IN La Place, La., a middle-aged white woman was ranting at a police officer, inching closer and closer as if bent on getting arrested. Jeanne Hall rarely exploded in rage, but she'd had it. First the cashier declined to sell tickets to Hall for the six children going to the movie with her. Recent rowdiness, the cashier explained, had prompted the theater to place restrictions on unaccompanied children entering the establishment after 7 p.m. Then the officer, called over by the cashier after Hall protested, told her she could take her daughter and two sons into the theater, but the three teenage black males could not be admitted because Hall was not their parent or guardian.

Never mind that the officer was upholding a theater rule, Hall was cursing him for refusing to accept her explanation that those three boys were around her house so much they might as well have been family. She was digging in for a fight, causing a commotion that startled other customers as they passed by. Then one of the boys, 16-year-old Ed Reed, stepped in. "Let's go," he calmly said to Hall. "We can rent a movie at home."

Even at that age Reed could read a situation and react deftly. He could see that the officer would never understand the relationship he had with this woman he called Mama as easily as she called him Son. It was time to move on. There were bigger obstacles to get past in life.

Early in his junior year he made a decision that would change his life: He asked Jeanne Hall, the secretary for the assistant principal at Destrehan, if he could move in with her family. Hall was a mother figure to many of the school's discipline cases, several of whom were athletes. She offered her home, a modest house in a middle-class neighborhood less than a mile from the Reeds', as an alternative to roaming the streets and getting into more trouble; it was a place where aimless kids could hang out and study, play video games or watch movies. "Ed didn't have the self-discipline to get his academics straightened out by himself," says Hall, who agreed to take him in. "He knew we would challenge him."

Now Reed had to persuade his parents to let him move out. Karen was 13 when she lost her mother to breast cancer and Ed Sr. was 19 when his father died of lung cancer. A close-knit family was important to both parents, but they also wanted the best for their children. Only a few months earlier Ed Sr. had told him, "Son, you don't ever want to make a living doing what I do." He and Karen realized Ed Jr. had a chance to go to college on a football scholarship, and they could see he wasn't going to make it unless his grades—and work habits—improved. After assuring his parents that he would come home often, Reed got their consent for the move. "It was hard to let Ed go, but I didn't want to tell him that," Karen says. "I knew Mrs. Hall, and I knew she wanted to help him."

Jeanne and her husband, Walter, a foreman at an oil refinery, provided Reed with a structured lifestyle. After football practice each night, for example, he usually napped until 9:30, then studied with Jeanne until midnight. His grades gradually improved. He was becoming more confident in his schoolwork, so much so that one night late in his junior year he shooed away Jeanne when she tried to help him with his math homework. When she checked his work later, Jeanne found all correct answers. "I actually can learn," Reed told her.

Since then, Reed says, he's been obsessed with realizing his potential. His motto became: Listen, learn, then lead. "There was something inside of me that [the Halls] brought out," Reed says. "And once I realized what I could do, I wanted to take it to another level. I saw if I did things right, people would follow me."

Reed was recruited by Miami, LSU and Tulane. He chose Miami, where he was a two-time All-America safety, helped the Hurricanes win the 2001 national title and graduated with a degree in liberal arts. By his senior year he had established himself as one of Miami's leaders, on and off the field. Each weekday morning before the season he would wake up at 5:30 and direct his teammates through their conditioning drills. At night he would join his friends and teammates at one of the area's many clubs, usually to make sure they avoided trouble.

After he was selected with the No. 24 pick in the 2002 draft, Reed gravitated to fellow Miami alum Ray Lewis. The two players watched game tapes for hours at Lewis's home, and they trained together in the off-season. Some teammates jokingly called Reed "Ray Jr.," but he didn't mind. He'd found another mentor, another Jeanne Hall.

Today Reed continues to speak almost daily with Hall, who is still generous with advice, and still calls Reed "her son." Last December, Hall and her 24-year-old daughter, Leslie, were waiting for Reed outside M&T Bank Stadium after the Ravens' 37–14 win over the Giants when Leslie's cellphone chimed. It was Reed, who asked them to walk down the street, where he was waiting in his Range Rover. He was worried that fans would recognize him and delay their exit. "Who do you think you are?" Leslie said with a laugh. "You act like you're somebody special."

But when Jeanne and Leslie finally reached the SUV, they heard shrieks and screams behind them. Leslie whirled and saw several fans racing toward Reed's vehicle. A few minutes later, with the stadium in Reed's rearview mirror, Leslie reluctantly apologized. "I have to give you your props, Edward," she said. "You really have become pretty important after all." ∎

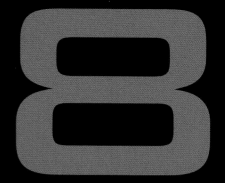

8

CHARLES WOODSON

RAIDERS 1998–2005, 2013–2015
PACKERS 2006–2012

> "Woodson broke in with the Raiders as a lockdown defender. As the leader of the Packers a decade later, he became a blitzer and freelance ball hawk." —TIM LAYDEN

≥ 2009 NFL DEFENSIVE PLAYER OF THE YEAR
≥ NINE-TIME PRO BOWL SELECTION

SITTING ON the couch in his town house, he gestures to the TV screen and says, "That's my man right there." He's referring to Victor Newman, his favorite character on *The Young and the Restless*, whom Woodson admires for obvious reasons. "The more critical the situation gets," says Eric Braeden, the actor who portrays Newman, "the more ice-cold Victor becomes." The scary thing is, Woodson expects to get colder as he gets older. He says his rookie year was "very average" and views the Hall of Fame as a plausible destination. "I don't think that's too heavy," he says. "I can't see it happening any other way." You look for a grin, a hint that the hyperbole is for effect, but instead his eyes narrow and his voice turns frosty. "Put a bull and a cat in an arena and have them run at each other," he says. "What do you think the bull is thinking? When I cover somebody, that's what I'm thinking."

—Michael Silver, SI, August 30, 1999

Woodson scored 11 touchdowns off interceptions.

PHOTOGRAPH BY JOHN BIEVER

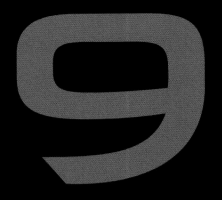

9

CHAMP BAILEY

REDSKINS 1999–2003
BRONCOS 2004–2013

" Bailey, an intelligent, lock-down cornerback, had 52 interceptions, and he also racked up nearly 800 tackles—proof of his willingness to get dirty. " —CHRIS BURKE

≥ THREE-TIME ALL-PRO
≥ 12-TIME PRO BOWL SELECTION

"YOU HAVE to watch him because Bailey can turn a game around," Giants coach Jim Fassel says. "I saw him as a rookie, when Michael Irvin went after him in Dallas, and he picked a ball off. Michael couldn't intimidate him, couldn't outmuscle him, couldn't do anything against him."

—*Josh Elliott, SI, August 20, 2001*

Bailey usually shadowed the opponents' top receiver.

PHOTOGRAPH BY WILLIAM PURNELL/ICON SPORTSWIRE

Tatum (32) personified Oakland's tough '70s defenses.

PHOTOGRAPH BY NEIL LEIFER

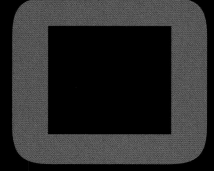

10

RAIDERS 1971–1979
OILERS 1980

❝ "The Assassin" was one of the most brutal tacklers from sideline to sideline in NFL history. Tatum's specialty was separating receivers from the football from his safety position. ❞ —GREG A. BEDARD

≥ THREE-TIME PRO BOWL SELECTION
≥ 37 CAREER INTERCEPTIONS

JACK TATUM

TATUM MADE Franco Harris look as if he had run into a wall. No gain. Tatum got up after the tackle and slammed Franco's feet to the rug. A rumble of disapproval rose from the stadium. . . . "He shoved me and I shoved back," Tatum said afterward. "I'm not a bad guy, like people say."

—Dan Jenkins, SI, October 3, 1997

THE 10

BEST COACHES

HERE'S A MEMO TO THE BRONCOS' VANCE JOSEPH, THE BILLS' SEAN MCDERMOTT, THE RAMS' SEAN MCVAY, THE CHARGERS' ANTHONY LYNN, AND THE 49ERS' KYLE SHANAHAN, ALL OF WHOM ARE BEGINNING THEIR NFL HEAD COACHING CAREERS IN 2017: IF YOU WANT TO BE CONSIDERED ONE OF THE ALL-TIME GREATS, THERE'S ONLY ONE WAY TO DO IT. YOU HAVE TO WIN A CHAMPIONSHIP. ACTUALLY, CHECK THAT: YOU NEED TO WIN MULTIPLE CHAMPIONSHIPS.

NOT THAT A PLAYER'S CASE FOR GREATNESS ISN'T AIDED BY A TITLE, BUT ONLY WITH COACHES DOES IT APPEAR TO BE A REQUIREMENT. AMONG OUR TOP QUARTERBACKS, FOR EXAMPLE, WE HAVE DAN MARINO, WHO NEVER WON A SUPER BOWL. THE MASSIVE FINGERS OF THIS BOOK'S NO. 1 OFFENSIVE LINEMAN ARE ALSO RING-FREE. COACHES, THOUGH, NEED TO SHOW UP WITH SOME JEWELRY.

HERE'S HOW STRICT THE ADMISSION POLICY IS: NO COACH WITHOUT A CHAMPIONSHIP RECEIVED A SINGLE VOTE IN ANY PANELISTS'S TOP 10. BUD GRANT AND MARV LEVY TOOK TEAMS TO FOUR SUPER BOWLS AND DIDN'T EARN A MENTION. NOR DID DON CORYELL, ONE OF THE GAME'S GREAT INNOVATORS. ONLY 12 MEN DREW VOTES FOR PLACES IN THE THE TOP 10 LIST, WHICH MEANS THAT THIS CATEGORY HAD THE MOST CONSENSUS OF ANY IN THE BOOK. ACROSS ERAS, TITLES ARE ONE STAT THAT IS EASY TO COMPARE.

1

VINCE
LOMBARDI

PACKERS 1959–1967
REDSKINS 1969

" If the NFL logo were a person, that person would be Vince Lombardi, the most iconic figure in the history of the league. He built the Packers into a model franchise. " —TIM LAYDEN

≥ WON FIVE NFL TITLES AND SUPER BOWLS I AND II
≥ WINNING RECORD IN EACH OF HIS 10 SEASONS

THE MAN who turned doubt into affirmation is Vince Lombardi, a moody, hoarse-voiced individual of great enthusiasms and lofty contempts. ("If you're within that circle of people important to him and his team," says a man etching circles on a white tablecloth in the Elks club, "there is nothing, absolutely nothing, he won't do for you. If you're not, he doesn't give a damn about you.") In less than two years as general manager and coach, Lombardi has taken a team which gave Green Bay its worst record in history (1-10-1 in 1958) and prodded it into distinction. "All those years of lookin' for somethin' and someone," says a man in a service station, "and this New Yorker"—the phrase was almost a profanity—"comes along and does it."

—*William Barry Furlong, SI, December 12, 1960*

Lombardi won his first NFL championship in 1961.

2

BILL BELICHICK

BROWNS 1991–1995
PATRIOTS 2000–PRESENT

" After inventing defensive schemes for the two-time Super Bowl champ iants a generation ago, he had a clunker of a head coaching trial in Cleveland. Patriots owner Bob Kraft smartly gave im a second chance. " —PETER KING

≥ FIVE SUPER BOWL TITLES
AS HEAD COACH
16 YEARS WITH 10 OR MORE
REGULAR-SEASON WINS

THE MOST amazing thing about the [21-game winning streak] is the ever-changing Patriots' roster. This is Belichick's fifth year as coach. At the start of every season he has had at least 10 starters who weren't in the opening day lineup the previous year, including a dozen guys in 2004 who didn't open the season for last year's title team. By comparison, the lineup for the 1972 Dolphins had only three changes from '71. "I think the Patriots' accomplishment in this era of free agency puts their streak on top of all the others," says Ron Wolf, the former Packers G.M. "The secret in today's football is that guys who can coach and teach, like Bill Belichick and his staff, are invaluable. Because if you're really good today, you've got to replace a $10 million player with a $400,000 player almost every year, and the Cadillac has to keep running."

—Peter King, SI, October 18, 2004

elichick holds the NFL mark for postseason wins (26).

RIGHT FROM THE START

The molding of the greatest coach in today's game began when Bill Belichick was nine years old and attending team meetings at the Naval Academy with his father

BY PETER KING

WOULD YOU LIKE TO see Bill's room?" The kindly voice belongs to Jeannette Belichick, a petite 82-year-old who is standing in the living room of her Annapolis, Md., home. Back when she taught Spanish at Hiram (Ohio) College, Jeannette spoke four languages fluently and understood seven, but now, as she says with a smile and a twinkle, "The only language I speak is football."

It's a short walk to the onetime bedroom of Steve and Jeannette Belichick's only child, now coach of the New England Patriots. The twin beds are made pristinely, as though awaiting military inspection. Two maritime paintings done by amateur painter Steve—hang on the walls. A high school graduation photo of Bill sits on the dresser. The bookshelf is crammed with volumes from his days at Annapolis High. *A Separate Peace*, by John Knowles. *Future Shock*, by Alvin Toffler. *The Case of the Screaming Woman*, a Perry Mason mystery by Erle Stanley Gardner. There's The Gettysburg Civil War Battle Game and a signed football from the 1963 Navy team and four trophies from Bill's childhood athletic triumphs. "That room hasn't changed in 40 years," Bill says when asked about it later.

The room is, to be frank, a little barren. "It's not a big deal," Jeannette says. "That's the way we live."

The contents of the room provide a window into the mind of Bill Belichick. They tell us that the hottest coach in the NFL is well-educated and uncluttered in his thinking. Through a roller-coaster coaching ride that has included a trying stint with the Cleveland Browns in the 1990s and a Captain Queeg–like performance in walking away from the New York Jets 24 hours after being promoted to head coach in January 2000, Belichick has in many respects remained unaltered. "I don't think he's changed from his Cleveland days," says good friend Jim Brown, the Hall of Fame running back, who remains close to the Browns' organization. "He's acquired some life experiences, but he's exactly the same man I knew 10 years ago."

As a coach, however, Belichick has continually educated himself, never allowing himself or his team to become too predictable. Less than a month after the Patriots beat the Carolina Panthers to claim their their second Lombardi Trophy, he flew to Baton Rouge and spent two days drawing up schemes with his former defensive coordinator in Cleveland, LSU coach Nick Saban. For the second straight year he traveled to the Florida Keys to pick the brain of fellow two-time Super Bowl winner Jimmy Johnson. During a vacation on Nantucket before training camp, he listened to audiotapes of a book by retired Navy captain D. Michael Abrashoff called *It's Your Ship: Management Techniques from the Best Damn Ship in the Navy*. He also found time for one of the Harry Potter tomes. Hey, even a guy as intense as Belichick has to have fun once in a while.

Even at age nine, Bill Belichick had football on the brain. He was devoted to his father, a longtime assistant coach and scout at Navy. Son joined Dad whenever he could. If Steve had to drive to the Baltimore airport to pick up films on that week's opponent, Bill rode with him. Once home, Bill not only watched the films but also saw how his father diagrammed plays. When Bill was nine or 10, he tagged along to the weekly Monday-night meeting, at which players were given the scouting report for the next game.

"He'd sit in the back of the room, maybe for 90 minutes a session," says Steve, now 85. "I never had to say a word to him about his behavior. He'd stare at the front of the room and not say a word."

When Bill was 10 or 11, the assistant in charge of the offensive game plan, Ernie Jorge, sent him an envelope every Thursday night. BILL'S READY LIST was written on the envelope, and inside was the game plan for the week, including all the plays. Before he was a teenager Bill knew terminology, formations, schemes. He also knew bona fide football stars from the time he spent at Midshipmen practices. When he was seven, Navy's biggest standout was running back Joe Bellino, the 1960 Heisman Trophy winner. "That was his first hero," Steve Belichick says. "Joe was the hero of a lot of kids in America then, and Bill was his friend."

To this day Bellino, who became an auto-auction executive in the Boston area, remembers playing catch on the practice field with Bill. "Imagine what Bill must have absorbed," says Bellino. "He'd sit in the back of the room listening to his father give the scouting report. He's a six-, seven-, eight-year-old youngster hanging out at the Naval Academy. Midshipmen in uniform, parades, the brass, the visiting presidents, the football team with two Heisman winners [Bellino and 1963 recipient Roger Staubach]. And he saw his father's work ethic. He saw everyone in that room soak up what his dad was telling us, believing if we did what he said, we could beat anybody."

As he got older and the Staubach era began, Belichick was able to do more. If Staubach wanted to work after practice on a pass he knew he'd be using that week, Belichick often served as his receiver. "Say Roger would be working on a sprint-out, throwing to the sideline," recalls Belichick. "I'd go to the spot on the sideline and practice the throw. Not a few. I'm talking 20, 30 of them. People ask me now why I do things a certain way. Look at the way I grew up. I grew up thinking, This is the way it's supposed to be." ∎

3

PAUL BROWN

BROWNS 1946–1962
BENGALS 1968–1975

" After he won four All-America Football Conference titles with his expansion Browns, his greatest achievement may have been Cleveland's first game in the NFL, in which the team clobbered the defending champion Eagles 35–10. Then he won three NFL titles in his first six seasons. " —PETER KING

≥ INNOVATOR CREDITED WITH REVOLUTIONIZING GAME PREPARATION AND SCOUTING THROUGH FILM STUDY
≥ FIRST COACH TO SEND IN PLAYS FROM THE SIDELINE

HIS OWN personal habits and table manners are impeccable. He expects the same from his players. "A few years ago we had a big end," Brown said. "I heard he chewed tobacco and spat it on the wall next to his bed. Can you imagine that?" He peered over his glasses. "I went to his room," he said. "I told him that I would fine him $500 if he didn't wash down the walls. Then I stood and watched him wash them. Can you imagine living with an animal like that?" The player went on to become All-Pro. Yet there was always, in Brown's mind, a reservation about him. "If they're sloppy, or drinkers, or chasers or whiners, it will show up eventually."

—Tex Maule, SI, September 10, 1962

Brown's career record was 222-112-9.

4

BILL WALSH

49ERS 1979–1988

" Remember, kids, before the Madden video game, there was Bill Walsh's College Football. Walsh is considered to be the mind behind the West Coast offense. In 10 years as head coach he won three Super Bowls. " —CHRIS BURKE

≥ REVOLUTIONIZED MODERN PASSING GAME
≥ 10 OR MORE WINS IN EACH NONSTRIKE SEASON FROM 1981 TO 1988

A SPRINT-OUT quarterback in college, Ken Anderson had never dropped straight back to pass. "I knew nothing," he says. Bill Walsh, then a Bengals assistant, showed him how to cradle the ball, how to move back into the pocket, how to set up. "We'd literally walk through the steps, counting out the numbers as we went," says Anderson. What Anderson got was the now famous Walsh teaching blitz, the intense reconstruction process Bengals quarterbacks Greg Cook and Virgil Carter had gotten before him and Dan Fouts, Joe Montana and others would get later. Walsh spoke quietly and rationally, joked a lot and emphasized restraint and discipline in throwing. "I don't advocate the discipline of a Marine drill sergeant," says Walsh. "What I try to get across is the discipline you'll see in a ballerina or concert pianist."

—Rick Telander, SI, January 25, 1982

Walsh was also a master drafter as 49ers G.M.

PHOTOGRAPH BY AL MESSERSCHMIDT

5

DON SHULA

COLTS 1963–1969
DOLPHINS 1970–1995

" Nobody did it better or longer than the only coach to lead his team to the Super Bowl in three decades. " —DON BANKS

≥ NFL RECORD 347 WINS
≥ SIX SUPER BOWL APPEARANCES, WITH WINS IN SUPER BOWLS VII AND VIII

SHULA HAS thrived in a world of pressure so intense that it has burned out even those who have succeeded at the highest level, or close to it. Joe Gibbs, Bill Walsh, Dick Vermeil, John Robinson, Don Coryell, John Madden—the list is long. Through it all, year after year, Shula marches on.

—Paul Zimmerman, SI, December 20, 1993

Shula celebrated the wins record in 1993.

PHOTOGRAPH BY GEORGE WIDMAN/AP

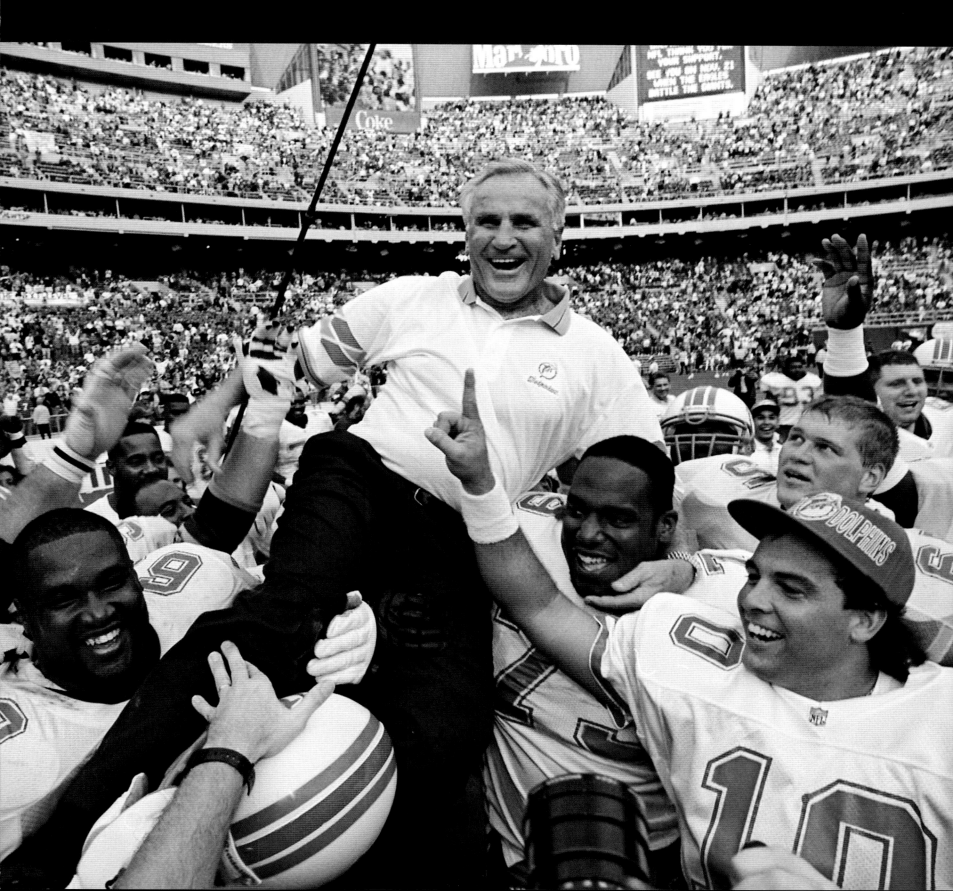

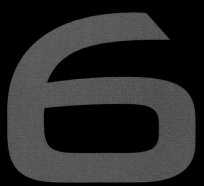

6

CHUCK NOLL

STEELERS 1969–1991

"During his 23-year run, Noll went 209-156-1, including 16–8 in the playoffs, which makes him seventh in career victories. He guided the most dominant team of the 1970s." —MARK GODICH

≥ WON FOUR SUPER BOWLS IN SIX YEARS
≥ DRAFTED FOUR FUTURE HALL OF FAMERS IN 1974, A RECORD FOR ONE CLASS

NOLL THE teacher has tended to overshadow Noll the innovator, mainly because Noll himself tends to downplay innovation. "If I had to choose between a coach who's a strategy guy and one who's a teacher, it'd be no contest," Noll says. "I'd take the teacher every time." They can go together. The Steelers threw three big offensive innovations at the Rams in the last Super Bowl. But "the key to everything was teaching," says Steelers linebacker Andy Russell. "You'd see him being stopped by some rookie after an afternoon practice during two-a-days, a kid he's got to know is going to be cut in a matter of days. The kid would say, 'Coach, I'm having trouble with this technique,' and Chuck would spend half an hour with him. I think he enjoyed it more than coaching the superstars. He just loves to teach."

—Paul Zimmerman, SI, July 28, 1980

Steelers' winning seasons were rare before Noll arrived.

PHOTOGRAPH BY WALTER IOOSS JR.

GEORGE HALAS

BEARS 1920–1929, 1933–1942,
1946–1955, 1958–1967
BEARS OWNER UNTIL 1983

" Nicknamed Papa Bear as the patriarch of the Bears franchise, he was the league's most enduring face as it transitioned from leather helmets to national TV contracts. " —TIM LAYDEN

≥ SIX NFL CHAMPIONSHIPS,
ONLY SIX LOSING SEASONS
IN 40 YEARS
≥ SECOND ON NFL'S ALLTIME
WINS LIST WITH 324

·

IT IS easy to forget that this man across the desk is a certified institution. Papa Bear was tackled by Jim Thorpe and struck out by Walter Johnson. He played six games in rightfield for the Yankees in 1919 (the Babe settled in that very realty the next season), and Halas was also there in Canton, Ohio, sitting on a running board in a Hupmobile showroom on Sept. 17, 1920 when pro football was created. It was a Friday, one of the last things to be created in just one day. And this fellow across the desk was right there, live. Then Papa Bear won 324 games, 12 more than Stagg, which at the time was more than anyone in the history of the pros or the colleges. He is the only man Vince Lombardi would embrace and one of the few he would call Coach.

—Frank Deford, SI, December 5, 1977

Halas's tirades were a trademark.

PHOTOGRAPH BY JOHN F. JAQUA

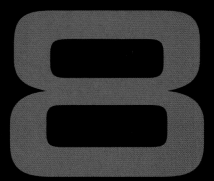

8

TOM LANDRY

COWBOYS 1960–1988

" No coach has ever done more with a modern expansion franchise, turning the nascent Dallas franchise into an every-year championship contender. He was instrumental in framing the 4–3 defense that ruled the NFL for two decades. " —TIM LAYDEN

≥ WON SUPER BOWLS VI AND XII
≥ 270 CAREER WINS,
THIRD-BEST ALLTIME

IN 1956, Landry coached the defense and Vince Lombardi oversaw the offense, giving the NFL champion Giants the most dynamic pair of assistant coaches ever to grace one staff. A visitor to the Giants that season described a walk down the corridor where the coaches' offices were located. "The first office I passed belonged to Landry," he said. "He was busy putting in a defense, running his projector, studying film. The next office was Vince Lombardi's. He was breaking down his own film, putting in an offense. The next office was head coach Jim Lee Howell's. He had his feet up on the desk, and he was reading a newspaper." Upon seeing the visitor, Howell quipped, "With guys like Lombardi and Landry in the building, there isn't much for me to do around here."

—*Paul Zimmerman, SI, February 21, 2000*

Landry made five Super Bowl appearances.

PHOTOGRAPH BY AP

9

JOE GIBBS

" A master strategist who specialized in offense, Gibbs is the only coach to win Super Bowls with three quarterbacks (Joe Theismann, Doug Williams and Mark Rypien)—and none of the three are in the Hall of Fame. " —GREG A. BEDARD

FLASH WAS never Joe Gibbs's style; he was as boring as a dog-eared Bible, the only book he may have read more often than the Washington playbook. But his fairness and diligence had a way of affecting even those who were nothing like him.

—*Rick Telander, SI, March 15, 1993*

≥ 17–7 IN POSTSEASON
≥ 171–101 CAREER RECORD

Gibbs instructed Joe Theismann in Super Bowl XVII.

PHOTOGRAPH BY NATE FINE/GETTY IMAGES

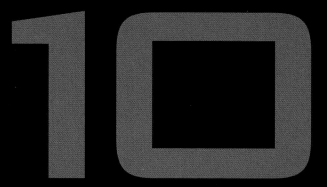

10

BILL PARCELLS

GIANTS 1983–1990
PATRIOTS 1993–1996
JETS 1997–1999
COWBOYS 2003–2006

" The Big Tuna embodied everything a coach is supposed to be. He was tough, exacting and demanded the highest standards. " —GREG BISHOP

≥ WON SUPER BOWLS XXI AND XXV
≥ ONLY COACH IN NFL HISTORY TO REACH PLAYOFFS WITH FOUR FRANCHISES

PARCELLS WAS brought up in an environment in which coaches got in athletes' faces. "Everybody who ever coached me was on me, coaching me hard," he says. "But, see, if you respect a player and he respects you, then you have a relationship, and in a relationship all commentary is allowed. I can say anything to Pepper Johnson, and he will understand where I'm coming from. Man, the things coaches used to say to me. . . ." Parcells is usually sparing in talking about his past. But, as coaches often do, he enjoys talking about *his* coaches, the men who shaped his life. With an almost childlike delight— and with laundered language—he remembers the day that a coach yelled to him during football practice, "Parcells, I wish you were a piece of crap out there because then at least somebody might slip on you."

—Jack McCallum, SI, December 14, 1998

Parcells was no sideline stoic.

PHOTOGRAPHS BY ANDY HAYT (LEFT) AND JERRY WACHTER

10 THE

BEST GAMES

THE HEADLINE THAT RAN WITH SI'S ORIGINAL STORY ON THE 1958 CHAMPIONSHIP BETWEEN THE COLTS AND THE GIANTS WAS "THE BEST FOOTBALL GAME EVER PLAYED." TWO WEEKS LATER THE MAGAZINE RAN A FOLLOW-UP WITH THE SOMEWHAT DEFENSIVE TITLE, "HERE'S WHY IT WAS THE BEST FOOTBALL GAME EVER." AND NOW, MORE THAN FIVE DECADES AND THOUSANDS OF GAMES LATER, THE JUDGMENT HAS BEEN REAFFIRMED. AN ALTERNATIVE TITLE FOR THIS CHAPTER: "IT'S STILL THE BEST GAME EVER."

OF THE 10 SELECTIONS IN THIS SECTION, SIX WERE LEAGUE CHAMPIONSHIP GAMES, AND ALL WERE FROM THE PLAYOFFS. THE TWO REGULAR-SEASON GAMES TO EARN VOTES DID A LITTLE EXTRA TO STICK IN THE MEMORY. THE 1968 JETS-RAIDERS GAME WAS CUT OFF BY A BROADCAST OF THE FILM *HEIDI*. THE '85 MIAMI-CHICAGO GAME WAS ALL ABOUT PERFECTION—THE BEARS' QUEST TO ATTAIN IT, AND THE DOLPHINS' MISSION TO PLAY SPOILER (AND PROTECT THE LEGACY OF THEIR UNDEFEATED '72 TEAM).

EVERY GAME THAT MADE A VOTER'S LIST—AS WELL AS ANYTHING THAT RATED A MENTION IN ANY OTHER CATEGORY—APPEARS IN AN APPENDIX IN THE BACK OF THIS BOOK. IT'S WORTH A PEEK, TO SEE WHAT MEMORIES COME SEEPING BACK.

1

1958 TITLE GAME

COLTS 23, GIANTS 17

" With 17 future Hall of Fame players and coaches involved, and the first sudden-death contest in NFL history, "The Greatest Game Ever Played" launched the league into the national consciousness, thanks to a TV audience estimated at 45 million viewers. " —GREG A. BEDARD

≥ COLTS TIED GAME ON FIELD
GOAL WITH SEVEN SECONDS
LEFT IN FOURTH QUARTER
≥ COLTS WON IN OVERTIME ON
80-YARD TOUCHDOWN DRIVE

JUST BEFORE the [winning] touchdown a deliriously happy Baltimore football fan raced onto the field during a timeout and sailed 80 yards, bound for the Baltimore huddle, before the police secondary intercepted him and hauled him to the sideline. He was grinning with idiot glee, and the whole city of Baltimore sympathized with him. Another Baltimore fan, listening on his auto radio, ran into a telephone pole when Steve Myhra kicked the tying field goal, and 30,000 others waited to greet the returning heroes. Ray Berry, a thin, tired-looking youngster still dazed with the victory, seemed to speak for the team and for fans everywhere after the game. "It's the greatest thing that ever happened," he said.

—Tex Maule, SI, January 5, 1959

Alan Ameche won the game with this one-yard run.

PHOTOGRAPH BY NEIL LEIFER

1967 TITLE GAME

PACKERS 21, COWBOYS 17

"With a trip to Super Bowl II on the line, Dallas and Green Bay squared off on New Year's Eve 1967 as the temperature at Lambeau Field dipped to -15°. After Vince Lombardi opted against a tying field goal attempt in the dying seconds, the Pack prevailed on Bart Starr's daring quarterback sneak for a touchdown." —MARK GODICH

≥ KNOWN AS "THE ICE BOWL"
≥ WITH WINDCHILL, TEMPERATURE WAS -48°

THE FIELD, now in the shadow of the stands, was fast becoming an iced-over pond. "I knew [running back] Donny [Anderson] wasn't getting any footing," Bart Starr said after the game. "I figured I wouldn't have as far to run and I wouldn't have as much chance to fumble, so I called the wedge to [guard Jerry] Kramer's side." "When he called the play, I knew he would be following me," Kramer explained. "[Cowboys defensive lineman Jethro] Pugh was playing on my inside shoulder—to my left—and I took my best shot at him. That may have been the biggest block I ever made in my life." The block moved Pugh in and back. Starr came hard behind him and slid into the end zone, and suddenly, for 50,000 people, spring came.

—*Tex Maule, SI, January 8, 1968*

Lambeau's "frozen tundra" earned its nickname.

PHOTOGRAPH BY NEIL LEIFER

3

SUPER BOWL III

JETS 16, COLTS 7

" From a dramatic standpoint, this game doesn't hold up, but that's insignificant. This one gave the AFL credibility and made Joe Namath a folk hero. " —TIM LAYDEN

≥ AFL TEAMS HAD LOST FIRST TWO SUPER BOWLS BY WIDE MARGINS
≥ ONE-LOSS COLTS WERE 18-POINT FAVORITES

BROADWAY JOE NAMATH is long hair, a Fu Manchu mustache worth $10,000 to shave off, swinging nights in the live spots of the big city, the dream lover of the stewardi—all that spells insouciant youth in the Jet Age. Besides all that, Namath is a superb quarterback who in the Super Bowl proved that his talent is as big as his mouth—which makes it a very big talent, indeed. Almost no one thought the Jets could penetrate the fine Baltimore defense, but Namath was sure of it and said so. "We're a better team than Baltimore," he said before the game. He was lying by the pool at the Gait Ocean Mile Hotel, where the Jets stayed, tanned and oiled against the sun. It was called loudmouthing, bragging, but as it turned out, Super Joe told it the way it was. In a surpassing display of passing accuracy and mental agility, he picked the Colt defense apart.

—Tex Maule, SI, January 20, 1969

Field general Namath was the game's MVP.
PHOTOGRAPHS BY WALTER IOOSS JR. (LEFT) AND HERB SCHARFMAN

4

SUPER BOWL XLII

GIANTS 17, PATRIOTS 14

" David Tyree made that helmet catch, sure. But before it, Eli Manning had to escape multiple defenders to make the throw. After, he still had to find Plaxico Burress to finish off the upset with a TD pass. " —CHRIS BURKE

≥ GIANTS MADE PLAYOFFS
AS WILD CARD
≥ UNDEFEATED PATRIOTS
WERE 12-POINT FAVORITE

IT WAS to have been a historic night. The Patriots would win their 19th consecutive game and become only the second NFL team to complete a season unbeaten and untied. They would fortify the legacy of a modern professional dynasty with a fourth Super Bowl title in seven years. They would prove themselves perfect. Instead, the Giants completed an unexpected and emotional postseason run. It was history cut from another cloth, a performance built on the sturdy underpinnings of a ferocious defensive effort, sustained when Eli Manning and David Tyree combined on one of the most memorable plays in NFL history. "It's just surreal," Manning said at the victory party. Past midnight he joined up with his oldest brother, Cooper, and together they sang. The selection, of course, was *New York, New York*.

—*Tim Layden, SI, February 11, 2008*

MVP Manning (left) surged while Tom Brady struggled.

5

1981 AFC PLAYOFFS

CHARGERS 41, DOLPHINS 38

"The lingering image of an exhausted Chargers tight end Kellen Winslow being almost carried off the field by two San Diego teammates tells you all you need to know about this overtime classic." —DON BANKS

≥ CHARGERS SURRENDERED
AN EARLY 24–0 LEAD
≥ MIAMI'S SCORING INCLUDED
A 40-YARD HOOK-AND-LATERAL
TOUCHDOWN TO
CLOSE FIRST HALF

IN OVERTIME Winslow searched for the oxygen behind the Chargers' bench. It was gone, removed for unknown reasons by maintenance men. When Rolf Benirschke finally kicked the winning field goal, Winslow was blocking and didn't see it. He dropped facedown on the sod, cramping from neck to calf, "ready to cry." He assumed the Chargers had won only because of the silence in the stadium. A Dolphins player asked Winslow if he wanted a hand getting up. Winslow said no thanks and stayed where he was. Eventually two Chargers helped him off the field. In the locker room, trainers covered him with cold towels to bring down his temperature, which was more than 100°, and Winslow fell asleep for a while. Despite drinking constantly throughout the game, he had lost 12 pounds.

—*Rick Telander, SI, September 1, 1982*

Winslow did everything except walk off on his own.

PHOTOGRAPH BY AL MESSERSCHMIDT

NO ONE SHOULD HAVE LOST

The Dolphins and Chargers battled to exhaustion, trading apparent knockout blows, but the game went on and on as their field goal kickers struggled to finish the job

BY JOHN UNDERWOOD

T IS THE ONE GREAT IRONY OF PROFESSIONAL football that magnificent games such as San Diego's wonderful, woeful 41–38 overtime AFC playoff victory over Miami are almost always decided by the wrong guys. Decided not by heroic, bloodied men who play themselves to exhaustion and perform breathtaking feats, but by men in clean jerseys. With names you cannot spell, and the remnants of European accents, and slender bodies and mystical ways. Men who cannot be coached, only traded. Men whose main objective in life, more often than not, is to avoid the crushing embarrassment of a shanked field goal in the last 30 seconds.

There, at the end, in a moist, numbed Orange Bowl still jammed with disbelievers after 74 minutes and 1,030 yards and 79 points of what San Diego coach Don Coryell called "probably the most exciting game in the history of pro football," was Dan Fouts. Heroic, bloodied Fouts, the nonpareil Chargers quarterback. His black beard and white jersey crusted with dirt. His skinny legs so tired they could barely carry him off the field after he had thrown, how many? A playoff-record 53 passes? And completed, how many? A playoff-record 33? For a playoff-record 433 yards? And three touchdowns? Fouts should have decided this game.

Or Kellen Winslow. There, at the end, his magnificent athlete's body battered and blued by a relentless—if not altogether cohesive—Miami defense, Winslow had to be carried off. Time after time during the game he was helped to the sidelines, and then, finally, all the way to the dressing room, the last man to make the postgame celebration. Staggering, sore-shouldered, one-more-play-and-let-me-lie-down Winslow, looking as if he might die any minute (the only sure way he could have been stopped), catching, how many? A playoff-record 16 passes? For a playoff-record 166 yards?

Winslow is listed as the tight end in the San Diego offense. The Dolphins know better. Like the 800-pound gorilla, Winslow plays just about wherever Winslow wants to play: tight end, wide receiver, fullback, wingback, slotback. Even on defense, as Miami discovered when he blocked what would have been the winning field goal and thereby spoiled what Dolphins guard Ed Newman called—another drum roll, please—"the greatest comeback in the history of professional football." Winslow should have decided this game.

Or there, on the other side, Don Strock, the gutty, heroic, 6' 5" Miami relief pitcher. Strock coming in with the Dolphins submerged at 0–24 and not only matching Smilin' Dan pass for pass, but doing him better than that for so long a stretch that it looked for sure the Dolphins would pull it out. Throwing (42 times, 28 completions) for 397 yards and four touchdowns, and getting Miami ahead and into position to win at 38–31, and then at the threshold of victory twice again at 38–38.

Strock is 31, a golden oldie amid Don Shula's youth movement, and in his 10th year as a Dolphin it is his business to bail out 23-year-old child star David Woodley. He did so again Saturday when Woodley suffered a first-quarter malaise—sacks, misfires, interceptions—right out of Edgar Allan Poe. In the end breakdowns not of his doing cost Strock exactly what Newman said it would have been—the greatest playoff comeback in the NFL's history. "Strock," said Fouts, "was awesome." Strock should have decided this game.

Fittingly, all of the above helped make it what Fouts himself called "the greatest game I ever played in." (See? It's catching.) But, typically, none of them had even a bit part in the final scene. Overtime games almost always come to that because the objective shifts to a totally conservative aim: The first team close enough tries a field goal. Be cool, play it straight, pop it in. Thus, after a day-into-night parade of exquisite offensive plots and ploys, the final blow was a comparative feather duster, struck by a former 123-pound weakling in a dry, spotless uniform. A tidy little 29-yard love tap that Rolf Benirschke put slightly right of center, 13 minutes and 52 seconds into overtime. It takes nothing away from him, however, to say that the denouement was more negative than positive, not a question of which team would deliver the knockout punch, but which team's kicker would not miss one more easy field goal.

Six minutes into the overtime Benirschke missed a 27-yarder that would have won it then and there. "Fortunately," he said, "I got a second chance." The Dolphins' Uwe von Schamann had two chances too. He missed both. With four seconds to play in regulation, Shula sent in Von Schamann to try a 43-yarder. Winslow, a defensive ringer, leaped and batted it away. Von Schamann went down to the far end of the Dolphin bench, away from everybody and meditated as the overtime started. After Benirschke's life-giving miss, he got his second chance. On fourth down at the Charger 17, in went Von Schamann. The snap was true, the hold good—but in his eagerness to get under the ball, Von Schamann dipped his left side a little too much and his right foot, sweeping across, scraped the ground behind the ball. Von Schamann turned away disgustedly almost as soon as he finished his follow-through. The ball disappeared into a sea of dirty white shirts.

San Diego's drive to the winning field goal was all the more impressive because it came at a time when Miami was apparently the stronger team. The setup play was a beauty. Wide receiver Charlie Joiner, in motion, cut across the field at the snap and saw that Miami had switched from a three-deep to a two-deep zone. He broke his pattern and split the defense up the middle. Fouts looked right, then left, then saw Joiner—"and I had all the time in the world to get it to him." The play covered 39 yards to the Miami 10, and Coryell immediately sent in Benirschke. Lights out, Miami. ∎

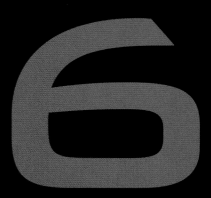

SUPER
BOWL LI

PATRIOTS 34, FALCONS 28

" Through 37 minutes, Atlanta led 28–3.
Then, the drama. In NFL playoff history,
teams with a lead of at least 19 points
entering the fourth quarter had been 93–0.
Now it's 93–1. " —PETER KING

≥ BIGGEST COMEBACK IN
SUPER BOWL HISTORY
≥ PATRIOTS SCORED 31
UNANSWERED POINTS

THE FALCONS still led 28–12, and
an offense that had scored the
seventh-most points in NFL history
had only 9:44 to kill. Yet that sense
of momentum shifting lingered. On
Atlanta's next possession linebacker
Dont'a Hightower barreled around left
end and knocked quarterback Matt
Ryan on his backside, jarring the ball
loose—just as defensive coordinator
Matt Patricia had drawn it up with
the No. 2 Dixon Ticonderoga pencil
stuck behind his right ear. Defensive
tackle Alan Branch recovered at
the Falcons' 25. Tom Brady needed
only five plays to throw another
touchdown, this one six yards to
wide receiver Danny Amendola,
and with the two-point conversion,
New England cut the deficit to one
score. Dot after improbable dot
connected. A victory started to
feel, to borrow a phrase from the
league's Deflategate investigation,
"more probable than not."

—Greg Bishop, SI, February 13, 2017

Julian Edelman's catch keyed the game-tying drive.

7

1981 NFC CHAMPIONSHIP

49ERS 28, COWBOYS 27

"Everyone remembers The Catch: Joe Montana to Dwight Clark, vaulting the 49ers to a 28–27 triumph. Lost to history: Clark actually made numerous catches that day. Eight, to be exact, for 120 yards and two scores." —GREG BISHOP

≥ CLARK CAUGHT MONTANA'S SIX-YARD TD PASS WITH 51 SECONDS LEFT
≥ DALLAS'S FINAL DRIVE WAS QUASHED BY A FORCED FUMBLE IN 49ERS TERRITORY

IT HADN'T been the 49ers' day. They had coughed the ball up six times, two of the turnovers leading to touchdowns. Two interference penalties against their brilliant rookie cornerback, Ronnie Lott (one of them on a very questionable call), had led to 10 more points. A tough game. The lead had already changed hands five times. The 49ers had moved smartly up and down the field, but Dallas had knocked them out of their last three playoffs, and as the 49ers took the ball on their own 11-yard line, down 27–21 with 4:54 left, a deep gloom settled over the Candlestick fans. "I looked down the field and I saw that patch of grass between our huddle and their goalposts," San Francisco center Fred Quillan said, "and I thought, 'That's it. That one patch of grass between us and the Super Bowl.'"

—*Paul Zimmerman, SI, January 18, 1982*

Montana's masterpiece concluded with Clark's catch.

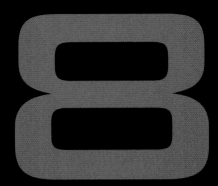

8

SUPER BOWL XLIX

PATRIOTS 28, SEAHAWKS 24

> " It's one thing for an all-time great quarterback to make two length-of-the-field drives in the fourth quarter against the top defense in football to win—and quite another thing for a player no one had ever heard of, Malcolm Butler, to shock the world with his goal-line pick in the last minute to win. Excellent game, and a wow ending. " —PETER KING

≥ SEAHAWKS LED 24–14 IN FOURTH QUARTER
≥ CIRCUS CATCH BY JERMAINE KEARSE GAVE SEAHAWKS A LATE FIRST-AND-GOAL

MARSHAWN LYNCH took a handoff and barreled to the one-yard line. With a minute left, a Seattle touchdown seemed imminent. On second down, as Seahawks coach Pete Carroll later tried to explain, the Patriots packed the line of scrimmage with defenders, forcing Seattle into a passing play. The idea, he said, was to throw the ball away if no receiver got open, then run on the next two downs. Instead, Russell Wilson tried to cram a pass to Ricardo Lockette on a slant route, and Malcolm Butler came down with the pick. "I'm as surprised as everybody else," said Brandon Browner, the cornerback the Patriots had signed away from the Seahawks. "You've got the best running back in the game. . . . Sometimes coaches get too smart."

—*Greg Bishop, SI, February 9, 2015*

Kearse (left) and Lynch took Seattle to the one-yard line.

9

1992 AFC WILD CARD

BILLS 41, OILERS 38

" The Bills proved all things were possible with a 32-point second-half comeback. " —DON BANKS

≥ BILLS STARTING QB JIM KELLY MISSED GAME WITH KNEE INJURY
≥ STEVE CHRISTIE HIT A 32-YARD FIELD GOAL TO WIN IT IN OT

FRANK REICH had thrown only 47 passes in the regular season, mostly in garbage time, so no one could have expected him to complete 21 of 34 for 289 yards and four touchdowns with one interception. Now he has the distinction of having led what at the time was the biggest major-college comeback in history as well as pro football's greatest comeback. He brought Maryland back from a 31–0 deficit at the Orange Bowl to beat Miami 42–40 on Nov. 10, 1984. "A lot of the thoughts I had that day came back today," he said, finally alone in the locker room after 90 minutes of bedlam. "I remember thinking the same thing I thought that day in Miami—one play at a time. You don't have to play bombs away. Your defense has to give the ball back to you every time, and you have to be protected well. Our defense was great, and my line was magnificent." Magnificent. A good word to describe the entire day.

—Peter King, SI, January 11, 1993

Reich's passes set up Christie's winning field goal.

PHOTOGRAPHS BY JOHN BIEVER

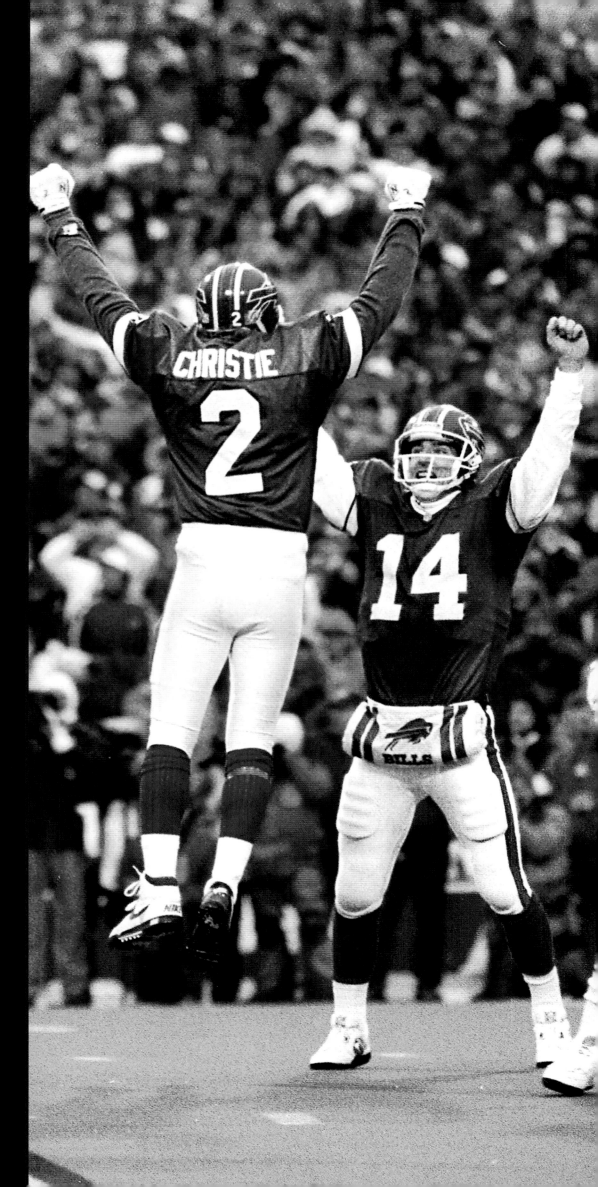

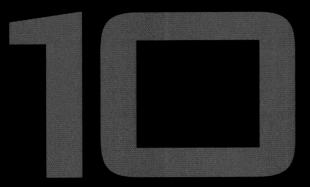

SUPER BOWL XIII

STEELERS 35, COWBOYS 31

> " Meeting in the Super Bowl for the second time in four years, the two best franchises of the era traded body blows, each scoring 14 points during a thrilling fourth quarter. The Steelers held on for their third championship in five seasons. " —MARK GODICH

≥ MVP TERRY BRADSHAW THREW FOUR TOUCHDOWNS
≥ JACKIE SMITH'S END-ZONE DROP HURT DALLAS

ALL GAME long it was Bradshaw who was the dominant presence, who was mainly responsible for turning XIII into the best Super Bowl game of all as well as the highest scoring. It was Bradshaw who took ferocious licks from a Dallas defense that sacked him four times. It was Bradshaw who kept playing with an injured shoulder. It was Bradshaw who kept finding Lynn Swann and John Stallworth and tight end Randy Grossman just when he needed them. And it was Bradshaw who escaped a Cowboy rush and improvised the touchdown pass to Rocky Bleier that put the Steelers ahead to stay 21–14 just before halftime. "Today I relaxed, felt good and had fun," said Bradshaw, who was the unanimous choice for MVP. "I just tried to go out there and help win a football game." Which he did—and how.

—Dan Jenkins, SI, January 29, 1979

Bradshaw escaped Dallas's Doomsday Defense.

10 THE

BEST PLAYS

AS ANYONE WHO HAS TAKEN HIGH SCHOOL HISTORY KNOWS, THE PASSAGE OF TIME CAN REDUCE GREAT SWATHS TO TINY BITS. THE FIRST HALF OF THE PREVIOUS MILLENNIUM OF WESTERN HISTORY IS REPRESENTED BY THE *MAGNA CARTA* AND THE GUTENBERG BIBLE. IT'S THE SAME WITH SPORTS HIGHLIGHT PACKAGES, IN WHICH THE 1970S BECOME LITTLE MORE THAN CARLTON FISK'S HOME RUN, SECRETARIAT'S BELMONT DASH AND LYNN SWANN'S LEAPING GRAB.

SWANN'S CATCH EXEMPLIFIES THE DISTORTING POWER OF THE HIGHLIGHT. SO ACROBATIC AND PICTURESQUE, IT IS SHOWN BEFORE EVERY SUPER BOWL. BUT READ SI'S ORIGINAL GAME STORY, AND YOU'LL FIND A DIFFERENT SWANN RECEPTION (WHICH IS NEVER SHOWN ANYMORE) DESCRIBED FOR PARAGRAPHS BECAUSE THAT WAS THE DECIDING SCORE, WHILE HIS HIGHLIGHT CATCH, WHICH ONLY SET UP A MISSED FIELD GOAL, MERITS A MERE SENTENCE.

IN RARE CASES IT'S A LACK OF DEFINING IMAGE THAT PROVES CAPTIVATING. THE IMMACULATE RECEPTION REPLAYS ARE NOTABLE FOR WHAT THEY DON'T SHOW, WHICH IS WHETHER THE CATCH WAS LEGAL. BACK THEN A CAROM FROM ONE OFFENSIVE PLAYER TO ANOTHER WITHOUT A DEFENDER TOUCHING THE BALL WASN'T A VALID CATCH. THE RAIDERS INSISTED THE BALL NEVER TOUCHED THEM. IT'S HARD TO VIEW THAT HIGHLIGHT AND NOT SEARCH ONCE AGAIN FOR THE PROOF THAT NEVER COMES.

1

MANNING-TO-TYREE

SUPER BOWL XLII

" Not only was David Tyree's third-and-five reception the most significant play in the Giants' taking down the unbeaten Patriots, it was a physically implausible act that would have been remarkable even if it had occurred in an exhibition game. " —TIM LAYDEN

≥ 32-YARD COMPLETION
≥ SET UP WINNING SCORE

THEY CAUGHT Eli Manning in a squeeze. He was a dead duck, but somehow he escaped. "My man had his jersey," left guard Rich Seubert said. "I yelled, 'Go, Eli, go!'" "I had a good view because nobody rushed over me," right guard Chris Snee said. "I turned around, and there were a couple of guys mugging Eli. Somehow that scrawny body got away." "No one pulled me down. . . . I felt a tug," Manning said. "I tried to stay small." He got off a pass that went 32 yards to Tyree, a special teams whiz and the No. 4 receiver. "I guarantee you," Peyton Manning said, standing by his brother's locker afterward, "there were guys on that Patriots defense who thought the play was already over. He gets sacked, that's it, it's over. Fourth-and-15." Giants fullback Madison Hedgecock said, "Most amazing play I've ever seen on a football field."

—*Paul Zimmerman, SI, February 11, 2008*

Manning's escape (left) set up Tyree's catch.
PHOTOGRAPHS BY BOB ROSATO (LEFT) AND DAMIAN STROHMEYER

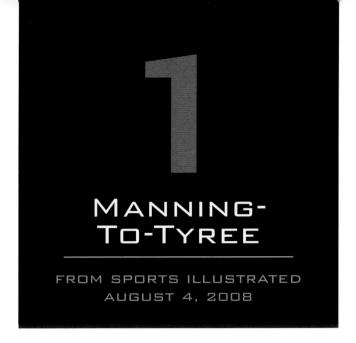
CONTINUING AMAZEMENT

Long after the Super Bowl XLII ended, players just couldn't wrap their heads around the catch that felled the Patriots

BY TIM LAYDEN

THE PLAY LIVES ON, SPRINKLING its magic over the weeks and months. Many of the New York Giants got their first clear look at it when they returned to Giants Stadium from Arizona after their epic Super Bowl victory; shouts and screams emanated from film rooms and bounced through the dark hallways. Some of them watched it again nearly three months later at a routine, off-season video session in late April, when players split up by positions to review cut-up digital video of offensive and defensive situations from the entire season.

On that day quarterbacks and wide receivers studied plays in which the Giants used four-wideout formations during their two-minute drill. In the middle of the session—"Just mixed in with the rest of them," says quarterback Eli Manning—up popped the play that defined a game and a season, and perhaps much more. A quarterback escapes a sure sack, a wideout leaps into the night, a football is pinned impossibly against the surface of a helmet and brought safely to earth. The Patriots' unbeaten season ends soon after.

Just as quickly, another play pops up on the screen. But the memory lingers. "The more you look at it," says David Tyree, the wide receiver who made the catch, "the more it doesn't make sense from a logical standpoint. The velocity of the throw, the defender draped all over me, the curved surface of the ball against a round helmet, the way we came down to the ground. It just doesn't make sense."

Manning sees it in simpler terms. As he watched the video in darkness, he measured the distance between victory and defeat. "If we don't make that play," he says, "it's fourth down and at least five yards, and you don't know what can happen then. You watch that play and you realize how close we came to not winning the Super Bowl."

Manning-to-Tyree was improvisational brilliance at best, sandlot good luck at worst. It still doesn't make sense, and that is part of its enduring beauty. "It's the greatest play in Super Bowl history," says Steve Sabol, the NFL Films president who has been chronicling the league since his father, Ed, started the company in 1962. Considering the play's stage and subplots, perhaps it's fair to see Sabol's claim and raise him: Call it the greatest play in NFL history.

A dull game suddenly turned riveting in the fourth quarter. A Manning-to-Tyree touchdown pass gave the Giants a 10–7 lead with 11:10 to play. After an exchange of punts, the Patriots took possession at their 20-yard line, chasing perfection against the clock with 7:54 to play. Twelve plays and just more than five minutes later, Tom Brady threw a six-yard touchdown pass to Randy Moss, and the Patriots led 14–10.

Then the Giants stuttered downfield. Eleven yards on a first-play completion from Manning to Plaxico Burress. . . . A stumbling two-yard run by Brandon Jacobs for a fourth-down conversion with 1:34 to play. . . . A five-yard scramble, then a near interception. The Giants faced third-and-five at their 44 with 1:15 left. The call came into Manning's helmet receiver: 62 Y Sail Union. "It's one of our basic two-minute plays," says Manning. "We probably ran it 10 or 12 times during the season."

Manning's first read was to the right, where free safety James Sanders lined up over Steve Smith and cornerback Asante Samuel over Tyree. If Sanders sat hard on Smith, Tyree needed only to get inside of Samuel and he'd be open to the post deep. "The safety sat pretty hard," says Manning. "I probably would have thrown it to David anyway."

In fact, Sanders and Samuel appeared to bungle the coverage. "Tyree and Smith were both open," says NFL Films senior producer Greg Cosell, who has watched the video many times.

Manning, however, had other concerns. At the snap Patriots linebacker Adalius Thomas beat Giants left tackle David Diehl with a speed rush to the outside, forcing Manning to step up early; nosetackle Jarvis Green beat center Shaun O'Hara to O'Hara's left; and right defensive end Richard Seymour looped to his left behind Green. O'Hara tried to come off Green and cut off Seymour, and left guard Rich Seubert tried to pick up Green. Both failed.

"They ran a three-technique inside, and we all got beat," says Seubert. "The nosetackle [Green] pretty much picked me off. They did a good job. I think everybody on their defense came free to Eli. [Not entirely true: Right tackle Kareem McKenzie controlled linebacker Mike Vrabel's outside rush.] At that point in the play, when I didn't get my job done, I'm thinking, Just throw it, Eli."

Seymour was the first to get to Manning, briefly grabbing the quarterback's jersey. Green's grip was more substantial—a meaty forearm across the top of Manning's back and then a handful of jersey as Manning tried to escape. Manning saw a flash of white shirt in front of him. "I was about to flip it to him," the quarterback says, "but then I saw it was [right guard] Chris Snee, so I thought, Don't do that."

Says Green, "It was a weird play, man. At first it was a perfect pocket push, with AD [Thomas] getting pressure on the outside and then a big push in the middle. I had my hand on his shoulder, then I had his jersey, and I think I could even feel it ripping a little bit. I thought Eli was going to go down for sure. Watching film on him all year long, somebody just touches him, he falls to the ground. But he got away."

History will remember Manning's great escape, but much credit on the play goes to Giants linemen O'Hara and Seubert, who were badly beaten initially but stayed with the play, heeding the order delivered on football fields every day: Play to the whistle. As Seymour grabbed Manning, O'Hara reached across under Seymour's chin and tried to drag him off Manning. Likewise, Seubert thrust a forearm under Green's left arm, making it more difficult for Green to get leverage on Manning.

The act of breaking free spit Manning out of the scrum and away from the line of scrimmage. He ran five steps to his right and back to the 33-yard line toward the Giants' sideline, caught a glimpse of Tyree, squared his shoulders and let fly. "If it had been the third quarter and that play happened, I would not have thrown the ball," says Manning. "You don't throw a 40-yard pass into the middle of the field, kind of up for grabs. But it was third-and-five, I almost got sacked, so you either throw it away or you give Tyree a shot. I gave him a shot."

Green turned, watched the play and heard a roar. "The whole thing was like slow motion," he says. "I said to myself, What in the hell just happened?" Green was raised in Donaldson, La., played at LSU and often visits New Orleans, where the Mannings are royalty. He has been hearing it since February: *How did you not get him down?*

At the snap Tyree had run at Samuel, planted his right foot and

turned toward the middle of the field. After clearing Sanders, the safety, he looked back over this left shoulder. "Eli had just stepped up," says Tyree, "and he was obviously struggling. I drifted back toward the line of scrimmage and a little toward the middle of the field. I felt open. But I knew I wasn't going to be open long."

He was the unlikeliest of heroes. Tyree grew up just seven miles from Giants Stadium, in Montclair, N.J., and in high school he was mired in a life of drugs and alcohol. "Every weekend I drank a 40-ounce bottle of malt liquor and a half-pint of Jack Daniel's and smoked a blunt of marijuana," says Tyree. It continued at Syracuse and in the NFL, until 2004, when he was arrested in possession of a half-pound of marijuana.

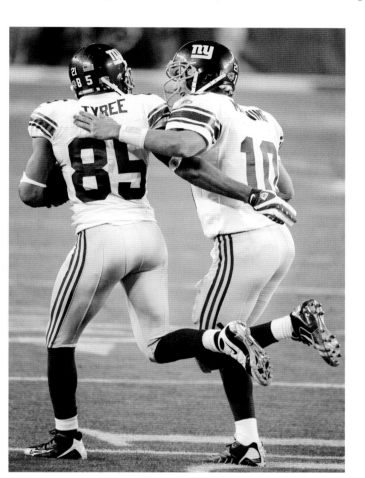

The incident scared him straight. He says he stopped drinking and smoking and reconciled with his girlfriend, Leilah, who had borne him one son and was pregnant with another. Tyree became a devout Christian. He married Leilah, and now they have four children (including twin girls born after the Super Bowl). On Dec. 15 Tyree's mother, Thelma, died of a heart attack in Florida at age 59. One day later the Giants' fourth receiver, Sinorice Moss, was injured. In five NFL seasons Tyree had established himself as a terrific special teams player but had seldom cracked the four-receiver rotation. "All of sudden, last two games of the year," he says, "I'm in the mix."

Manning's throw traveled 42 yards in the air, and it was no moon ball. "People said it hung up," says Tyree. "Take a look. It was a pretty hard throw." On the sideline Giants defensive end Justin Tuck watched the throw and cringed. "'Oh, my lord, this is just up in the air,'" he remembers saying. "I just put my head down."

Tyree went nearly straight up and got two hands on the ball. Patriots strong safety Rodney Harrison first tried to bat the ball through Tyree's hands, pushing it against the receiver's helmet. Then Harrison took Tyree down by his right biceps, which had the effect of clamping the ball tighter against the headgear. "As it was happening, I almost felt like I could hear music," says Tyree. "It was fast, but it was slow too."

Tyree ran off the field as tight end Kevin Boss was inserted into the game. The crowd gasped as the play was rerun on the stadium's huge video screens. "I knew it was a good play," says Tyree. "I didn't know the degree. But I would be a hypocrite to take credit. That goes to God."

Four plays later Manning threw 13 yards to Burress for the game-winning TD, a play that was climactic and at the same time anticlimactic.

Shortly after the game ended, Sabol boarded a private plane for the trip back to New Jersey, where work on the official Super Bowl film would begin early the next day. He fretted on the flight—"flop sweats," he says—over whether NFL Films cameras had fully captured the Tyree catch. His memory went back to 1972, when Ernie Ernst was the only NFL Films cameraman to get footage of Franco Harris's Immaculate Reception.

He was in his office at 5 a.m. on Monday and watching video of the Super Bowl by seven. Three tape machines unspooling action. Eight people in the room. "We went right to the Tyree catch, before anything else," says Sabol. The angles were covered. The pictures were good. And the play was unlike anything they had ever seen. ∎

The names of Manning and Tyree will be forever linked.

2

IMMACULATE RECEPTION

1972 AFC PLAYOFFS

" Franco Harris's last-minute touchdown reception against Oakland not only launched the Steelers dynasty, but remains the most famous, and disputed, play in NFL history. " —DON BANKS

≥ STEELERS WERE BEHIND 7–6 AND ON THEIR OWN 40
≥ OAKLAND ARGUED THE CATCH WAS A CAROM FROM ONE RECEIVER TO ANOTHER, WHICH WAS ILLEGAL THEN

SCRAMBLING, TERRY BRADSHAW spotted Frenchy Fuqua at the Oakland 35 and desperately heaved the ball in his direction. Fuqua and Oakland safety Jack Tatum collided. The Steelers' hopes were dashed, the game was over . . . until, suddenly, from out of nowhere, came rookie fullback Franco Harris. "When the play got messed up," Harris later said, "I was running toward Fuqua, hoping he'd get the ball and I could block for him." The ball headed right for Harris, who, in full stride, scooped it up just above the grass. He raced down the left sideline and scored. Raiders coach John Madden, for one, was a disbeliever and argued— in vain—with officials. "Tomorrow morning when I wake up and read the paper," said Madden, "I still won't believe it."

—Steve Wulf, SI, October 16, 1991

Harris's fourth-down catch came with 22 seconds left.

3

THE
CATCH

1981 NFC CHAMPIONSHIP

" There have been hundreds of thousands of receptions in NFL history, but there is one "Catch." Had Dwight Clark mistimed his jump or even been 6' 3" instead of 6' 4", the arrival of the 49ers' dynasty may have been delayed by the Cowboys. " —CHRIS BURKE

≥ THE CATCH WAS THE 13TH PLAY OF AN 89-YARD-DRIVE
≥ THE SIX-YARD PASS CAME ON THIRD-AND-THREE WITH 58 SECONDS REMAINING

CLARK REMEMBERS only fragments of The Catch—the fear he'd jumped too soon; the way the ball bounced off his fingertips, obliging him to recatch it; the thought that maybe Montana was heaving the ball out-of-bounds. The Catch propelled San Francisco into the Super Bowl and has made a famous and much-photographed man of the dashing, white-toothed Clark. He still can't quite get a handle on what happened that day, on how a midair 10th of a second could mean so much to so many. But whenever the crush of the autograph hounds and the praise of the writers and the flacks threaten to inflate Clark's opinion of himself, he knows enough to ask himself one question. "I just say, 'Dwight, what if you'd dropped that thing?'"

—Rick Telander, SI, September 1, 1982

Clark was Montana's second option on the play.
PHOTOGRAPH BY WALTER IOOSS JR.

4

BUTLER'S INTERCEPTION

" Seattle was one yard and 25 seconds away from back-to-back Super Bowl titles when unheralded and undrafted rookie cornerback Malcolm Butler jumped in front of receiver Ricardo Lockette at the goal line. " —GREG A. BEDARD

≥ PATRIOTS HAD COME BACK FROM 10 POINTS DOWN ≥ JUGGLING CATCH BY JERMAINE KEARSE HAD MOVED SEATTLE NEAR END ZONE

BUTLER LINED up three yards deep in his end zone. "Just like anybody else would feel," he recalls thinking, "I felt like the game was on me." And then he noticed: In a situation where most teams— especially one with Marshawn Lynch—would run, the Seahawks lined up in a formation that screamed pass, a shotgun with three receivers to the right. Butler had seen it before, in a midweek practice, and wideout Josh Boyce had burned him. He wasn't going to let Seattle's Ricardo Lockette do the same. "I knew it was coming," Butler says, "so I beat him to the spot." This was a gamble, but when you have maybe one shot to hold on to a victory, you take your chances. As Seattle QB Russell Wilson said after the game, "It was going to be a touchdown."

—Joan Niesen, SI, February 9, 2015

Butler snared an interception and saved New England.

PHOTOGRAPHS (FROM TOP) BY JOHN BIEVER ; JOHN IACONO; JOHN W. MCDONOUGH; AND JOHN IACONO (RIGHT)

MUSIC CITY MIRACLE

" The Titans turned a desperation kick return into a 75-yard score that featured a handoff and a pass across the field—in a playoff game. " —GREG BISHOP

≥ BILLS HAD JUST TAKEN
A 16–15 LEAD
≥ 16 SECONDS REMAINED

AFTER VIEWING a replay for the first time, Titans coach Jeff Fisher put down his wine glass, dropped his head and looked humbled by the magnitude of the feat. Yet Kevin Dyson's 75-yard catch and dash—which came after fullback Lorenzo Neal had fielded a short, high kickoff and handed off to tight end Frank Wycheck, who ran to his right before throwing across the field to Dyson behind a wall of blockers along the left sideline— was anything but supernatural. True to his methodical nature, Fisher had anticipated just such a situation, chosen a viable escape route, made sure his team knew the drill and practiced the play at the end of each Saturday's special teams session. "Another one of Jeff Fisher's crazy setups," quipped Blaine Bishop, the Titans' veteran free safety. "You name the situation and we'll practice it. Guys'll be tired and rolling their eyes, saying, 'Yeah, like this'll ever come up.'"

—*Michael Silver, SI, January 17, 2000*

Once Dyson caught Wycheck's pass, he had a free run.

PHOTOGRAPH BY BOB ROSATO

6

The Holmes TD

SUPER BOWL XLIII

> " Santonio Holmes caught the pass while falling, nearly parallel to the ground, to finish off a game-winning 78-yard drive engineered by Ben Roethlisberger. " —TIM LAYDEN

≥ SIX-YARD CATCH GAVE PITTSBURGH A 27–23 LEAD
≥ 35 SECONDS REMAINED

FIRST-AND-GOAL, 48 seconds to play. Roethlisberger whistled a pass to the back of the end zone that slipped through the leaping Holmes's hands. On the next play, with the Steelers' line keeping the Cardinals' rush at bay, Roethlisberger had time to run through his progression. His first read, running back Willie Parker, was covered in the flat. His second option, receiver Nate Washington, also had too many red jerseys around him. So Roethlisberger looked to his third option, Holmes, and saw him racing to the right corner of the end zone. Three defenders were in front of the receiver, but Roethlisberger fired the ball anyway, high and outside. Holmes snagged it with his fingertips and touched the grass with both sets of outstretched toes. His fourth catch of the drive and ninth reception of the night was the game-winner.

—Damon Hack, SI, February 9, 2009

Holmes was named Super Bowl MVP.

SWANN'S CATCH

SUPER BOWL X

> *" Lynn Swann's acrobatic catch came on a ball that he tipped to himself after it was deflected by Cowboys cornerback Mark Washington. "* —MARK GODICH

≥ SWANN'S 53-YARD GRAB HELPED STEELERS OUT OF BAD FIELD POSITION
≥ SWANN WAS NAMED GAME MVP AND HAD FOUR CATCHES FOR 161 YARDS

FOR ALL of those gaudy things that happened throughout the afternoon, memories of the 1976 Super Bowl will keep going back to the Pittsburgh Steelers' Lynn Swann climbing into the air like the boy in the Indian rope trick, and coming down with the football. He didn't come down with very many passes last Sunday, really, only four, but he caught the ones that truly mattered. That is why it will seem that he spent the day way up there in the crisp sky, a thousand feet above Miami's Orange Bowl, where neither the Dallas Cowboys nor even a squadron of fighter planes could do anything to stop him. When it was all over Lynn Swann and the Steelers had won 21–17 and had repeated as the champions of professional madness.

—Dan Jenkins, SI, January 26, 1976

Swann and Washington both tipped the ball.

PHOTOGRAPHS BY KEN REGAN/CAMERA 5 (LEFT) AND HEINZ KLUETMEIER

JONES'S TACKLE

SUPER BOWL XXXIV

" Shotgun. Six seconds left. Steve McNair back to pass, complete to Kevin Dyson, driving for the goal line. Linebacker Mike Jones lunges, grabs Dyson by the legs, and they stop churning, and Dyson reaches, reaches, reaches . . . but he's about 40 inches short of the goal line. " —PETER KING

≥ TITANS HAD BALL ON THE 10-YARD LINE
≥ RAMS LED 23–16

TENNESSEE CALLED its final timeout with six seconds remaining, and the season came down to one precious play. The Titans sent tight end Frank Wycheck into the end zone, hoping to draw several defenders to the area and hit Kevin Dyson on an underneath slant with room to run. Dyson, whose kickoff return off a Wycheck lateral had given Tennessee a stunning wild-card victory over the Buffalo Bills, had another Music City Miracle in reach. He caught the ball in stride inside the five and had only one man between him and the first overtime game in Super Bowl history. Mike Jones, however, wrapped up the wideout, and Dyson's lunge for the goal line fell short. "It seemed like slow-motion," Jones said. "I couldn't see McNair throw the ball, but I could feel it."

—*Michael Silver, SI, February 7, 2000*

Jones, a career journeyman, made a textbook tackle.
PHOTOGRAPH BY JOHN BIEVER

HAIL MARY

" Cowboys quarterback Roger Staubach launched a heave to wideout Drew Pearson in the final seconds that the receiver somehow caught for the winning score. " —GREG BISHOP

≥ 50-YARD PASS GAVE DALLAS A 17–14 WIN
≥ STAUBACH: "I CLOSED MY EYES AND SAID A HAIL MARY"

USUALLY IT only happens in those novels written for young readers. It is cold and gloomy and all hope seems to be gone, but the good guy who loves his wife and family and country has gone back to try one more long pass against the evil villains who throw bottles and garbage at football officials. The ball sails high and far, straining to be seen against the feeble lights that glow through the gray Minnesota sky. Now the ball is coming to earth as the scoreboard flickers away the final seconds of the game. There are two men underneath the ball and suddenly one of them slips and falls, and the one who is supposed to catch it and complete the grandest of comebacks and upsets and fairy tales does exactly that. Roger Staubach has thrown a pass to Drew Pearson, and the Dallas Cowboys have used up a lifetime of good fortune in a single play.

—*Dan Jenkins, SI, January 5, 1976*

The Vikings argued that Pearson (88) had pushed off.

10

MIRACLE AT THE MEADOWLANDS

NOVEMBER 12, 1978

"The play changed the way teams close out games and helped make Herman Edwards famous." —DON BANKS

≥ GIANTS LED 17–12
WITH 31 SECONDS LEFT
≥ EAGLES HAD NO TIMEOUTS

"JUST FALL on it" his teammates implored in the huddle. The game was over, for God's sake. But Joe Pisarcik had no choice. A week earlier, in a loss to the Washington Redskins, Giants offensive coordinator Bob Gibson had screamed at his quarterback for changing a play. So on this frigid afternoon at Giants Stadium, Pisarcik followed Gibson's instructions and called a handoff to the fullback. Pisarcik mishandled the ball and made a clumsy handoff to Larry Csonka, who dived for the football after it bounced off his right hip and fell to the turf. Eagles cornerback Herman Edwards picked it up and raced 26 yards into the end zone. Now the game was over. "It was just one play," Pisarcik says, "but it changed the fortunes of an organization, and it changed people's lives." The play's greatest victim was Gibson, who was canned the day afterward and never worked in football again.

—Albert Chen, SI, July 2, 2001

Edwards ran in the third-down fumble by Pisarcik (9).

THE 10

BEST SINGLE-SEASON TEAMS

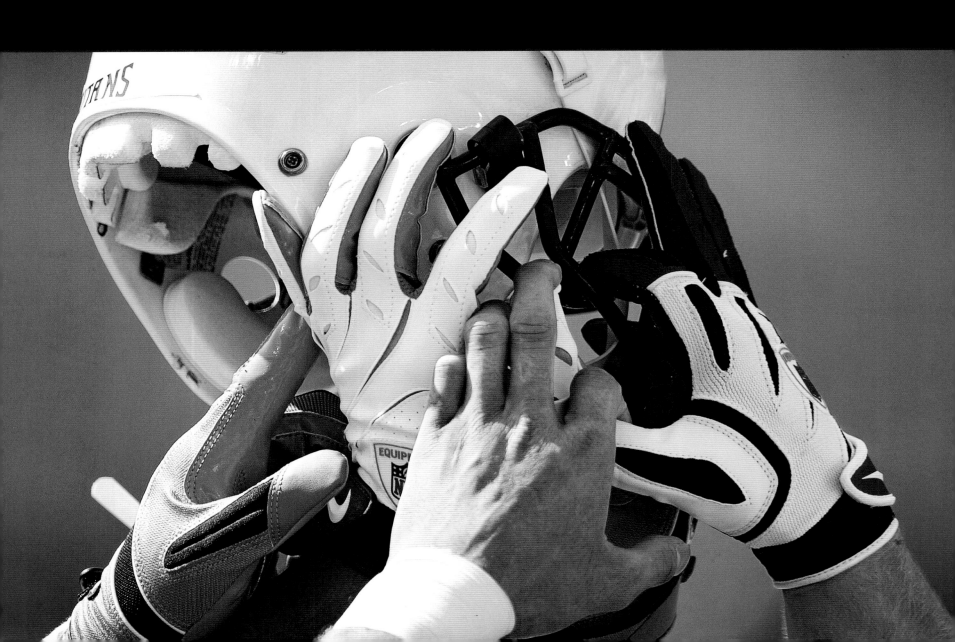

SHOULD ONE BAD SUNDAY DEFINE A SEASON? NOT ACCORDING TO OUR PANEL. THE GROUP WAS FORGIVING OF THE OCCASIONAL STUMBLE, AND NOT JUST IN WEIGHING THE CLASSIC FAN'S DEBATE AT THE TOP OF THE POLL, BETWEEN THE UNDEFEATED BUT UNSPECTACULAR 1972 DOLPHINS AND THE MORE DOMINANT, ONE-LOSS 1985 BEARS.

THE LENIENCY ALSO SPILLED OVER TO THE 2007 PATRIOTS, WHO PLOWED THROUGH 18 STRAIGHT WINS UNTIL THEY RAN INTO DAVID TYREE AND HIS MAGIC HELMET. THE PATRIOTS MAKE THE LIST, BUT THE GIANTS TEAM THAT KNOCKED THEM OFF DIDN'T RECEIVE A SINGLE VOTE.

THAT PATRIOTS LOSS INSPIRES HEATED FEELINGS, AS THEIR FANS WILL TELL YOU THAT IF CORNERBACK ASANTE SAMUEL HADN'T DROPPED AN INTERCEPTION JUST BEFORE TYREE'S CATCH, THE 2007 GROUP WOULD BE AT THE TOP OF THE POLL. BUT TO DISCOUNT ONE TEAM'S CRITICAL MISPLAY IS TO CRAWL INTO A RABBIT HOLE. THE 1984 49ERS LOST ONE REGULAR-SEASON GAME, BY THREE POINTS—CAN THEY PICK A PLAY TO DO OVER? THE '98 VIKINGS, BUT FOR A SHANKED FIELD GOAL IN THE NFC TITLE GAME, MIGHT HAVE HAD A SHOT AT THIS LIST TOO. RESULTS ARE ABOUT WHAT HAPPENED, NOT WHAT MIGHT HAVE HAPPENED.

1

1985 BEARS

15–1 REGULAR SEASON

" Widely considered the best defensive unit in NFL history, the '85 Bears allowed a scant 12.4 points per game, introduced the world to the Super Bowl Shuffle and carried Chicago to within one loss of an undefeated season. Every great defense since then has been compared to those Bears —and often not favorably. " —GREG BISHOP

≥ DEFENSE HAD 64 SACKS, FORCED 64 TURNOVERS
≥ SECOND IN SCORING OFFENSE

IT WILL be many years before we see anything approaching the vision of hell that Chicago inflicted on the poor Patriots in Super Bowl XX. It was near perfect, an exquisite mesh of talent and system, defensive football carried to its highest degree. It was a great roaring wave that swept through the playoffs, gathering force and momentum, until it finally crashed home in New Orleans' Superdome. The game wasn't exciting. So what? Go down to Bourbon Street if you want excitement. The verdict on Chicago's 46–10 victory was in after two Patriot series. Don't feel cheated. Louis-Schmeling II wasn't very competitive, either. Nor was the British cavalry charge at Balaklava, but Tennyson wrote a poem about it.

—Paul Zimmerman, SI, February 3, 1986

Jim McMahon (left) and William Perry (72) shone for Chicago.

2
1972
DOLPHINS

14–0 REGULAR SEASON

" The only team in the Super Bowl era to win the championship with a perfect record. " —GREG A. BEDARD

≥ LED NFL IN TOTAL OFFENSE AND DEFENSE
≥ LARRY CSONKA AND MERCURY MORRIS BOTH HAD 1,000-YARD RUSHING SEASONS

ALMOST EVERYWHERE across the pro football landscape there was a heartfelt vote for the Pittsburgh Steelers, a team so snakebitten that it had suffered its whole long life, 40 years, without a single championship. But after weeks of favoring her with bountiful blessings, the fairy godmother suddenly failed to touch Cinderella with her magic wand. Instead, she strung along with the inexorable Miami Dolphins, that acquisitive bunch of opportunists that she has been dating steadily.

And so it is the Dolphins who will now meet Washington in the Super Bowl. This was Miami's 16th consecutive victory. To the very end it seemed that Pittsburgh might be able to employ the same kind of wicked lightning that it had used in the last seconds to execute the Raiders. But Miami's No-Name Defense precluded another miracle by twice intercepting Terry Bradshaw in the waning minutes of the game.

—Ron Reid, SI, January 8, 1973

Csonka ran for 112 yards in Super Bowl VII.

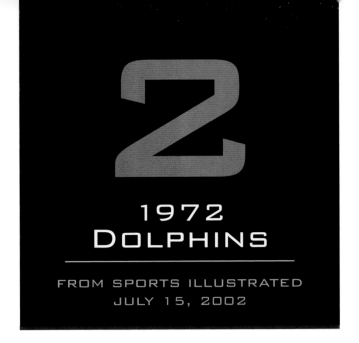

NOBODY'S PERFECT (EXCEPT US)

If you don't believe the only team to go undefeated is also the best in the history of the NFL, just ask men who played on it

BY MICHAEL SILVER

A S TIME HAS PASSED, THE perfect season's impeccable beauty has been tinged with less-pleasant associations. The unabashed glee displayed by some of the '72 Dolphins when other undefeated teams falter is a turnoff to many fans. This doesn't seem to bother those Miami players who, almost to a man, believe they have been slighted by history's hand. "We don't get the respect we deserve," says Hall of Fame quarterback Bob Griese, who in 1998 angered some Denver Broncos by openly rooting for them to lose after a 13–0 start—even though Griese's son, Brian, was the team's third-string quarterback. "We don't get mentioned as one of the greatest teams of all time, so being the only one that had a perfect season is what makes us special."

The '72 Dolphins have no use for decorum or, some would argue, dignity. Thirty years after they ran the table, nine of them can sit at a banquet table at Shula's Steakhouse in Miami Lakes, as they did recently, and rail on everyone—from SI's Rick Reilly to NFL Films president Steve Sabol—who has ever denied them their due. "Hey, give this to Rick Reilly for me," says former tight end and current team broadcaster Jim Mandich, offering a middle-finger salute that cracks up his dining companions. "He called us bitter old men, but this is the kind of record you want to hold on to."

The unbeaten Dolphins were feeling dissed even before Super Bowl VII. Consider that the Redskins, who went into the game with three defeats—two of them to New England and Buffalo, teams against whom Miami had gone 4–0—were nonetheless favored to beat the Dolphins.

Even after Miami's 14–7 victory, which was far more decisive than the score suggests, the team received no White House invitation from embattled President (and Skins supporter) Richard Nixon.

Before Don Shula arrived in 1970, the Dolphins were a national joke. Co-owned by comedian Danny Thomas upon its launch as an expansion team in '66 (he later sold his interest to Joe Robbie), Miami went a combined 15-39-2 in its first four seasons and, says Hall of Fame linebacker Nick Buoniconti, "the team was known as the Floating Cocktail Party." Shula, who had coached the Baltimore Colts to NFL Championship Game and Super Bowl appearances, changed everything. "He was a strong disciplinarian, almost to the point of tyranny," Csonka says. Modern-day players who complain about two-a-day practices in training camp, take note: In his first preseason, Shula put the Dolphins through four daily workouts in the muggy South Florida heat.

Though there was a nucleus of talented players, mostly on offense, this was a major building project, and Shula and his staff did a masterly job. Consider that offensive line coach Monte Clark, who was later head coach of the San Francisco 49ers and the Detroit Lions, fielded five starters in '72 who had been discarded by at least one other NFL team. Two of those castoffs, center Jim Langer and guard Larry Little ended up in the Hall of Fame.

Miami went 10–4 in Shula's first season, then made its surprising Super Bowl run in '71, where it lost to Dallas 24–3 in New Orleans. The Dolphins' stink bomb against the Cowboys left Shula fighting a stigma—unable to win the big one—since he had also been on the wrong side of the New York Jets' Super Bowl III shocker. "In New Orleans, I had tried to stress that they had plenty of time to celebrate after the game, but sometimes you have to feel that emptiness for yourself," says Shula, who was inducted into the Hall of Fame in '97, two years after his retirement. "What it did was give us that sense of purpose for the next season."

The '72 team set an NFL single-season record with 2,960 rushing yards, as the rugged Csonka and slashing halfback Eugene (Mercury) Morris became the first teammates to hit the 1,000-yard plateau in the same year. The team's other halfback, Jim Kiick, was a punishing blocker and gifted receiver who ran for 521 yards. Wideout Paul Warfield was a superstar, later elected to the Hall of Fame, but he and possession receiver Howard Twilley were both underused. Even after Griese went down in the fifth game with a broken right ankle—he shocked even himself by returning to play in the AFC Championship Game and the Super Bowl—his 38-year-old backup, Earl Morrall, was a resplendent replacement, averaging 9.1 yards per pass.

Csonka, a 6' 3", 237-pound moose of a man, set the tone for Miami's ball-control attack. For those of you too young to remember him as anything but a ham-it-up *American Gladiators* cohost, think of every old-school cliché in the book, then add piss and vinegar. "True story," says Shula. "We're in Buffalo, and Csonka's running toward the sideline when a guy runs over from the secondary. Zonk throws a forearm and knocks him cartwheeling back. The official throws a flag and calls unnecessary roughness on him. I said, 'What, for hitting the poor tackler too hard?'"

Though not overpowering, the Dolphins were plenty tough on the other side of the ball as well. Under coordinator Bill Arnsparger, the No-Name Defense—a term coined before Super Bowl VI when Dallas coach Tom Landry described the Miami defenders as Buoniconti and a bunch of no names—allowed just 171 points and a league-low 235.5 yards per game. In addition to standouts like Buoniconti and defensive tackle Manny Fernandez, the unit boasted one of the great safety tandems in history in Dick Anderson and Jake Scott.

Before Shula and Griese arrived, the Dolphins were seen as a joke.

Oddly enough it was placekicker Garo Yepremian who produced the most memorable play of the perfect season. With 2:07 remaining in Super Bowl VII, Yepremian, an immigrant from Cyprus who had learned football on the fly, lined up for a 42-yard field goal. The Dolphins had dominated the Redskins all day, and the kick, fittingly, could have made the final score 17–0. But Yepremian, whose 51-yarder at Minnesota in Week 3 had helped Miami survive its closest call, had his low kick blocked right back to him, and his subsequent attempt to pass the ball resembled a sea lion trying to shotput a half-melted block of ice. Defensive back Mike Bass intercepted the pass and went 49 yards for Washington's only score.

After his retirement in 1981, Yepremian launched a second career as a motivational speaker. The fact that the gaffe became so famous—and that Yepremian has made light of it in his speeches—still enrages some Dolphins, most notably Kuechenberg, who says, "It was an act of cowardice." Says Morris, laughing, "Garo says, 'I know Kuechenberg doesn't like me.' I tell him, 'Garo, it's not that he doesn't like you. He wants to kill you.'"

Every family has its strife, and the Dolphins are no exception. Teammates say that Scott, the MVP of Super Bowl VII, remains bitter toward

Shula for the '76 trade that sent him to the Redskins. Mostly, though, the Dolphins' bonds have remained strong. Several extended financial assistance to wideout Marlin Briscoe, who after leaving football in the late '70s became addicted to crack cocaine—L.A. dealers nicknamed him 17 and 0—and once was kidnapped by Crips because of a drug debt. He now works for the Watts/Willowbrook Boys and Girls Club. Another rallying point has been the Miami Project to Cure Paralysis, initiated by Buoniconti after his son, Marc, broke his neck while playing football for The Citadel in 1985 and became a quadriplegic. Nick Buoniconti says his family and teammates have helped raise more than $100 million.

Buoniconti and his teammates chafe at having been supplanted by the Pittsburgh Steelers, who won four Super Bowls from the '74 through '79 seasons, as the team of that decade. The Dolphins believe their five-year run from '70 through '74 was comparably dominant, and they may have a point: When Miami (15–2) mauled the Vikings in Super Bowl VIII, it was the team's 32nd victory in 34 games. The Dolphins had a shot at reaching their fourth consecutive Super Bowl in '74, but they lost their playoff opener to the Raiders on the so-called Sea of Hands catch—Clarence Davis's improbable, last-minute touchdown grab. Then Csonka, Kiick and Warfield left Miami for the riches promised by the World Football League's Memphis Southmen, and that was the end of the Dolphins' run.

When NFL Films staged a computer-generated mock tournament involving the greatest teams of all time, the '72 Dolphins dropped a 21–20 decision to the '78 Steelers in the title game. "That's why Shula hates Steve Sabol," Kiick says. "He called up Sabol and reamed him out." Explains Shula, "I don't see how there could be a program that would cause a computer not to pick our team." Detractors point out that in the regular season Miami played only two teams that finished with winning records, and both went 8-6.

The men who produced the perfect season believe the numbers 17 and 0 should end all debate. Thirty years later, they are still a team: undefeated, untied and unbowed. In '85, when the 12–0 Bears traveled to Miami for a Monday night game, Csonka, at Shula's behest, gave a stirring pregame speech. Then Csonka and many of his former teammates stood on the sideline. The Dolphins won 38–24, and Chicago finished 18–1.

Showing support for their old team was one thing, but the Miami players' blatant joy over other teams' failures took on gauche overtones. After the 11–0 Redskins lost in '91, Anderson and Buoniconti initiated an annual champagne toast that accompanies the demise of the league's last remaining undefeated team.

Like most of his former teammates, Csonka has grown to value the perfect season more as the years have passed and team after team has failed to duplicate the feat. "I don't want to think that anyone can," Csonka says, his bushy mustache practically sinking into his chin. "We're the only team that has ever been perfect, and there's a certain serenity and pride in having done that. Every year, when another team wins a few games without losing, we're reborn, and our spirits rise up out of the ground." ■

3

2007 PATRIOTS

16-0 REGULAR SEASON

" While the Giants and David Tyree ruined their bid for a historic 19–0 season, Tom Brady led a record-breaking Patriots offense that demolished almost everything in its path. " —DON BANKS

≥ SCORED 589 POINTS, THEN AN NFL RECORD
≥ OUTSCORED OPPONENTS BY RECORD 315 POINTS

THEY SHRUGGED off the blowback from the Week 1 Spygate controversy and averaged more than 40 points a game in the first half of the season, prompting accusations that coach Bill Belichick was needlessly running up scores on defenseless opponents. The last month's more difficult victories have provided a true measure of the franchise's culture. The Pats caught America's attention with glitz and big scores, but have kept it with solid performances more emblematic of their foundation. They do not court Football Nation's affection or scrutiny, but inside their walls they embrace the simplest concepts—selflessness, rigor, tunnel vision—until they are reflex. The concepts are not novel. Every football team at every level from Pop Warner to the NFL seeks the same discipline, but the Patriots have come closest to achieving it.

—Tim Layden, SI, January 28, 2008

Brady (left) and LB Tedy Bruschi flirted with perfection.

4

1962
PACKERS

13–1 REGULAR SEASON

"The best team in the Lombardi dynasty, this version of the Packers led the league in offense, defense and scoring margin." —TIM LAYDEN

≥ OUTSCORED OPPONENTS
415–148
≥ 10 HALL OF FAME PLAYERS

PARTLY BECAUSE of the weather and often because New York coach Allie Sherman and his players wanted to prove that they could whip the Packers where the Packers are best, the Giants ran against the right side of the Packers line—Henry Jordan at right tackle and Bill Quinlan at right end. It was the Giants' misfortune that they did not succeed. Jordan and Quinlan played heroically, and the Packers linebackers—Ray Nitschke, Dan Currie and Bill Forester—were, as they have been all year, the best in the league. Giants backfield coach Kyle Rote pointed that out. "The Packers won because they have a fine offense and a great line," he said. "But most of all, they have three magnificent linebackers. After everyone else had gone home, Sherman said his farewell: "We weren't humiliated. There was no humiliation this year." There wasn't. The Giants were good. Green Bay simply was better.

—Tex Maule, SI, January 7, 1963

Bart Starr led the NFL with a 90.7 passer rating.

5

1989
49ERS

14–2 REGULAR SEASON

"George Seifert took over for Bill Walsh as coach, and the defending Super Bowl champions didn't miss a beat. The Niners outscored their three playoff opponents by 100 points." —MARK GODICH

≥ NFL'S TOP SCORING OFFENSE, THIRD-BEST SCORING DEFENSE
≥ DEFEATED BRONCOS 55–10 IN SUPER BOWL XXIV

WE ARE sailing in uncharted waters with these 49ers. We are seeing power football, defensive brilliance, and execution so precise it's scary. . . . So what must coach George Seifert fear as his Niners head to the Super Bowl? Complacency? A false sense of invincibility? All the evils the rich and powerful are heir to? He'll take them, as long as he can keep Montana on his side. "Joe's been phenomenal all year," said Seifert, "but it seems that he's elevated his performance for the playoffs. His concentration, his 'into-it-ness'—it's mind-boggling. You look at him from the sidelines, and you're almost in awe. You find yourself watching like a fan would. You fight to get out of a mode like that. In this game if you let your guard down, pretty soon you're fighting for your life. But today, in the heat of battle, I couldn't help saying, 'Damn, we're pretty good.'"

—Paul Zimmerman, SI, January 22, 1990

WR John Taylor (left) and RB Roger Craig added power.

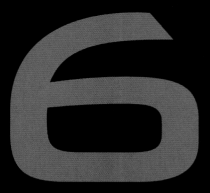

6
1991
REDSKINS

" The Redskins were five points from an undefeated season. They scored 30.3 points per game and allowed just 14, then steamrolled through the playoffs by a combined score of 102–41. " —CHRIS BURKE

≥ LED NFL IN SCORING OFFENSE
≥ SECOND IN SCORING DEFENSE

MAYBE WE should reflect on the simple fact of Washington's superiority for just a moment. The Skins won 17 games this season and lost only twice. They whipped their NFC playoff foes, the Falcons and the Lions, by a combined score of 65–17. They have the premier offensive line in the league, the best trio of wide receivers (Gary Clark, Art Monk and Ricky Sanders) and the best coach (Joe Gibbs). "If we'd scored before the half," said Bills center Kent Hull after their 37–24 loss in the Super Bowl, "we could have won." No, they couldn't have. The Redskins are a team of remarkable strength and determination. Boring, perhaps, but disciplined and smart. "If the rest of Washington ran as efficiently as this football team, there wouldn't be any deficit," said Skins center Jeff Bostic, while ripping tape off his knees after the game and puffing on a big cigar.

—Rick Telander, SI, February 3, 1992

Mark Rypien won Super Bowl MVP after a stellar season.

PHOTOGRAPH BY JOHN BIEVER

7

1978
STEELERS

14–2 REGULAR SEASON

" Not the most dominant defensive unit Chuck Noll had, but the team with the most offensive firepower by far—with 33, 34 and 35 points scored in its three playoff games. This season, and this postseason, proved Terry Bradshaw and the Pittsburgh passing game were as formidable as the Steelers running attack ever was. " —PETER KING

≥ NINE HALL OF FAME PLAYERS
≥ BRADSHAW WON NFL MVP

AT THE start of 1978, the Steelers' defense was considered over the hill. It was even suggested—perish the thought—that the Steel Curtain should be dismantled and replaced by a 3-4 defense. So the Curtain regrouped and had an intimidating year. The Steelers allowed the fewest points in the NFL (195). A year ago, for the first time in four seasons, Joe Greene didn't play in the AFC Championship Game. Instead he sat home and watched Oakland and Denver play on TV. During the telecast a camera focused on a sign in the stands in Mile High Stadium that read, JOE MUST BE GREENE WITH ENVY. Quietly, Greene got his two Super Bowl rings out and placed them on top of his television set. Now he plans to add a third ring to that collection.

—Joe Marshall, SI, January 15, 1979

Franco Harris scored in Super Bowl XIII (left).

PHOTOGRAPHS BY TONY TOMSIC (LEFT) AND JOHN IACONO

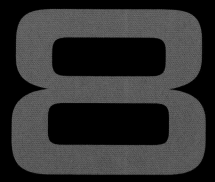

8

1984
49ERS

15–1 REGULAR SEASON

" In the heart of the Walsh-Montana-Rice-Lott dynasty, the Niners lost only once and swept through the postseason, winning playoff games by an average of almost 20 points. They were a model of efficiency on offense and led the league in scoring defense. " —TIM LAYDEN

≥ NFL'S FIRST TEAM TO WIN
15 REGULAR-SEASON GAMES
≥ ALL FOUR STARTING DBS
MADE PRO BOWL

THEY'RE EFFECTIVE on any level, from working on a cerebral plane, with Joe Montana running one of the NFL's most complicated passing attacks, to brutalizing opponents with a very rough and effective ground game. There's only one thing missing. The magic. The beautiful rose-colored glow of 1981, when the 49ers came from nowhere and won it all. The Bay Area gasped at their play. In a way it's unfair to compare the two teams. What can compare with your first kiss, your first sip of wine? "Ask anyone and he'll tell you there's no question that this team's better than the one we had in '81," says defensive back Ronnie Lott. "And it's fun now too . . . don't get me wrong . . . but it's more professional. In '81 it was a different kind of fun, bubbly fun, rookie fun, you know what I mean?"

—Paul Zimmerman, SI, November 26, 1984

WR Freddie Solomon snagged one in the NFC title game.

PHOTOGRAPH BY RICHARD MACKSON

1966
PACKERS

12-2 REGULAR SEASON

"The first-ever Super Bowl winner won its fourth NFL championship in the span of six years. By this point Lombardi's Packers were a finely tuned machine." —DON BANKS

≥ QB BART STARR WAS
NAMED NFL MVP
≥ DEFEATED CHIEFS 35–10
IN SUPER BOWL I

HAVING LIVED luxuriously on poise and control all season, the Packers won their second straight NFL championship in Dallas by defeating the Cowboys 34–27 in a flamboyant display of football histrionics. For pure suspense and unremitting excitement no championship game has approached it for at least eight years. . . . After the win the Packers were too tired to think ahead to the Super Bowl. But in chilly Buffalo, after the Chiefs had defeated the Bills 31–7 to win the AFL championship, Kansas City coach Hank Stram let himself be carried away by the wonder of it all. "Pour it on, boys," he burbled. "There'll be lots more when we tear apart the NFL in two weeks." Told of this rather optimistic statement, Packers guard Fuzzy Thurston shrugged. "Hank Stram can think what he wants," he said. "We just play the game and win."

—*Tex Maule, SI, January 9, 1967*

Paul Hornung (5) blocked for Jim Taylor (31).

PHOTOGRAPH BY WALTER IOOSS JR.

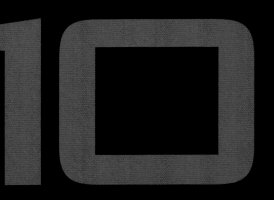

2004
PATRIOTS

14-2 REGULAR SEASON

" This team won New England's third title in four years and completed a 21-game win streak that began in the previous season (with many of the same players). " —GREG A. BEDARD

DEFEATED EAGLES 24-21
IN SUPER BOWL
OUTSCORED OPPONENTS BY
11.1 POINTS PER GAME

"FIVE YEARS ago, when I was about to hire Bill [Belichick], we were having dinner at the Capital Grille in Chestnut Hill," Patriots owner Robert Kraft recalled. "I said, 'Promise me that when we have success that you won't change,' and he has been true to that promise." The coach demands similar humility from his players, who in the words of backup linebacker and special teams ace Matt Chatham, are "all drinking the Kool-Aid. Everybody buys into the team concept, and we'd be stupid not to." "When you work together— when you embrace words like dignity, integrity and unselfishness—great things can be accomplished," said linebacker Tedy Bruschi. Realizing that he, too, was falling into a familiar trap, the ninth-year linebacker caught himself and laughed. "And if you've got some ballers in your locker room," Bruschi added, "you'll win a lot of Super Bowls."

—Michael Silver, SI, February 14, 2005

on Branch (11 catches, 133 yards) was Super Bowl MVP.

PHOTOGRAPH BY HEINZ KLUETMEIER

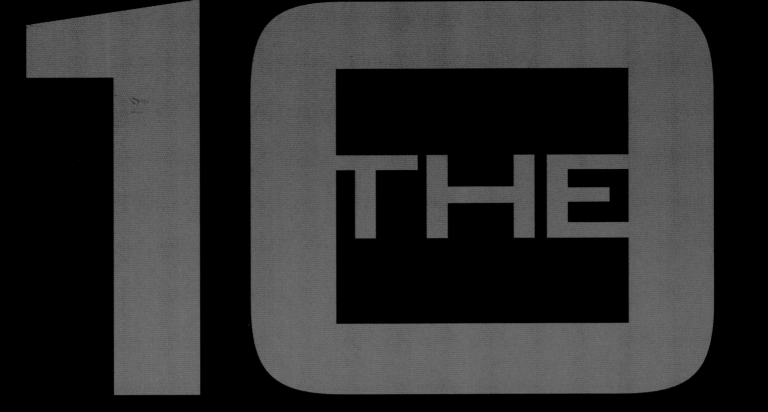

10 THE

BEST STADIUMS

THE MOST UNORTHODOX CHOICE OF ANY PANELIST IN ANY CATEGORY WAS TIM LAYDEN'S VOTE FOR THE NO. 1 NFL STADIUM. IT CAME, ALMOST LITERALLY, OUT OF LEFTFIELD. THAT IS, HE CHOSE YANKEE STADIUM. HIS EXPLANATION: "DOZENS OF THE MOST IMPORTANT GAMES IN BUILDING THE FOUNDATION OF THE LEAGUE TOOK PLACE HERE, WITH PLAYERS KICKING UP CLOUDS OF DUST ON THE BASEBALL INFIELD AND DISAPPEARING INTO DARK CORNERS OF THE BUILDING AFTER TOUCHDOWNS."

LAYDEN'S VOTE WASN'T ENOUGH TO PUT YANKEE STADIUM IN THE TOP 10. BUT VOTERS LARGELY MADE CHOICES WHICH EMBRACED HIS BASIC LOGIC, WHICH WAS THAT HISTORY AND CHARACTER SHOULD BE MORE IMPORTANT THAN THE MODERN REFINEMENTS FOUND IN TODAY'S FOOTBALL-SPECIFIC STADIUMS.

OUR TOP PICK, LAMBEAU FIELD, IS LONG ON HISTORY—HOME TO THE ICE BOWL, WHERE MALFUNCTIONING HEATING COILS RESULTED IN A FROZEN FIELD. BUT IT HAS CONTEMPORARY TOUCHES TOO. A 2013 RENOVATION ADDED A NEW LEVEL WHICH FEATURES CHAIRS WITH BACKS, INSTEAD OF THE BENCHES IN THE STADIUM'S LOWER STRATA. THE STADIUM ALSO HAS A STATE-OF-THE-ART VIDEO BOARD. THIS MEANT THAT FANS AT THE '15 PLAYOFF GAME AGAINST DALLAS COULD SCRUTINIZE THE VIDEO AND SEE IF, IN FACT, DEZ BRYANT CAUGHT THAT BALL. WHAT WOULD A LIVE GAME BE WITHOUT REPLAY?

1

LAMBEAU FIELD

GREEN BAY

" What Fenway Park and Wrigley Field
are to baseball, Lambeau Field
is to football. " —GREG A. BEDARD

≥ FIRST GAME HELD IN 1957
≥ CAPACITY HAS EXPANDED
FROM 32,500 TO 81,435

THERE WAS a time when the Green
Bay Packers' Lambeau Field wasn't
the quaint anomaly it is today.
Everyone played football on grass,
and there were no Teflon roofs to
shut out the midday sun, no domes
to block the late-autumn wind.
When mud-spattered linemen
Forrest Gregg and Jerry Kramer
hoisted coach Vince Lombardi onto
their shoulders in 1961 for his first
NFL title ride, only God's gray sky
hung overhead. Why, the world
hadn't even heard of turf toe when
Lombardi stalked Lambeau's frozen
sidelines in his trademark overcoat,
shrieking, "Hey! Whaddaya doin'
out there?" in his best Brooklynese.
"With Lombardi it was never cold
here," says former All-Pro Fuzzy
Thurston, who played guard for
Green Bay from 1959 to '67. "Before
games he'd just say something like,
'Men, it's a little blustery out there
today.' Blustery, see? Then he'd say,
'It's our kind of day. Now get out
there and strut around like
it's the middle of July.' "

—Johnette Howard, SI, January 13, 1997

At Lambeau, it's always football weather.

PHOTOGRAPH BY SIMON BRUTY

2

ARROWHEAD STADIUM

KANSAS CITY, MO.

" The sea of red displayed on game
day at Arrowhead always speaks
to how beloved the Chiefs remain
in their home market. It's still
one of the loudest outdoor venues in
the NFL. " —DON BANKS

≥ OPENED IN 1972
≥ CAPACITY: 76,416

WHY YOU DON'T NEED TO REMEMBER JOE
CAHN'S NAME Because he goes by
Commissioner of Tailgating. WHY
HIS TITLE MAKES SENSE Each football
season since 1996 the Commish,
54, has logged 30,000 miles in
his Monaco Signature coach,
visiting about 50 of the nation's
finest stadium parking lots. WHY
SERIOUS 'GATERS SHOULD INVITE HIM
TO HELP OUT AT THE HIBACHI Cahn
founded the New Orleans School
of Cooking (which he's since sold)
and has prepared king salmon at
a Seattle tailgate and Cuban pig
in Miami. He always wears the
home team's colors, and he can
spin a good travel yarn—like the
time John Madden invited him into
the Madden Cruiser for a pregame
bite of barbecue. HEAVEN IS Kansas
City's Arrowhead Stadium. "They
know their barbecue, know their
football, and they have a lot of
porta-potties out there."

— *Sports Illustrated, September 16, 2002*

Arrowhead is one of the NFL's loudest stadiums.

3

AT&T STADIUM

ARLINGTON, TEXAS

Some worried, but in-game punts have never hit the TV.

PHOTOGRAPH BY GREG NELSON

" Built at a cost of $1.3 billion and opened in 2009, the stadium features a retractable roof and a video board that stretches from one 25-yard line to the other. " —MARK GODICH

≥ CAPACITY IS 80,000, PLUS ANOTHER 20,000 IN STANDING ROOM
≥ WORLD'S LARGEST HIGH-DEFINITION VIDEO BOARD

OURS IS BIGGER! proclaimed T-shirts, and this was of course true; the stadium is the largest column-free structure in the world. Before kickoff a series of photos appeared on the video board: the Pyramids, the Parthenon, the Great Wall, the Taj Mahal, the Colosseum and, finally, Cowboys Stadium.

— *Chris Ballard, SI, September 28, 2009*

THE KING OF TEXAS

Jerry Jones, who built his fortune by taking outsized risks, positively glowed as he oversaw—and underwrote—construction of America's largest and most expensive football palace

BY RICHARD HOFFER

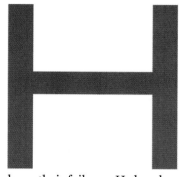

IS "TOLERANCE FOR AMBIGUITY"— his phrase—is high enough to register somewhere between impudence and daredevilry. Where else would you put it? When the big oil companies, who are hardly in the business of prudence, abandoned their dry holes in the late '60s, it was Jerry Jones who offered to lease their failures. He barely understood their caution anyway. Spending $14 million to drill, say, 18,000 feet and then just walking away because of something called budget—was that any way to find oil or gas? "Unthinkable," he says. "That's just unthinkable."

Jones, an independent operator and not answerable to anything like budget, kept drilling, and who knows how many times he embarrassed the big oil companies with his finds. A dry hole, after all, is simply a gusher without conviction. Jones, then as now, supplied all the conviction necessary. Maybe if he hadn't made 12 strikes in his first 13 tries—drilling between dry holes in Oklahoma's Red Fork Wells—he'd have had less of it. Then again, we're talking about a guy who, as a 23-year-old in 1966, nearly bought the San Diego Chargers from Barron Hilton with money he didn't have. (Jones had arranged for a letter of credit from a labor union.) "You sure are young," Hilton told Jones, who was born with all the conviction he'd ever require.

But let's not make him sound pathological, either, as if he lacked a mortal's ability to recognize consequence. He never actually drilled to the center of the earth for oil, and the times he came close he sweated it. When he pledged his wealth and all receivables to buy the floundering Dallas Cowboys—America's Team or not, this was a failing outfit in 1989—he needed two hands to steady a cup of coffee. Who wouldn't? In those days Dallas was the epicenter for one of the oil industry's worst depressions. Titans were being wiped out, banks closed, skyscrapers shuttered. Loans were being sold for a nickel on the dollar.

Of course his hands shook. Even beyond the economic climate, the deal was punishing, a sophisticated form of extortion, really. It was bad enough that he had to pay a $65 million for the Cowboys (quite literally America's Team, considering the federal government owned 12% of the franchise after a lending bank failed). The team was not very good, and, after three losing seasons, home sellouts were even harder to come by than victories. But—here's the extortion part—he was forced to absorb the $75 million leasing rights on Texas Stadium as well. (The total purchase price was a record for an NFL team.) In those days NFL stadiums were essentially rentals, some place you visited on Sundays. They had no income or marketing worth to NFL owners.

The deal done, Jones barely had time to count the empty suites, consider the previous season's 3–13 record, and get over the surprising fact that the Cowboys had lost $9.5 million on just $41 million in revenues the year before, when the bills began to come in. They totaled $105,000 a day. "If you want to get motivated," Jones suggests, "strap that on."

O.K., that was then, and now here's Jones in his splendid office at Valley Ranch in Irving, the three Super Bowl trophies always in his line of sight. That pitiful team he bought is valued by *Forbes* at $1.2 billion, and he has turned that albatross of a stadium into his biggest revenue producer. But what's the fun of this business, really, if your hands aren't shaking?

"Let's go see the stadium," Jones says, and we're off to 140 acres of mud. This is the latest, possibly the greatest, edifice to be constructed for the people's entertainment in this great land of ours, maybe the final frontier in sports-related architecture.

Jones, who did not answer to budget here any more than he did in the Oklahoma oil fields, did not stint on anything, even when the original cost of $650 million ballooned to $1 billion. The city of Arlington's share was capped at $325 million, meaning that Jones pays for every add-on doodad—such as two 60-yard-wide flat screens hanging over the field—out of his pocket, 100%. "And I'm an adder-oner," he says.

It turns out Jones is a bit of a stadium freak as well, going way back. Before playing Nebraska in the 1965 Cotton Bowl, his Arkansas team stayed in Houston and got a tour of the new Astrodome. "When we saw that thing—glistening—I couldn't stand it," he says. "It sucked the air right out of you." Many years later (he won't say when because it embarrasses him to admit how old he was on his first visit to New York City) Jones paid a cab driver to take him to Yankee Stadium first thing. He got out, touched it and returned to business.

When it became obvious to him that simply renovating 36-year-old Texas Stadium—"And by the way," he says, "I didn't have to do even that"—wouldn't cut it, he plunged into the new venture with his usual gusto. He got the idea for his giant screens while watching a Celine Dion show at Caesars Palace. He was visually discombobulated by the screens behind her, redundant to the Canadian songbird's performance, but mesmerized all the same. "You didn't know what you were seeing," he says, "but you knew it must have been good."

Jones actually seems to delight in the possibility of failure, however slim it really is. As he conducts a tour of his pile—"There," he points to some concrete at field level, "is where the players will come onto the field. Through a stadium club!"—you can enjoy a secondhand exhilaration. *This is what it's like to commit $1 billion!* "I'm writing a one-million-dollar check every day," Jones says, aggrandizing his risk the way any gambler would, the way he always has, the tab just higher these days. "That will keep your eye on the ball." He couldn't seem any happier. ∎

4

MILE HIGH STADIUM

DENVER

❝In a Denver-Houston playoff game early in my career, John Elway was rallying the Broncos in the fourth quarter, the noise was deafening, and the ground actually started shaking. I couldn't believe it. And from the horrified look on Oilers defensive end Sean Jones's face, he couldn't believe it either. Denver won.❞ —PETER KING

≥ STOOD FROM 1948 TO 2002
≥ CAPACITY GREW FROM 18,000 TO 76,123

YEAH, THAT'S your seat, that little 16-inch-deep stretch of wood covered by that bleached-out skin of orange fiberglass. Yeah, it's a little small for the modern backside, especially when everybody's wearing a ski parka against the cold, but scrunch up. Everybody does. Get your breathing in sync with the rest of the folks in the row and enjoy. You're in the group now. Let me tell you about it. The south stands have room for 8,096 backsides, and 8,096 backsides have filled those spaces for 33 years. All these seats are for season tickets, most of them owned by the same people for most of that time. If you're a stranger, you stand out like a kicker's clean jersey, like Jason Elam in the fourth quarter on a rainy, muddy afternoon.

—*Leigh Montville, SI, December 25, 2000*

Mile High, as seen from a mile higher.

5

CenturyLink Field

SEATTLE

" The best of the new class of NFL stadiums, the Seahawks' new home features spectacular views of downtown Seattle to the north and Mount Ranier to the south. The 3,000-seat bleacher section called the "Hawks Nest" helps make the stadium one of the loudest in the league. " —DON BANKS

≥ DESIGNED TO BOUNCE NOISE OFF ROOF
≥ CHEERING FROM MARSHAWN LYNCH'S 2011 PLAYOFF TD AGAINST NEW ORLEANS REGISTERED AS A MEASURABLE SEISMIC EVENT

WITH THE help of smelling salts and the urgings of 67,837 fans, linebacker Lofa Tatupu played three-plus quarters with what was later diagnosed as a mild concussion and helped the Seahawks complete a declawing of the Panthers that reverberated from Grungeville all the way to Motown.... Sometimes Tatupu's signals weren't easy to hear, as the boisterous crowd celebrated a team it hopes can win Seattle's first major professional sports championship since the SuperSonics won the 1978–79 NBA title. "This is the craziest crowd I've ever seen in this town," said a man who should know, Pearl Jam bassist Jeff Ament.

— *Michael Silver, SI, January 30, 2006*

Seattle retired the number 12 in honor of their fans.

HEINZ FIELD

PITTSBURGH

" To watch a Steelers game there is to be overwhelmed by Terrible Towels and the history of the franchise, making Heinz Field one of the best home-field advantages in sports. " —GREG BISHOP

≥ OPENED IN 2001
≥ CAPACITY: 68,400

ROB RUCK, a Pittsburgh native and senior lecturer in history at the University of Pittsburgh, says "It's impossible to overstate how Pittsburgh was battered by the collapse of the steel industry. The Steelers replaced steel as the city's identity." Pittsburgh has remade itself in subsequent years as a finance and technology center, but the relationship forged between the fans and the team has endured. Terrible Towels conceived in 1975 by writer-broadcaster Myron Cope still fill Heinz Field. The Steelers trail only the Cowboys and the Giants in sales of officially licensed merchandise, and a 2007 survey by Turnkey Sports and Entertainment ranked them number 3 among 122 professional sports franchises in fan loyalty. "As soon as you come here, you can sense that the franchise is revered in this city," says Jerome Bettis, a Steeler from 1996 to 2005. "And you know it was that way years and years before you came here."

—Tim Layden, SI, February 2, 2009

The stadium was built with 12,000 tons of steel.

7

SOLDIER FIELD

CHICAGO

"The lakefront stadium has been home to more than the Bears. Some 104,000 witnessed the Tunney-Dempsey Long Count fight in 1927, and a Notre Dame–USC game later that year drew 120,000, still a record for a college football game." —MARK GODICH

≥ OPENED IN 1924
≥ BEARS BEGAN PLAY
THERE IN 1971

AH, CHICAGO. It is a city built on stamina, endurance and stoicism. For more than a century waves of immigrants fleeing the poverty of European ghettos found their way to Lake Michigan's shore, there to endure the suffocating summers and savage winters, but never yielding to despair. The Bears, even when they are the recipients rather than the dispensers of violence, are a metaphor for the city itself. So for that matter is Soldier Field, its brightly painted seats and Astro Turfed surface a shining facade that distracts from but does not conceal the cracks in its ancient concrete and the 12-by-12-foot wooden beams that prop up its crumbling structure, just as the lakeshore Gold Coast stretches a thin, glamorous skin over a carcass as excruciatingly ugly as the bare-ribbed remnants of a rhinoceros.

— *Richard W. Johnston, SI, December 9, 1974*

After years with artificial turf, grass returned in 1988.

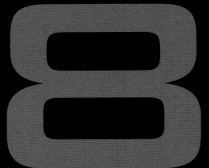

8

WASHINGTON, D.C.

> "One of the great old barns in which I always felt honored to cover a game. It oozed football. It smelled like football. And when the Redskins were rolling, it was my favorite stadium in the league." —PETER KING

≥ REDSKINS HOME, 1961 TO 1996
≥ RENAMED FROM DISTRICT OF COLUMBIA STADIUM IN 1969

RFK
STADIUM

IN WASHINGTON, the fans have made a federal case out of the Hogs. A pig was brought to the stadium Saturday. Hog signs were everywhere: HOGTIE THE VIKINGS. WE'RE IN HOG HEAVEN. WE'RE HOG WILD OVER THE REDSKINS. THE HOGS THAT ATE MINNESOTA. This Hog business could get to be a boar.

—*Steve Wulf, SI, January 24, 1983*

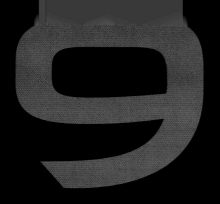

ORANGE BOWL

" Five of the first 13 Super Bowls took place in Flipper's home. The Dolphins went undefeated there in 1972. It stood and decayed in downtown Miami, but it represents some of the most significant moments in the history of the league. " —TIM LAYDEN

≥ STOOD FROM 1937 TO 2008
≥ DOLPHINS HOME STADIUM, 1966 TO 1986

AS THE site of 14 national championships and five Super Bowls, it served as a national proving ground. Joe Namath became a New York legend, Doug Flutie a Boston legend, Bear Bryant an Alabama legend, Kellen Winslow a San Diego legend—all because of their exploits in the neighborhood now known as Little Havana.

—S.L. Price, SI, November 12, 2007

Super Bowl III was one of the stadium's high points.
PHOTOGRAPH BY NEIL LEIFER

CITY OF MIAMI ORANGE BOWL STADIUM

0 COLTS • 5:32 JETS 16
DOWN 3 10 TO GO BALL ON 37 QTR 4

The scoreboard reads:

QUARTER	1	2	3	4	TOTAL
CHIEFS	0	10	0		10
PACKERS	7	7	14		28

K C BALL ON 33 YARD LINE

3 DOWN 25 YARDS TO GO
FIRST DOWNS K C 15 GB 14
TIME-OUTS LEFT 3 3
ATTENDANCE 63 036

LOS ANGELES

The Coliseum hosted Super Bowls I (above) and VII.

PHOTOGRAPH BY WALTER IOOSS JR.

" New and beautiful? No. Historic? Absolutely. The Coliseum has twice served as the Rams' home, the franchise's arrivals separated by 70 years (1946 and 2016). The Raiders played there, too, for more than a decade, not to mention the AFL Chargers. " —CHRIS BURKE

REGAINING THEIR glory days may be a vain hope no matter how good the Rams become. In those wonderful old days of splendid memory when they drew 21 crowds of more than 80,000 from 1950 through '58, the Rams did not have ticket competition with the Dodgers, the Angels and the Lakers.

— Edwin Shrake, SI, October 3, 1966

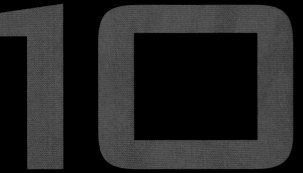

10
MEMORIAL COLISEUM

≥ OPENED IN 1923
≥ CAPACITY: 80,000

10

THE

BEST FRANCHISES

THE NFL BEGAN PLAY IN 1920 WITH TEAMS LIKE THE MUNCIE FLYERS AND THE COLUMBUS PANHANDLES IN ITS LINEUP. SADLY, OF THOSE 14 ULTRAORIGINALS, ONLY TWO, THE DECATUR STALEYS (WHO BECAME, IN 1922, THE CHICAGO BEARS) AND THE CHICAGO CARDINALS, WHO EVENTUALLY MIGRATED TO ARIZONA, SURVIVED LONG ENOUGH TO SEE THEIR FOOTAGE BROKEN DOWN BY RON JAWORSKI ON ESPN.

BUT WHILE MOST OF THE FOUNDING TEAMS FOLDED, NEW FRANCHISES ENTERED THE FRAY. PAGING THROUGH THIS SECTION AND NOTING THE DATES OF EACH TEAM'S INAUGURAL SEASON, YOU CAN SEE THE KEY CHARACTERS COMING TOGETHER, EACH ADDING AN ESSENTIAL ELEMENT TO THE LEAGUE.

THE VOTE FOR THIS CATEGORY'S TOP SPOT WAS THE CLOSEST IN THE BOOK, WITH THE STEELERS NIPPING THE PACKERS BY THE NARROWEST OF MARGINS (AND BOTH FINISHING WELL AHEAD OF DALLAS AT NO. 3). THE STEELERS AND THE PACKERS HAVE MUCH IN COMMON: BOTH HAVE BEEN AROUND A LONG TIME; THEY EACH ENJOYED A DECADE OF DOMINANCE (THE PACKERS IN THE 1960S, THE STEELERS IN THE '70S); THEY PLAY IN MARKETS THAT ARE RELATIVELY SMALL; AND HAVE STABLE LEADERSHIP. AND WITH EACH FRANCHISE, THERE'S PLENTY FOR FANS OF OTHER TEAMS TO APPRECIATE AND TO ENVY.

1

THE STEELERS

FOUNDED 1933

" After decades in the wilderness during
their early years, the Steelers have set
the standard with six rings in the
Super Bowl era and a franchise stability
that is unmatched. " —DON BANKS

≥ MADE PLAYOFFS IN
29 OF LAST 45 SEASONS
≥ THREE COACHES SINCE 1969

THE LITTLE black notebook has
been called Art Rooney's private
office. It contains the most detailed
information about some of his
principal interests: the Steelers, the
grain market, the whereabouts of his
running horses, the state of affairs at
Shamrock, his thoroughbred breeding
farm of 387 acres in Sykesville, Md.
There was a time when Rooney was
able to run all his business out of
the black notebook—football, fight
promoting, political maneuvering
as Republican boss of Pittsburgh's
22nd Ward, big-time wagering on
horses. But the black book does not
suffice today. Rooney finds he must
call upon the familiar accoutrements
of modern business—lawyers and
accountants, mouthpieces and
peace-mouthers. Yet he clings to the
little book just the same and yearns for
the old days when a handshake was
enough to commit a man to
a business deal or put a few grand
riding on the nose of a horse.

—*Gerald Holland, SI, November 23, 1964*

The spirit of founder Art Rooney Sr. (left) carries on.

PHOTOGRAPHS BY HARRY CABLUCK (LEFT) AND SCOTT BOEHM/AP

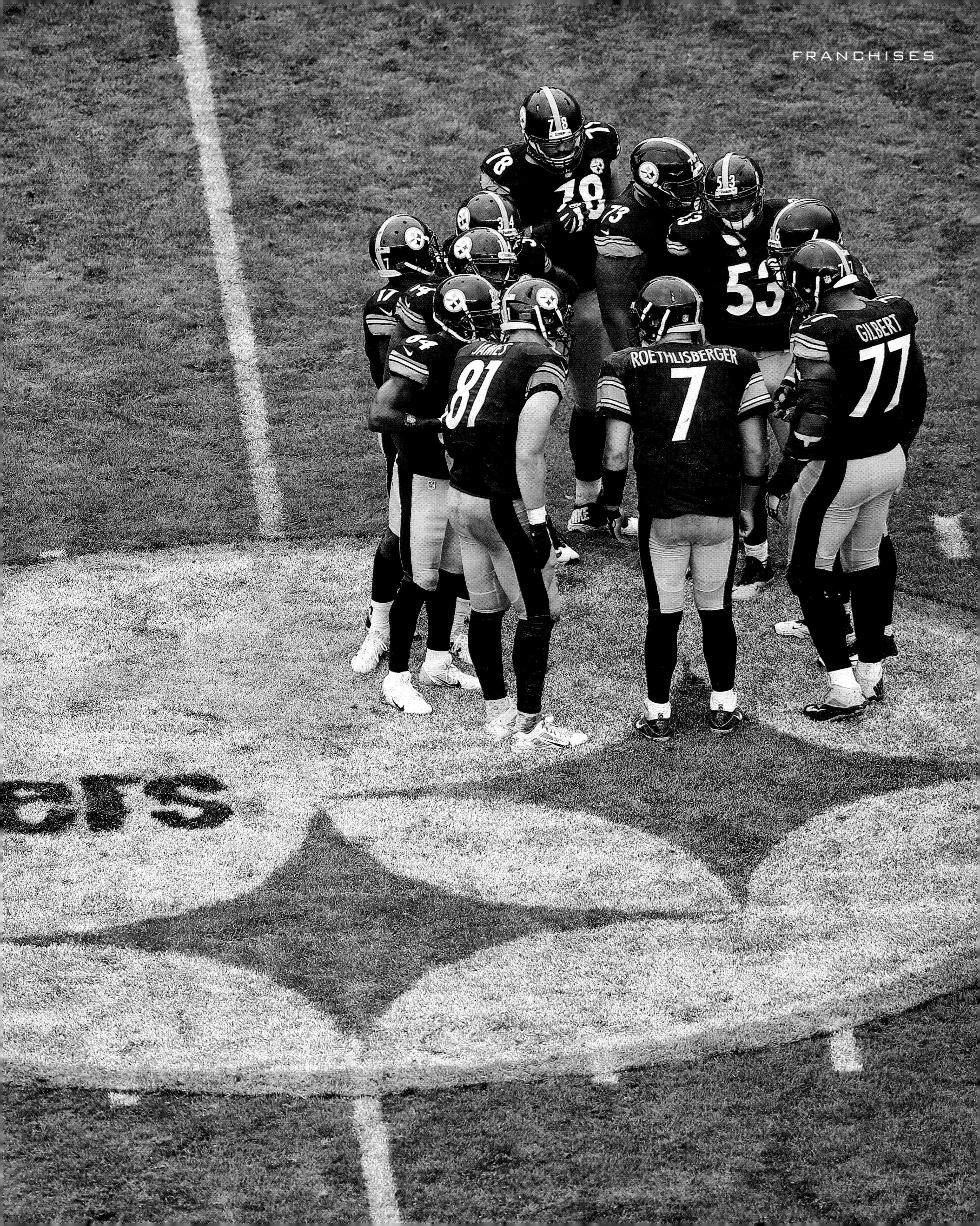
78
78
73
53
JAMES
81
ROETHLISBERGER
7
GILBERT
77

2
THE
PACKERS

FOUNDED 1919

" The only nonprofit, community-owned major league professional sports team in North America, the Packers have been a symbol of excellence for most of their 98 years. " —GREG A. BEDARD

≥ JOINED NFL IN 1921
≥ 13 CHAMPIONSHIPS

A MAN in his early 50s, with tattoos on his biceps and a nose that had been punched out of shape long ago, walked into the sauna in Green Bay wearing a bathing suit and looked around curiously, touching the walls and the benches to see if they were indeed hot. "This is the first motel I was ever in," he said. "My first vacation in 36 years. We got 11 kids, nine still home, some of 'em big full-grown kids that don't believe in work but only in stealing everything I got. So I says all right, I am going to take off a week and drive up here and see the Packer game. And my wife says she has to stay home and take care of the kids. That means I got to travel with my sister, who tells me I smoke too much and do everything wrong. But what the hell, here I am in a motel sauna bath in Green Bay, and I'm gonna see the Packers in real life. In case you don't know it, football is what made this town. Who would ever have heard of Green Bay if it wasn't for the Packers?"

—Edwin Shrake, SI, August 25, 1975

Donald Lee was one of many to take the Lambeau Leap.

PHOTOGRAPH BY JOHN BIEVER

The cheerleaders helped keep all eyes on Dallas.

PHOTOGRAPH BY BILL FRAKES

FOUNDED 1960

" The best expansion team in history, by far. Dallas expanded the NFL into a new frontier when the league needed it. "America's Team" is a misnomer, but it's no small task to become the team that everyone loves . . . or hates. " —TIM LAYDEN

≥ FIVE SUPER BOWL VICTORIES
≥ NFL'S MOST VALUABLE FRANCHISE

THE GLAMOROUS Cowboy image that G.M. Tex Schramm loves to promote is displayed nowhere so openly as it is by the Dallas cheerleaders. In their sexy, foxy way, they're a mirror image of what Cowboy football represents: entertainment dealt with as very serious business.

—William Oscar Johnson, SI, September 1, 1982

THE COWBOYS

4

THE GIANTS

" The Giants won their first NFL championship in 1927. They've played at the Polo Grounds, Yankee Stadium and the Meadowlands. This franchise is a walking encyclopedia of football history. " —CHRIS BURKE

≥ EIGHT CHAMPIONSHIPS
≥ 19 HALL OF FAMERS

JERRY REESE, Tom Coughlin and John Mara have the same philosophy as predecessors George Young, Bill Parcells and Wellington Mara a generation ago: Get big people up front on both sides of the ball, run the ball late when the weather gets dodgy, and find a quarterback whose passes can cut through that weather.

—*Peter King, SI, April 30, 2012*

Phil Simms collected two Super Bowl rings in New York.
PHOTOGRAPH BY RICHARD MACKSON

5

THE PATRIOTS

"Since being purchased by Robert Kraft in 1994, the franchise's fortunes have improved dramatically, and the Bill Belichick–Tom Brady tandem has made New England the envy of the NFL both on and off the field." —DON BANKS

≥ FIVE SUPER BOWL VICTORIES
≥ NFL-RECORD 21-GAME WINNING STREAK, INCLUDING PLAYOFFS, IN 2003–04

"IN THIS game," Kraft said on Sunday night, after the Patriots had arrived in Indianapolis for their sixth Super Bowl under his ownership, "you better take some risks—or you'll have a nice team, and once every 10 or 20 years you'll be good. That's not what I want to be about."

—Peter King, SI, February 6, 2012

Kraft showed fans the bounty from Super Bowl XXXVIII.

PHOTOGRAPH BY JULIA MALAKIE/AP

FOUNDED 1920

Ditka consulted with Papa Bear, George Halas.

PHOTOGRAPH BY NEIL LEIFER

6

THE BEARS

" The Bears won titles in the '20s, '30s, '40s, '60s and '80s. George Halas is on the Mount Rushmore of NFL architecture. I asked one G.M. candidate two years ago what team he'd most like to steward, he said, "The Bears. That's the gold standard." " —PETER KING

≥ NINE CHAMPIONSHIPS
≥ 27 HALL OF FAMERS

MIKE DITKA drafts and trades for and teaches only those players who are Bears. Ask Ditka to name his most cherished accomplishment over his football career and the answer is not the Super Bowls (two as a player, three as an assistant coach) or the All-Pro teams, but this: "I am proudest of being a Bear."

—*Curry Kirkpatrick, SI, December 16, 1985*

7

THE 49ERS

FOUNDED 1946

" With four Super Bowl championships in the 1980s, the Niners had one of the greatest runs in NFL history. " —MARK GODICH

≥ FIVE SUPER BOWL VICTORIES
≥ 15 HALL OF FAMERS

THE NINERS lost the way Chicagoans voted—early and often: 5–9 the first year of Eddie DeBartolo's ownership, 2–14 in 1978. . . . On Monday, Nov. 27, 1978, San Francisco mayor George Moscone and city supervisor Harvey Milk were shot to death by Dan White, a depressed former supervisor. The Niners were playing Pittsburgh at home that night, and G.M. Joe Thomas wanted to cancel the game, but for the wrong reason. He was worried about his own safety. "I knew then that I had to make a change," says DeBartolo. He hired the anti-Thomas, Bill Walsh of Stanford, as coach and general manager. Walsh, DeBartolo, sanity and a little luck helped launch a dynasty. "What should we do with this Notre Dame kid?" Walsh teased DeBartolo, a Fighting Irish alum, when the 82nd pick came up in the third round of the '79 draft and Joe Montana was available. "What the heck," said DeBartolo. "He's a Notre Dame kid. How can you go wrong?"

—Rick Reilly, SI, September 10, 1990

Montana, Steve Young and Jerry Rice are all in Canton.

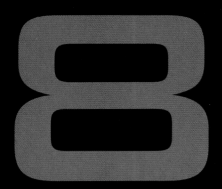

8

THE RAIDERS

FOUNDED 1960

> "Al Davis was always an easy target for ridicule, especially in the last years of his life. But he protected the name of the Raiders fiercely and ensured that the silver and black always had its own persona." —TIM LAYDEN

≥ ONE AFL TITLE
≥ THREE SUPER BOWL VICTORIES

DAVIS'S RAIDERS won with a panache that fully justified their skull-and-bones fashion line: Using castoffs (Lyle Alzado, John Matuszak) and overlooked prospects (Fred Biletnikoff, Howie Long)—"He never had normal players," said Tom Keating, a defensive tackle during the glory years—Davis brought a heightened sense of physical jeopardy to the game. As he once said (when he wasn't saying, "Just win, baby"), he would rather be "feared than respected." And Davis was, although not only for the physical mayhem that players like safety Jack (the Assassin) Tatum and linebacker Ted (the Mad Stork) Hendricks visited on their opponents. Davis's dedication to winning was so exaggerated that rivals felt certain he was capable of almost anything. If he was willing to hang around celebrity golf tournaments to gauge the availability of prospects, what else might he do?

—Richard Hoffer, SI, October 17, 2011

Davis rose from coach and general manager to owner.

THE MASTER BUILDER

In a freewheeling chat, Raiders architect Al Davis talked about the secrets of his black-and-silver magic, and lamented that no one ever leaves their heart in Oakland

BY DAN JENKINS

N FEAR OF DROWNING, THE WRITER TESTS THE carpet in the office of Al Davis to see if it has been watered down the way they say the field is for all home games of the Oakland Raiders. Al Davis laughs. Being a genius, a winner, rich and powerful, he can afford to laugh. The writer explains that he has been sentenced to pro football this year and he has come to Oakland on a vacation to get away from it all. He likes what they're doing with the marsh areas.

"Hey, can I say something?" says Al Davis. "I don't know what I'm doing here today. . . . See, John Madden's the coach. . . . "

The writer didn't catch the last name. John who?

"That's the thing," says Al Davis. "Here's a guy who's got the best record in pro football next to Don Shula. To be a head coach, you've either got it or you don't. John's got it. All he does is win. . . . "

The writer wonders why everybody in the world thinks Al Davis is still the coach, nevertheless.

"When have I got time to coach?" says Davis, who sits in a silver and black office in his suburban Oakland marsh. "I'm too busy watering down the field."

Al Davis performs miracles. Stadiums get built in Oakland, leagues merge, the Raiders win more football games than anybody over a 12-year period, unknown players become stars, a fairly young ex-coach and ex-commissioner becomes a "managing general partner"—the majority owner—and it has to be because he's a combination genius and devil.

"I'm just an organization guy," Davis claims. "I like to think I've put together a good thing here. I don't go to workouts. I don't send plays down from the top of the stadium."

Why does Al Davis think John Madden can't get enough credit?

"I don't know," he says. "It's an image thing. People know me. They didn't know him. I talk a lot. I've been around a long time. The war between the leagues, the merger. Maybe everybody thought I was too young to quit coaching, so they can't believe I have. But I have."

The writer wonders if it is a lot of trouble to water down the Oakland Coliseum's natural dirt.

Al Davis says, "We play at least nine out of 14 games a year on turf. Seven here and one each against Denver and San Diego on the road. And we win. So we must be good mudders, I don't know. A few years ago the Coliseum had a drainage problem. It's been fixed. With Cliff Branch, we'd really be smart to slow him down, wouldn't we?"

Davis does things differently. He ridicules the computer technique, scouting pools, publicizing individual players, believing the draft is a cure-all. His coach was young and anonymous, his director of player personnel, Ron Wolf, was a youthful journalist and now his quarterback, Ken Stabler, is lefthanded. What does he have against pro football?

"Take Ron Wolf," he says. "I hired him when he was 21. He loves college football. He knows every player, every statistic. I needed a guy who would read everything and tell me everything. He gets to know the kids. Is he a leader? Can he play in cold weather?"

Ron Wolf is a secondary genius. Of the 47 players on the Raiders' current roster, 34 are draft choices, and 24 of them have come in the past six years. Oakland doesn't get old.

"We like kids who come from winners," says Davis. "Kenny Stabler quarterbacked the best team Alabama ever had. He's a leader."

And what is the secret of drafting if you never get to draft higher than 19th?

"We work hard at it," says Davis. "Without computers. We take a punter [Ray Guy] in the first round, and he's a hell of a weapon."

The writer wants to know about Al Davis paying off the Bay Area sportswriters. Was it in cash or free fishing licenses for the Lake Oakland Coliseum?

"We give 'em a gift every Christmas," he says. "We've given binoculars, TVs, stereo . . . it's something I want to do. I guess some other teams do it. A little appreciation for the guys who live with us. Instead of a gift certificate, I gave a guy a check. He showed it to his sports editor. He gave it back. No big deal. He didn't get fired. There's no scandal."

Al Davis laughs.

"You know how to buy good publicity?" he says. "By winning, like John Madden does. We don't get the best of it around here. Nobody left their heart in Oakland."

Was he serious about the Super Bowl changing to a two-out-of-three playoff?

"I don't think that's impossible," he says. "You get the best team as your champion that way. None of this 'on any given day' stuff, which happens to be true. I'd like to see two-out-of-three."

What would he do with television?

"I'd go Sunday afternoon, Sunday night and Monday night. Give all three networks their shot," he says. "Everybody has their own turf. The public gets the best."

How much have the players changed?

"They've changed," Davis says. "There's not so much of this 'I'll do it because the coach says to do it.' They're smarter. You tell 'em why, and if it makes sense, they'll do it."

Al Davis believes in winning, and he doesn't understand the athlete who questions that motivation.

"Football is a game you play to win," he says. "Otherwise, like they say, why do we keep score? You play, you win, the money comes; and the recognition, if that's what you want. I didn't make up those rules. That's the way life is."

∎

Elway (7) has powered Denver on and off the field.

THE
BRONCOS

" Since John Elway became their quarterback in 1983, the Broncos have been among the NFL's most successful teams. Both versions of Mile High Stadium have been among the toughest venues for visiting teams to emerge with a victory. " —GREG A. BEDARD

≥ THREE SUPER BOWL VICTORIES
≥ EIGHT AFC CHAMPIONSHIPS

IN 2011, Broncos owner Pat Bowlen hired Elway as his vice president of football operations. "We could have given him a ceremonial role," says Joe Ellis, Denver's CEO. "But he did not take kindly to that [idea]. John never took a half-baked approach to anything."

—Greg Bishop, SI, February 15, 2016

10

THE REDSKINS

FOUNDED 1932

" The franchise is known for its controversial nickname as well as its on-field success, of which it has had plenty. " —GREG BISHOP

≥ FIVE CHAMPIONSHIPS
≥ 19 HALL OF FAMERS

RICHARD M. NIXON, erstwhile District resident and Redskins fan: "The trouble is, Washington is a city without identity. Everybody comes from someplace else. Anywhere else people say, 'I'm from Cincinnati, I'm from New York, I'm from Topeka.' You never hear people say that about Washington. Deep down, they still think they're back home. But you take any hometown boy— well, these days I guess you have to say hometown 'person'—and they come to Washington for politics, but they need an identity with the city. And the Redskins provide that. The Redskins are the only thing in Washington that the people think of as 'ours.' Nobody in Washington gives a tinker's dam about the Kennedy Center or the Washington Symphony." . . . In 1972, the year the team reached the Super Bowl, *The Washington Post* dispatched a staff of 13 to cover the event— twice as many as covered the first moonwalk and 11 more than it took to topple a President.

—*Frank Deford, SI, July 2, 1979*

QB Joe Theismann and RB John Riggins enjoyed the '80s.

PHOTOGRAPH BY JOHN IACONO

10 THE

BEST ENTERTAINERS, SPECIAL TEAM PLAYERS, INTIMIDATORS, MOVIES, REGULAR-SEASON PLAYS, BROADCASTERS, UNITS AND THE FULL RESULTS

A PANEL IS A WONDERFUL WAY TO DEVELOP A CONSENSUS, BUT IT TENDS TO TRAMPLE PERSONAL POINTS OF VIEW. SO FOR THIS SECTION OUR PANELISTS WERE ALL INVITED TO CREATE A LIST THAT REPRESENTS THEIR OPINIONS ALONE.

SOME LISTS REFLECT INDIVIDUAL EXPERIENCE—NO ONE BUT PETER KING, FOR EXAMPLE, CAN MAKE A LIST OF PETER KING'S MOST ENTERTAINING PLAYERS. SENIOR EDITOR MARK GODICH CONTRIBUTED A LIST OF THE NFL'S GREATEST ANNOUNCERS, AND THAT TOPIC IS AS SUBJECTIVE AS IT GETS. EVEN THE MOST BELOVED BROADCASTERS HAVE VIEWERS WHO WILL DECLARE, "I CAN'T STAND THAT GUY."

THIS SECTION CONCLUDES WITH A RUNDOWN OF EVERY VOTE IN EVERY CATEGORY—AND THERE YOU'LL FIND SOME OF THE CHOICES THAT DIDN'T MAKE THE LARGER LISTS. IF YOU WERE STUNNED THAT MARSHAWN LYNCH'S BEAST MODE RUN IN THE 2011 PLAYOFFS WASN'T NAMED A TOP 10 PLAY, YOU CAN SEE HERE THAT IT WAS NOT ENTIRELY FORGOTTEN. FANS OF THE BILLS, BROWNS, EAGLES AND LIONS CAN TAKE HEART THAT THOSE TEAMS RECEIVED VOTES FOR BEST FRANCHISE, DESPITE A COLLECTIVE ZERO SUPER BOWL WINS. AS THEY SAY IN HOLLYWOOD, IT IS AN HONOR JUST TO BE NOMINATED.

THE 10 MOST ENTERTAINING PLAYERS

SI senior writer PETER KING names
the players who have amazed with exuberance,
unpredictabilty and exceptional talent

1. JOE NAMATH

Imagine it's two days before the Super Bowl. You're in Fort Lauderdale. You're walking by a pool, and you find the quarterback of one of the teams, on a chaise lounge, talking to eight or 10 media members, with no PR person around to hand-wring over what he's saying. This happens the day after, while at a banquet honoring him as pro football's most outstanding player, that same quarterback guaranteed his team would win the game. And then the game comes and he pulls off this great upset. Joe Namath did that with the Jets at Super Bowl III. Also, since this list should be about a little more than football: Namath once very famously had his legs shaved and did a commercial displaying those lovely gams wearing nylons. A gem, folks.

2. BRETT FAVRE

I have covered football for 33 years, and there's no question that Favre was the most fun player I've covered, on and off the field. He threw underhanded. He threw left-handed. He shovel-passed. On the night after his father died, positive that his dad would have wanted him to play, he threw four TD passes, through his tears (there were some, on the field), to beat Oakland. But my favorite Favre story was the night I dined with him before a game, and he'd just seen *Sling Blade*, and he conversed for much of the evening in Billy Bob Thornton's voice from the movie. Perfect. And though he swore he'd seen the film only once, he had paragraphs of dialogue down pat. Now that's entertainment.

3. BRONKO NAGURSKI

The rare running back/professional wrestler. He played football for the Bears for eight years in the 1930s and made the Pro Football Hall of Fame; Nagurski threw a trick touchdown pass to account for the only touchdown in the first "championship game" in NFL history in '32. That was a game scheduled between the top two teams in the league, Chicago and Portsmouth, and won by the Bears 9–0. As a wrestler Nagurski won the world heavyweight title twice, and quit pro football after the '37 season—he returned for one year in '43 when the Bears were shorthanded during World War II—because wrestling was more lucrative.

4. DEION SANDERS

He scored 22 NFL touchdowns. He hit 39 major league home runs. He hit a home run and scored a touchdown in the same week in 1989. He batted .533 with five stolen bases in the '92 World Series, playing with a broken bone in his foot. He high-stepped down the sideline in a vaudevillian act like no one in football had ever seen. When checking into hotels he protected his anonymity with a hilarious alias: MR. REDD FOXX. And for the record, he was best cover corner of the last 25 years, and maybe ever.

5. TIM ROSSOVICH

I always remember the Eagles linebacker as the guy who ate glass. All kinds of glass. From John Underwood's story in SPORTS ILLUSTRATED in 1971: "The stories are told—in locker rooms, at bowling lanes, over long-distance phones—by almost anyone who knows or has ever met Tim Rossovich and by Rossovich himself. Only those who feel insecure around him, like coaches who think his life-style is a threat to the Republic, try to keep his wondrous light under a bushel. Tim Rossovich eats lightbulbs. He wears tie-dyed shirts and shower-of-hail suits, Dracula capes and frontier buckskins and stands on his head in hotel lobbies. Sometimes when he stands on his head his head is in a bucket of water."

6. LESTER HAYES

One of the great quotes in NFL history, and one of the great corners. When Al Davis drafted him as a college safety, he saw something very quick in Hayes and moved him to corner—though Hayes begged him not to do it. He feared not being good enough to be a cornerback. But he was. He was great. And he made the NFL outlaw Stickum after using it to improve a pair of bad hands that dropped too many balls. He told the *Houston Chronicle* in 2004: "These hands were clubs and claws. I could not catch a cold buck naked in Antarctica. But Fred Biletnikoff taped my fingers with about a half ounce of Stickum in our first game and it set me free. I could catch a football behind my back on one knee."

7. SAMMY BAUGH

No player ever—and the NFL could play till 2117 and this still won't be topped—had a better season than Baugh had for Washington in 1943, when he was the league's best quarterback, safety and punter. In a game against Detroit, he threw for four touchdowns, intercepted four passes and booted an 81-yard punt.

8. BOBBY LAYNE

The Lions have been awful for 60 years, mostly. The last time they were consistently good, in the 1950s, they won three championships, and their quarterback was Bobby Layne. In '54, after they lost the title game to Cleveland 56–10, Layne famously said, "I slept too much last night." As great a player as Layne was, he was known as much for his hard life off the field and for his ability to perform so well after drinking all week. He became such a celebrity in Detroit that when he went out at night, he got away with parking his car on the sidewalk outside bars.

9. JULIO JONES

The Falcons receiver is a quiet, blend-in-the-crowd guy. He barely watches football when he's out of uniform. And I put him on this list as much for what he is going to do as for what he has done. So this is for actual football, and only football, and it comes after a catch in Super Bowl LI that should never be forgotten. Matt Ryan left the pocket in the fourth quarter, looking for Jones, and he threw it deep down the right sideline, and the ball was impossibly high, just above the fingertips of a blanketing Patriots cornerback Eric Rowe, and Jones somehow caught this ball, dunked his two feet on the last couple of blades of fake green grass by the white stripes on the sidelines, and bounced off the turf, holding onto the ball. Good catch. One of the greatest under pressure in NFL history. Oh, and about his 300-yard receiving game against Carolina earlier in the 2016 season . . .

10. DARREN SPROLES

Year after year for his 11 seasons with the Chargers, Saints and Eagles, I keep saying this little guy cannot continue to be a ping-pong back with Gale Sayers quickness and survive—but survive he does. For my money, the 5' 6", 181-pound Sproles is the most durable, exciting, game-changing running back/returner I have seen. And that merits a place on my list.

Namath basked in both the sun and the media attention before his Jets upset the Colts in Super Bowl III.

Jones's eye-popping agility was on display in this fourth-quarter catch in Super Bowl LI.

10

THE

BEST SPECIAL TEAMS PLAYERS

SI senior writer TIM LAYDEN identifies the players who excelled most while the offense and defense watched from the sideline

1. DEVIN HESTER

The most dangerous return man in NFL history, Hester took a combined 19 punts (14) and kickoffs (five) to the end zone, including 11 return touchdowns in his first two years of his career. He played 11 seasons, mostly with Chicago, and at the peak of his powers, opposing coaches preferred a poor kick to putting the ball in Hester's hands.

2. STEVE TASKER

The prototype of the fearless cover man, Tasker, who played 12 of his 13 seasons with the Bills, was the rare player who could not only inspire teammates with his effort, but also influence field position and strategy with his speed and tackling skills. He was named to the Pro Bowl seven times from 1987 to '95.

3. ADAM VINATIERI

Certain to someday join the short list of kickers in the Pro Football Hall of Fame, Vinatieri is the only kicker to win a Super Bowl with a field goal twice, and he also won the notorious, snowy 2002 Tuck Rule game for the Patriots with a three-pointer in a blizzard. Now with the Colts, he ranks third in NFL history with 530 field goals made and 2,378 points scored, and he could lead both categories before he retires.

4. GALE SAYERS

The "Kansas Comet," who also made this book's list of best running backs, played only three full seasons before horrific knee injuries diminished his mercurial greatness. But in those three years, he returned eight punts and kickoffs for touchdowns, and his mud-splattered 85-yard punt return against the 49ers in 1965 stands as one of the most spectacular plays in the game's history.

5. DEION SANDERS

Known for his lockdown skills as a cornerback, for playing two pro sports and for his brand-establishing flamboyance, Sanders was also a game-breaking kick returner. In 14 seasons spent mostly with the Falcons and Cowboys, Sanders returned six punts and three kickoffs for touchdowns and filled with the stadium with an electric anticipation every time he received a kick.

6. TOMMY DAVIS

A kicker-punter, Davis played his entire 11-year career for the 49ers, from 1959 to '69. His net average of 44.5 yards per kick is more than a half yard better than any other kicker in history. Here's how SI's Paul Zimmerman once described Davis's kicks: " . . . that sweet KABOOM! as he rockets another one into the gusts in the windiest stadium in the league. A high hanger into the wind, 48 yards from scrimmage, 4.8 on the stopwatch. Week after week of that, game after game."

7. JAN STENERUD

The first pure kicker elected to the Hall of Fame, Stenerud was in the first wave of so-called "soccer style" kickers and played the first 13 of his 19 years with the Chiefs. Despite playing from 1967 to '85, in a time of poorer surfaces, Stenerud made 66.8% of his field goals and retired as the NFL leader in field goals.

8. LARRY IZZO

The eight-time special teams captain from the first wave of the Bill Belichick dynasty in New England (2001–08), Izzo was a tremendous coverage tackler from the middle of the field. The three-time Pro Bowler, originally a Dolphin, finished his career with the Jets in '09.

9. RAY GUY

The first punter elected to the Hall of Fame, Guy was seen as such a potential weapon that Al Davis' Raiders selected him in the first round of the 1973 draft. Over his 14-year career, Guy controlled field position with cloud-scraping kicks.

10. BRIAN MITCHELL

The most prolific return man in NFL history, Mitchell set league records for the most kickoff and punt returns, and return yardage. He also brought back 13 for touchdowns over his 14-year career.

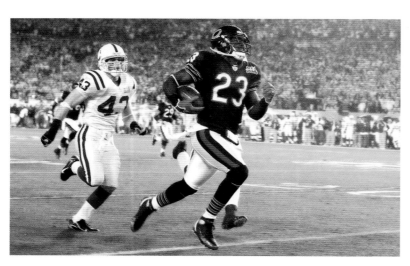

Hester opened Super Bowl XLI with a kick return for a touchdown.

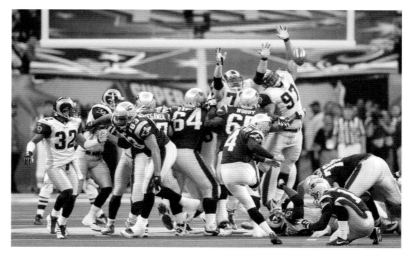

Vinatieri hit two Super Bowl game-winners, including this one against the Rams.

1. LAWRENCE TAYLOR

The Giants linebacker scared opposing offenses so much that he changed football. The West Coast offense, with all those short, precise passes, was a direct response to how quickly LT came off the edge, how easily and savagely he sacked quarterbacks. He was the rare defensive player to win an MVP (1986) and was the best player on his Giants Super Bowl teams.

2. JACK TATUM

Nicknamed "the Assassin," the Raiders' safety in the 1970s was once described by *The New York Times* as a "symbol of a violent game." Indeed. Few hit harder than the player who embodied an era and was named to the Pro Bowl three times. Tatum made each hit count.

3. JIM BROWN

The Cleveland running back was capable of running around defenders, but Brown often chose to plow over them instead. He remains as punishing an offensive player as the league has ever known, a bruising back who carried linebackers into end zones and charged through defensive ends as if they were tackling dummies.

4. BARRY SANDERS

The 5' 8", 200-pound Lions back wasn't physical in the way that Brown was, but the shifty Sanders terrified defenders for 10 seasons with the prospect that he would leave them tackling air. He could elude players of all size and skill, and spin and juke his way through any defensive alignment. He will be remembered as the toughest tackle in league history–proof that intimidation comes in all sizes.

5. DICK BUTKUS

The punishing Bears linebacker defined toughness as he attacked ballcarriers, twice winning defensive player of the year honors and making the league's All-Decade team in both the 1960s and '70s. Any list of the NFL's greatest hits surely includes a Butkus tackle–or 14.

6. CHUCK BEDNARIK

The Eagles linebacker and center played in an era well before the days of concussion protocols and pass-oriented offenses. Despite playing both ways, "Concrete Charlie" missed just three games in 14 seasons while doling out punishment to linebackers and running backs alike. In his postplaying days Bednarik, who died in 2015, lamented how soft the game had gotten and how delicate players had become.

7. JACK YOUNGBLOOD

The longtime Rams end played in the 1979 NFC championship game and Super Bowl XIV with a broken fibula. How's that for intimidating? Unofficially, Youngblood registered 151½ sacks in 14 seasons with the Rams, even as teams threw multiple blockers at him.

8. DEACON JONES

Jones's patented pass rush move was a slap to the head, and he did that so often that opposing offensive linemen reportedly sharpened their helmet buckles in response. The NFL eventually outlawed the head slap, but the Rams defensive end still managed, by unofficial count, 173½ sacks—a term he is credited with coining—in 14 seasons.

9. DICK LANE

When your nickname is "Night Train," it's safe to say you resided in your opponents' nightmares. In addition to receivers, Lane also scared opposing quarterbacks. The 14 interceptions he snagged his rookie season (1952) set a league record.

10. JERRY RICE

It's hard to be scarier than Rice was for opposing defenses, despite his lithe, 6' 2", 200-pound frame. Rice was simply impossible to cover over two decades, intimating defenses with his ability to get open, run after the catch and turn short completions into big scores.

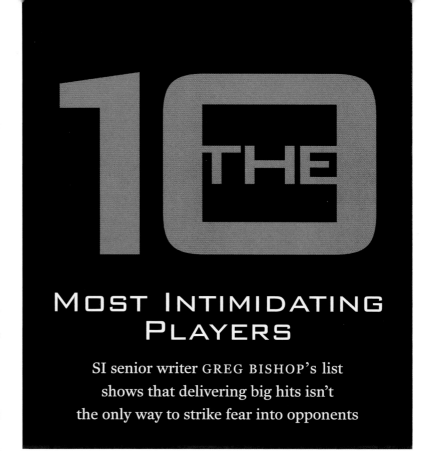

THE 10 MOST INTIMIDATING PLAYERS

SI senior writer GREG BISHOP's list shows that delivering big hits isn't the only way to strike fear into opponents

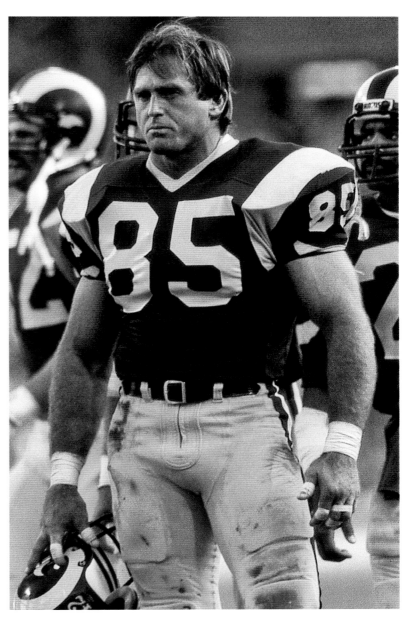

Youngblood played in an NFC title game and a Super Bowl on a broken leg.

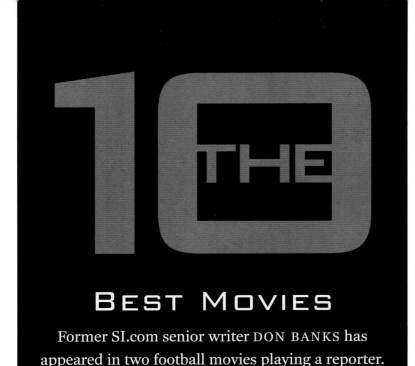

10 THE

BEST MOVIES

Former SI.com senior writer DON BANKS has appeared in two football movies playing a reporter. He graciously includes only one on his Top 10 list

The happy times don't last for Caan (left) and Williams in *Brian's Song*.

1. BRIAN'S SONG (1971)

For guys of my generation, just hearing a halting Billy Dee Williams (as Gale Sayers) struggle to get through that "I love Brian Piccolo" scene at the awards banquet brings a lump to the throat every time. James Caan is superb as the wise-cracking Piccolo, and Jack Warden makes for a memorable George Halas, but it's the story of friendship and ultimate tragedy that grabs you and never lets you go. I can still remember almost everything about the night I first watched *Brian's Song* on television in November 1971. How many movies leave that kind of mark so many years later?

2. THE LONGEST YARD (1974)

Burt Reynolds had played a little football at Florida State, and it showed in this gritty yet entertaining story about a group of ragtag inmates who got to stick it to the man by beating the prison guards on the gridiron. Packers great Ray Nitschke was superb as an intimidating guard/linebacker, and Eddie Albert made for one evil prison warden. The remake in 2005 starred Adam Sandler in Reynolds's quarterbacking role, with Reynolds playing a prisoner who coaches the inmates team, but it didn't begin to recapture the look and feel of the original.

3. CONCUSSION (2015)

This eye-opening bio drama tells the story of Bennet Omalu, the doctor who discovered the brain trauma known as CTE (Chronic Traumatic Encephalopathy) in former football players. Will Smith gives Omalu intensity and an inherent sense of righteousness without lapsing into melodrama as the forensic pathologist seeks to share his findings with the skeptical and uncooperative NFL hierarchy. A story centered on the potential life-and-death risks of football doesn't make for light fare, but this is an entertaining and well-done issue movie on an important topic.

4. NORTH DALLAS FORTY (1979)

Based on the seminal autobiographical novel by ex-NFL receiver Pete Gent, the movie showed pro football fans the seamy underside of the game as never before, in the way that Jim Bouton's book *Ball Four* did for baseball. Nick Nolte stars as Phil Elliott, an aging and pain-pill-popping receiver for a North Dallas Bulls team that sounds more than a little bit like the Cowboys clubs that Gent played for. Former Oakland Raiders' wild man John Matuszak is memorably cast as one of Elliott's freewheelin' and fun-loving teammates.

5. GLEASON (2016)

This acclaimed documentary of New Orleans Saints special teams standout Steve Gleason's battle against ALS is as real and intimate as any film you will ever see, and it's painful to watch in spots due to its frank depiction of how the disease has decimated the body of the former NFL star. The film plays out through four years worth of his family's video journals after he is diagnosed in 2011, shortly before his 34th birthday. It's a powerful portrait of the devastating effects of ALS. This is one movie that leaves an indelible mark.

6. EVERYBODY'S ALL-AMERICAN (1988)

This underrated Taylor Hackford film might not make everyone's top 10, but I've always loved the way the story evokes the romance and feel of big-time college football in the 1950s, with Dennis Quaid starring as fictitious LSU running back Gavin Grey, "The Grey Ghost." Quaid plays the football scenes very believably and even broke his collarbone during the filming. Based on the book of the same name by legendary SPORTS ILLUSTRATED writer Frank Deford, the story follows Grey over the span of 25 years, through his heroic days at LSU and into the NFL. But in the rest of his football career and postretirement life, Grey can never quite match the magic he created on field in his glory days in college.

7. JERRY MAGUIRE (1996)

Until Kurt Warner showed up in the desert, the fictitious receiver Rod Tidwell was widely regarded as the best player in Phoenix/Arizona Cardinals history. Sure, the Tom Cruise–led and Cameron

Nolte (clockwise) pals with Mac Davis in *North Dallas Forty*; Cuba Gooding Jr. asks Cruise to show him the money in *Jerry Maguire*; Quaid coaches Brown in *The Express*.

Crowe–directed movie is more about the sports agent business and affairs of the heart than football, but it did add the phrase "Show me the money" to our pop culture lexicon, and I'm still partial to Jerry Maguire's plea to Tidwell, "Help me, help you."

8. THE EXPRESS (2008)

Sorry, fans of the 2014 movie *Draft Day*, but my nod to the Cleveland Browns' cinematic history goes to this underrated biopic of Ernie Davis (played by Rob Brown), the charismatic Syracuse running back who in 1961 became the first African-American to win the Heisman Trophy. While most of the film centers on Davis's time at Syracuse with coach Ben Schwartzwalder (Dennis Quaid), the Browns play a key role in this tragic story. The Browns acquired Davis in a trade a week after Washington had made him the first black player to be drafted first overall, and Cleveland's plan was to pair Davis in a backfield with Jim Brown. But Davis was diagnosed with a highly toxic form of leukemia and never played a down for Cleveland, dying in May 1963 at age 23. The Browns honored Davis by retiring his number 45 jersey.

9. INVINCIBLE (2006)

If you look really quickly and really closely, I'm actually in some background shots of this Mark Wahlberg vehicle, quite credibly playing a mid-'70s-era sportswriter in a salmon-colored blazer and gray bell bottoms. But that's not why this movie made my list. (Well, not the entire reason, anyway). Wahlberg is a convincing Vince Papale, the tough kid from Philly who made the 1976 Eagles roster as a long shot with no college experience, bringing his Rocky-like story to real life. Plus, the period soundtrack kicks butt.

10. PAPER LION (1968)

Does this book-inspired film look a bit creaky and dated almost five decades out? Sure, but many classics do. A hopelessly young-looking Alan Alda gives a great performance as author George Plimpton, who took participatory journalism to new heights by spending a training camp with the Detroit Lions, even playing in an intrasquad scrimmage. Lions defensive tackle Alex Karras launched a nice little acting career playing himself in the film, and *Paper Lion* is interesting time-capsule look at the NFL in the late 1960s.

HONORABLE MENTION: LEATHERHEADS (2008)

This film has always struck me as the pro football counterpart to the baseball movie *The Natural*. This George Clooney vehicle does a super job of recapturing the look and feel of the game in its struggling, formative stages, with Clooney as Jimmy (Dodge) Connelly, the captain of the almost bankrupt Duluth Bulldogs. The movie is set in 1925, and although the story is fictional, it has echoes of the George Halas-signs-Red Grange story with a collegiate football star joining the Bulldogs in order to bring legitimacy to both the team and the sport itself.

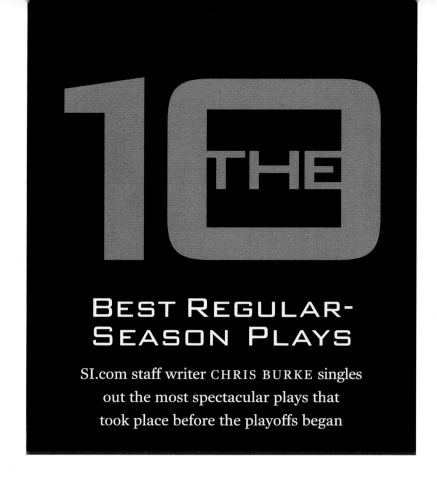

THE 10

BEST REGULAR-SEASON PLAYS

SI.com staff writer CHRIS BURKE singles out the most spectacular plays that took place before the playoffs began

1. THE HOLY ROLLER (SEPT. 10, 1978)

How many plays have led the NFL to rewrite its own rule book? Down by six points with 10 seconds left at the Chargers' 14-yard line, Oakland quarterback Ken Stabler was about to take a game-ending sack when he fumbled the ball forward, setting off a crazed scramble in which another Raiders player, Pete Banaszak, batted the ball forward. Then tight end Dave Casper, after batting and kicking the ball, fell on it in the end zone for the score. The touchdown resulted in a Raiders win and an off-season change by the NFL which said that in the last two minutes of a game, only the fumbling player can recover and advance the ball.

2. ODELL BECKHAM'S CATCH (NOV. 23, 2014)

Every season produces its share of extraordinary catches, but this one seemed to suspend the laws of physics. Despite being grabbed by Cowboys cornerback Brandon Carr (who was called for pass interference), Beckham extended as far as the human body can go to reach out with one hand and nab Eli Manning's 43-yard pass and pull the ball into his stomach for a touchdown.

Jackson's miraculous return deep-sixed punter Dodge (6).

3. ANTONIO FREEMAN'S OT WINNER (NOV. 6, 2000)

The only person in Lambeau Field who seemed to know that Brett Favre's deflected overtime pass against Minnesota on Monday night had not hit the turf was the man who caught it (and the game's officials, who let the play continue.) Both Freeman and Minnesota cornerback Cris Dishman went up for the ball, which was tipped into the air and bounced off the prone Freeman's back. The receiver somehow rolled to his side and snagged the ball out of the air, and then got up and took off for the end zone.

4. TONY DORSETT'S 99-YARD RUN (JAN. 3, 1983)

This was a busted play in which the Cowboys had only 10 men on the field—and the missing man was fullback Ron Springs, who was supposed to get the ball but was on the sidelines because he misunderstood the call. But perhaps most mind-boggling aspect of Dorsett's record-setting run is that despite all this he was touched only twice—by Minnesota cornerback John Swain at the Dallas 15, then by corner Willie Teal about 60 yards farther downfield. Hustling Dallas wide receiver Drew Pearson helped fend off Teal on the score. Dorsett's dash remains the only 99-yard running play in NFL history.

5. THE RIVER CITY RELAY (DEC. 21, 2003)

All that was missing here was the Stanford band coming onto the field. The Saints' final play of regulation in Jacksonville went 75 yards, the first 42 or so coming on a pass from quarterback Aaron Brooks to Donte' Stallworth. The receiver then lateraled to Michael Lewis, who lateraled to Deuce McAllister, who tossed it to Jerome Pathon, who ran in the final 20 yards for the score. But the play was not the triumph it should have been because kicker John Carney blew the extra point, his first miss in four years, and the Saints lost by one. The defeat eliminated New Orleans from playoff contention.

6. AARON RODGERS'S WALK-OFF HAIL MARY (DEC. 3, 2015)

Rodgers's majestic, 61-yard bomb against Detroit, made after he scrambled out of the pocket to avoid a sack, stands as the longest game-winning Hail Mary in NFL history. The catch, made by tight end Richard Rodgers in front of a group of defenders, erased a two-point deficit, and was especially crushing because the game should have ended the play before. Green Bay was running a desperation multi-lateral play when the Lions were flagged for a face mask (against Devin Taylor, for pulling down quarterback Rodgers, to whom the ball had come back) as time expired. The penalty gave the Packers an extra play on an untimed down.

7. MIRACLE AT THE NEW MEADOWLANDS (DEC. 19, 2010)

Like the original "Miracle at the Meadowlands"—Herm Edwards's last-second fumble recovery to beat the Giants in 1978—this one involved an improbable Philadelphia comeback. This play came in a game in which the Eagles had erased a 21-point fourth quarter deficit to tie the score at 31–31. With 14 seconds left DeSean Jackson fielded a punt, bobbled the ball to the turf, picked it up and streaked 65 yards for a touchdown, running parallel to the goal line to make sure time expired before he turned into the end zone. As the Eagles celebrated, Giants coach Tom Coughlin berated rookie punter Matt Dodge, who had been instructed to kick the ball out-of-bounds. Dodge was cut by New York before the following season.

8. MIRACLE AT THE MET (DEC. 14, 1980)

This is really two plays that felt like one. With 14 seconds, trailing by one, the Vikings found themselves 80 yards from the end zone against the Browns at Minnesota's Metropolitan Stadium. A hook-and-lateral with a short pass that set up a long run by fullback Ted Brown moved the ball to the Cleveland 46. Then on the next play quarterback Tommy Kramer threw a high, arcing Hail Mary that was tipped by Browns defenders and caught by Ahmad Rashad, who stepped into the end zone for a win. The play was especially climactic because is clinched the NFC Central title for the Vikings.

Beckham made his one-handed, 43-yard catch despite pass interference on the play from Dallas cornerback Carr.

9. STEVE YOUNG'S 49-YARD TD RUN (OCT. 30, 1988)

Three years before he would become a full-time starter, Young, filling in for an injured Joe Montana, willed the 49ers to a win over Minnesota with a mesmerizing scramble. With 1:58 left and San Francisco down by four, Young escaped a collapsing pocket and broke seven tackles before nearly tripping over his own feet at the five-yard-line, and then stumbling across the goal line.

10. DAN MARINO'S FAKE SPIKE (NOV. 27, 1994)

Marino threw for 61,361 yards in his NFL career, but this eight-yard touchdown pass against the Jets was his most memorable play. The Dolphins had trailed 17–0 before closing to 24–21 in the final moments. With 38 seconds left, Marino came to the line and yelled "Clock! Clock! Clock!" as if he was going to throw the ball into the ground. Then, with the Jets' defense off guard, he fired a pass to Mark Ingram just past the pylon to cap the comeback.

HONORABLE MENTION: ANTONIO CROMARTIE'S 109-YARD FIELD-GOAL RETURN (NOV. 4, 2007)

Cromartie literally could not have gone any deeper in the end zone to field this kick, which came in the closing seconds of the first half of a game between his Chargers and the Vikings. He caught Minnesota kicker Ryan Longwell's miss while tip-toeing the end line under his own goal posts, a fantastic play in itself, and then streaked up the middle of the field, made a hard cut to his right, and raced up the sideline untouched for the shocking score.

Rodgers pulled in the record-long Hail Mary.

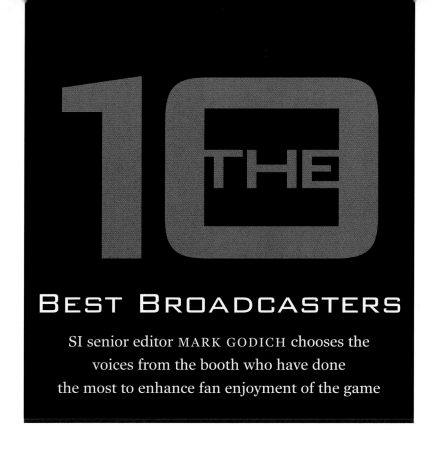

10 THE
BEST BROADCASTERS

SI senior editor MARK GODICH chooses the
voices from the booth who have done
the most to enhance fan enjoyment of the game

1. JOHN MADDEN
The former Raiders coach took analysis to a new level with lively commentary and use of the Telestrator, a device he helped popularize. He was sometimes rambling but never dull, and his passion for the game echoed off the television screen as he broadcast for CBS, Fox, ABC and NBC. Madden was authentic in every sense of the word.

2. AL MICHAELS
The best play-by-play broadcaster the sport has seen, Michaels is a technician, fluidly describing the action while seamlessly engaging and setting up partners such as Madden or Cris Collinsworth to deliver pertinent analysis. He worked *Monday Night Football* for two decades on ABC before leading *Sunday Night Football* for NBC.

3. PAT SUMMERALL
We'll keep this brief, as that's the way the man who worked 16 Super Bowls would have wanted it. Over a career that spanned 40 years, the former Giants, Cardinals and Lions kicker was the most respected voice of his time—succinct yet authoritative.

4. DICK ENBERG
One of NBC's most respected broadcasters across sports for almost a quarter century, Enberg picked his spots carefully and knew he could enhance the game with what he didn't say. And he was behind the mike for eight Super Bowls between 1981 to '98. Oh my!

5. CRIS COLLINSWORTH
The NBC analyst is adept at breaking down the action, often explaining why a play was or wasn't successful based on what happened away from the ball. Plus, his analysis manages to be both detailed and simple at the same time, and the former Bengals All-Pro receiver's conversational tone conveys how much enjoys what he's doing.

6. HOWARD COSELL
Love him or hate him, The Mouth That Roared always let you knew where he stood. He was a member of ABC's *Monday Night Football* booth for 14 years, beginning at the show's inception in 1970, and his opinionated takes on everything from football to world politics helped make that program a cultural phenomenon.

7. CURT GOWDY
The lead voice of NBC Sports for a generation, Gowdy, who called seven early Super Bowls, was renowned for his low-key approach. "I'm no cheerleader," said the Wyoming native, who began his career calling local six-man football for a Cheyenne radio station. "Besides, you have to instill confidence in your listeners."

8. RAY SCOTT
Scott began calling football in the days when broadcasters were assigned to specific teams, and he was the voice of the Green Bay Packers through the Vince Lombardi era, including the first two Super Bowls and the Ice Bowl. CBS then made Scott part of a lead national broadcast team, in which he was paired with Paul Christman and then Pat Summerall, and called two more Super Bowls.

8. JACK BUCK AND HANK STRAM
This pair gets a slot because for two decades starting in the late 1970s, they were the premier radio tandem in the NFL, calling everything from Monday night games to the Super Bowl. Buck deftly handled the play-by-play and Stram's analysis was insightful, but what set the two apart was their chemistry and spontaneity.

10. MERLIN OLSEN
A defensive tackle on the Rams' Fearsome Foursome unit, the gentle giant made a natural transition to the small screen, both as an actor and a commentator. He called five Super Bowls, four with Enberg.

HONORABLE MENTION. JOHN FACENDA
This Philadelphia radio and TV newsman never called an NFL game, but he was the narrator of NFL Films for almost 20 years. With his distinctive baritone, Facenda was football's "Voice of God."

Michaels (left) and Madden were a pairing of all-time greats on Monday nights.

Enberg (right) and Olsen called four Super Bowls together with gentlemanly style.

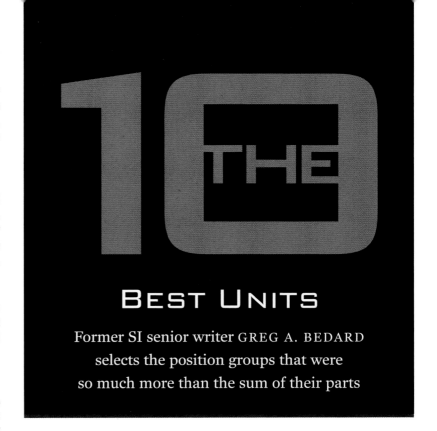

10 THE

BEST UNITS

Former SI senior writer GREG A. BEDARD
selects the position groups that were
so much more than the sum of their parts

1. PACKERS OFFENSIVE LINE, 1960S

The unit—left tackle Bob Skoronski, left guard Fuzzy Thurston, center Jim Ringo (later Bill Curry), right guard Jerry Kramer and right tackle Forrest Gregg—keyed the Packers' dominant run under coach (and former college guard) Vince Lombardi. Gregg and Ringo are in the Pro Football Hall of Fame, and Kramer has been a finalist 10 times.

2. PURPLE PEOPLE EATERS

The Vikings' defensive line produced 19 Pro Bowl selections and led the team to four Super Bowl appearances. Tackle Alan Page and end Carl Eller are in the Hall of Fame. End Jim Marshall and tackle Gary Larsen (later, Doug Sutherland) and were no slouches on a defense gave up the fewest points in the NFL three years in row (1969 to '71).

3. RAIDERS OFFENSIVE LINE, 1970S

Four members of this line's best incarnation are in the Hall of Fame: center Jim Otto, guard Gene Upshaw, and tackles Bob Brown and Art Shell. (Guard George Buehler rounded out the unit.) These Oakland teams were perennial powers and won two Super Bowls.

4. THE HOGS

Joe Jacoby, Russ Grimm, Jim Lachey, Raleigh McKenzie, Jeff Bostic, Mark Schlereth, George Starke and Mark May were the heart of an eclectic group on the Washington offensive line in the 1980s and early '90s. The group, winners of three Super Bowls, became so popular that they earned their own cheering section: The Hogettes, who were a dozen men wearing dresses and pig noses.

5. PERFECT BACKFIELD

Running backs Larry Csonka, Jim Kiick and Mercury Morris dominated the early 1970s and led Miami to its perfect season in '72. If only the short-lived World Football League hadn't broken up the group by signing Csonka and Kiick (and receiver Paul Warfield) for the '75 season. Miami's offensive line (Hall of Famers Jim Langer and Larry Little, plus six-time Pro Bowler Bob Kuechenberg), wasn't bad in those days either.

6. GREATEST SHOW ON TURF

The Rams featured future Hall of Famers at QB (Kurt Warner) and RB (Marshall Faulk), but from 1999 to 2001 the Greatest Show on Turf really ran on the outstanding receiving corps of Isaac Bruce, Torry Holt, Az-Zahir Hakim and Ricky Proehl.

7. LEGION OF BOOM

Never has the NFL seen such a suffocating secondary. Led by safeties Earl Thomas and Kam Chancellor and cornerbacks Richard Sherman, Brandon Browner and Byron Maxwell, this Seattle unit shut down the highest scoring offense in league history (the 2013 Broncos) in Super Bowl XLVIII, and nearly delivered a championship repeat the next year against Tom Brady's Patriots.

8. SOUL PATROL

With cornerback Willie Brown and safety Jack (the Assassin) Tatum as the backbone, aided by corner Skip (Dr. Death) Thomas and safety George (the Hitman) Atkinson, Al Davis's 1970s Raiders featured as menacing a secondary as the league has ever seen.

9. DOME PATROL

From 1987 to '92, the Saints attacked offenses with a ridiculously talented and swarming linebacker group. In '92 Rickey Jackson, Vaughan Johnson, Sam Mills and Pat Swilling were all named to the Pro Bowl, making the Patrol the only linebacking unit ever to pull off that feat.

10. 1970S STEELERS LINEBACKERS

You could take your pick of units on those Steel Curtain teams that won four Super Bowls. I'm going with the linebackers. Jack Ham and Jack Lambert are among the greatest of all time at their position. Andy Russell, passing for this group's lesser light, went to seven Pro Bowls.

Csonka (top) and Kiick were two of the gems in Miami's Perfect Backfield.

THE FULL RESULTS

IF THEY WERE LISTED ON A PANELIST'S BALLOT, THEY MAKE IT HERE TOO, IN THIS FULL RANKING OF EVERYONE WHO RECEIVED A VOTE IN EVERY CATEGORY

QUARTERBACKS
1. TOM BRADY
2. JOE MONTANA
3. PEYTON MANNING
4. JOHNNY UNITAS
5. OTTO GRAHAM
6. JOHN ELWAY
7. DAN MARINO
8. BRETT FAVRE
9. SAMMY BAUGH
10. BART STARR
11. ROGER STAUBACH
12. DREW BREES
13. STEVE YOUNG
14. SID LUCKMAN
15. NORM VAN BROCKLIN

RUNNING BACKS
1. JIM BROWN
2. WALTER PAYTON
3. BARRY SANDERS
4. EMMITT SMITH
5. O.J. SIMPSON
6. ERIC DICKERSON
7. GALE SAYERS
8. EARL CAMPBELL
9. LADAINIAN TOMLINSON
10. ADRIAN PETERSON
11. RED GRANGE
12. MARION MOTLEY
13. TONY DORSETT
14. MARCUS ALLEN
15. CURTIS MARTIN
16. BRONKO NAGURSKI

WIDE RECEIVERS
1. JERRY RICE
2. DON HUTSON
3. RANDY MOSS
4. LANCE ALWORTH
5. RAYMOND BERRY
6. LARRY FITZGERALD
7. TERRELL OWENS
8. MARVIN HARRISON
9. STEVE LARGENT
10. PAUL WARFIELD
11. TIM BROWN
12. CRIS CARTER
13. MICHAEL IRVIN
14. CALVIN JOHNSON
15. ELROY HIRSCH
16. HINES WARD
17. FRED BILETNIKOFF
18. DANTE LAVELLI
19. STEVE SMITH

TIGHT ENDS
1. TONY GONZALEZ
2. JOHN MACKEY
3. KELLEN WINSLOW
4. SHANNON SHARPE
5. MIKE DITKA
6. ROB GRONKOWSKI
7. OZZIE NEWSOME
8. ANTONIO GATES
9. DAVE CASPER
10. JASON WITTEN
11. MARK BAVARO
12. JACKIE SMITH

OFFENSIVE LINEMEN
1. ANTHONY MUÑOZ
2. JOHN HANNAH
3. FORREST GREGG
4. BRUCE MATTHEWS
5. LARRY ALLEN
6. MIKE WEBSTER
7. JIM PARKER
8. JONATHAN OGDEN
9. MEL HEIN
10. DWIGHT STEPHENSON
11. WALTER JONES
12. JIM OTTO
13. CLYDE TURNER
14. GENE UPSHAW
15. ORLANDO PACE
16. ROOSEVELT BROWN
17. RUSS GRIMM
18. ART SHELL
19. MIKE MCCORMACK
20. RANDALL MCDANIEL
21. JOE DELAMIELLEURE
22. JOE STALEY
23. JOE THOMAS

DEFENSIVE LINEMEN
1. REGGIE WHITE
2. DEACON JONES
3. JOE GREENE
4. BRUCE SMITH
5. BOB LILLY
6. ALAN PAGE
7. MERLIN OLSEN
8. GINO MARCHETTI
9. MICHAEL STRAHAN
10. RANDY WHITE
11. DWIGHT FREENEY
12. WARREN SAPP
13. BUCK BUCHANAN
14. J.J. WATT
15. LEO NOMELLINI
16. LEE ROY SELMON
17. CARL ELLER
18. JOHN RANDLE
19. HOWIE LONG
20. LEO ROBUSTELLI

LINEBACKERS
1. LAWRENCE TAYLOR
2. DICK BUTKUS
3. RAY LEWIS
4. JACK LAMBERT
5. MIKE SINGLETARY
6. DERRICK THOMAS
7. CHUCK BEDNARIK
8. JUNIOR SEAU
9. JACK HAM
10. WILLIE LANIER
11. BRONKO NAGURSKI
12. JOE SCHMIDT
13. RAY NITSCHKE
14. DEMARCUS WARE
15. BOBBY BELL
16. BILL GEORGE
17. BRIAN URLACHER
18. DERRICK BROOKS

DEFENSIVE BACKS
1. RONNIE LOTT
2. DEION SANDERS
3. ROD WOODSON
4. DICK LANE
5. MEL BLOUNT
6. DARRELL GREEN
7. ED REED
8. CHARLES WOODSON
9. CHAMP BAILEY
10. JACK TATUM
11. EMLEN TUNNELL
12. WILLIE WOOD
13. TROY POLAMALU
14. DARRELLE REVIS
15. CLIFF HARRIS
16. KEN HOUSTON
17. HERB ADDERLEY
18. JIMMY JOHNSON
19. WILLIE BROWN
20. PAUL KRAUSE
21. MEL RENFRO

COACHES
1. VINCE LOMBARDI
2. BILL BELICHICK
3. PAUL BROWN
4. BILL WALSH
5. DON SHULA
6. CHUCK NOLL
7. GEORGE HALAS
8. TOM LANDRY
9. JOE GIBBS
10. BILL PARCELLS
11. CURLY LAMBEAU
12. JIMMY JOHNSON

GAMES
1. 1958 NFL TITLE GAME, COLTS-GIANTS
2. 1967 NFL TITLE GAME, PACKERS-COWBOYS
3. SUPER BOWL III, JETS-COLTS
4. SUPER BOWL XLII, GIANTS-PATRIOTS
5. 1981 AFC PLAYOFFS, CHARGERS-DOLPHINS

6. SUPER BOWL LI,
   PATRIOTS-FALCONS

7. 1981 NFC
   CHAMPIONSHIP,
   49ERS-COWBOYS

8. SUPER BOWL XLIX,
   PATRIOTS-SEAHAWKS

9. 1992 AFC WILD CARD,
   BILLS-OILERS

10. SUPER BOWL XIII,
    STEELERS-COWBOYS

11. 1986 AFC
    CHAMPIONSHIP,
    BRONCOS-BROWNS

12. SUPER BOWL XXXVI,
    PATRIOTS-RAMS

13. SUPER BOWL XLIII,
    STEELERS-CARDINALS

14. SUPER BOWL XXXIV,
    RAMS-TITANS

15. SUPER BOWL XXIII,
    49ERS-BENGALS

16. 2006 AFC
    CHAMPIONSHIP,
    COLTS-PATRIOTS

17. 1990 NFC
    CHAMPIONSHIP,
    GIANTS-49ERS

18. DOLPHINS-CHIEFS,
    1971 AFC PLAYOFFS
    (NFL'S LONGEST GAME
    AND CHRISTMAS DAY)

19. 1972 AFC PLAYOFFS,
    STEELERS-RAIDERS
    (IMMACULATE
    RECEPTION)

20. SUPER BOWL XXXII,
    BRONCOS-PACKERS

21. 1998 NFC PLAYOFFS,
    49ERS-PACKERS

22. 2001 AFC PLAYOFFS,
    PATRIOTS-RAIDERS
    (TUCK RULE)

23. 1932 NFL TITLE GAME,
    BEARS-SPARTANS

24. RAIDERS-JETS,
    NOV. 17, 1968
    (HEIDI GAME)

25. DOLPHINS-BEARS,
    DEC. 2, 1985

PLAYS

1. MANNING-TO-TYREE,
   SUPER BOWL XLII

2. IMMACULATE RECEPTION,
   1972 AFC PLAYOFFS

3. THE CATCH,
   1981 NFC PLAYOFFS

4. BUTLER'S
   INTERCEPTION,
   SUPER BOWL XLIX

5. MUSIC CITY MIRACLE,
   1999 AFC WILD CARD

Brees, who has led the NFL in passing yards seven times, ranked 12th among quarterbacks.

6. THE HOLMES TD,
   SUPER BOWL XLIII

7. SWANN'S CATCH,
   SUPER BOWL X

8. JONES'S TACKLE,
   SUPER BOWL XXXIV

9. HAIL MARY,
   1975 NFC PLAYOFFS

10. MIRACLE AT THE
    MEADOWLANDS,
    EAGLES-GIANTS,
    NOV. 19, 1978

11. ALAN AMECHE TD,
    1958 NFL TITLE GAME

12. JAMES HARRISON'S
    RUNBACK,
    SUPER BOWL XLIII

13. TOM BRADY
    "TUCK RULE,"
    2001 AFC PLAYOFFS

14. CHUCK BEDNARIK HIT
    ON FRANK GIFFORD,
    EAGLES-GIANTS,
    NOV. 20, 1960

15. BART STARR SNEAK,
    1967 NFL TITLE GAME

16. DAVE CASPER
    "HOLY ROLLER"
    FUMBLE RECOVERY,
    RAIDERS-CHARGERS,
    SEPT. 10, 1978

17. JOHN ELWAY
    HELICOPTER SPIN,
    SUPER BOWL XXXII

18. STEVE GLEASON
    PUNT BLOCK,
    FALCONS-SAINTS,
    SEPT. 25, 2006

19. ADAM VINATIERI
    SNOW FIELD GOAL,
    2001 AFC PLAYOFFS

20. SCOTT NORWOOD WIDE-
    RIGHT KICK, SUPER
    BOWL XXV

21. MARSHAWN LYNCH
    BEAST MODE TD RUN,
    2010 NFC PLAYOFFS

22. ANTONIO FREEMAN
    MONDAY NIGHT
    MIRACLE CATCH,
    VIKINGS-PACKERS,
    NOV. 6, 2000

23. TOM DEMPSEY
    63-YARD
    FIELD GOAL,
    SAINTS-LIONS,
    NOV. 8, 1970

SINGLE-SEASON TEAMS

1. 1985 BEARS
2. 1972 DOLPHINS
3. 2007 PATRIOTS
4. 1962 PACKERS
5. 1989 49ERS
6. 1991 REDSKINS
7. 1978 STEELERS
8. 1984 49ERS
9. 1966 PACKERS
10. 2004 PATRIOTS
11. 1975 STEELERS
12. 1979 STEELERS
13. 1992 COWBOYS
14. 1996 PACKERS
15. 1950 BROWNS
16. 1971 COWBOYS
17. 1986 GIANTS
18. 1955 BROWNS
19. 1998 BRONCOS
20. 1975 STEELERS
21. 1999 RAMS
22. 1940 BEARS
23. 2013 SEAHAWKS
24. 1976 RAIDERS
25. 2000 RAVENS
26. 1994 49ERS

STADIUMS

1. LAMBEAU FIELD
2. ARROWHEAD STADIUM
3. AT&T STADIUM
4. MILE HIGH STADIUM
5. CENTURYLINK FIELD

6. HEINZ FIELD
7. SOLDIER FIELD
8. RFK STADIUM
9. ORANGE BOWL
10. MEMORIAL COLISEUM
11. TEXAS STADIUM
12. GIANTS STADIUM
13. NEW ERA FIELD
14. MEMORIAL STADIUM
15. YANKEE STADIUM
16. OAKLAND COLISEUM
17. THREE RIVERS STADIUM
18. LUCAS OIL STADIUM
19. METROPOLITAN
    STADIUM
20. SUPERDOME
21. PAUL BROWN STADIUM
22. NISSAN STADIUM
23. LINCOLN
    FINANCIAL FIELD
24. COTTON BOWL

FRANCHISES

1. STEELERS
2. PACKERS
3. COWBOYS
4. GIANTS
5. PATRIOTS
6. BEARS
7. 49ERS
8. RAIDERS
9. BRONCOS
10. REDSKINS
11. COLTS
12. DOLPHINS
13. BROWNS
14. BILLS
15. EAGLES
16. LIONS

John Mackey (88), SI's second-ranked tight end, huddles with his 1968 Colts.

THIS BOOK DRAWS FROM THE EFFORTS of a legion of SPORTS ILLUSTRATED writers, reporters, editors and photographers who have covered the NFL since the magazine's inception in 1954. Special thanks goes to Steve Hoffman, Josh Denkin and Geoff Michaud for their work on the first incarnation of this product; to Liana Zamora, Eric Marquard, Ed Truscio, Karen Carpenter, Prem Kalliat, Will Welt, George Amores, Gary Stewart and Allie Adams for their generous help on this edition; and to Dan Larkin and the rest of the SI Premedia group for their tireless efforts on this project.

PHOTO CREDITS

COVER: FRONT (left to right, from top): Damian Strohmeyer, Mickey Pfleger, Neil Leifer, Walter Iooss Jr., Neil Leifer, Robert Beck, Simon Bruty, Damian Strohmeyer, John Biever, Brian Bahr/Getty Images, David E. Klutho, Tom Lynn. BACK (left to right, from top): John Biever (2), Damian Strohmeyer, Robert Beck, Peter Read Miller, John Iacono, Jon Soohoo/Getty Images, John Biever, Walter Iooss Jr., John W. McDonough, Heinz Kluetmeier. SECTION OPENERS: Page 24: Bill Frakes; Page 42: Peter Read Miller; Page 60: Bill Frakes; Page 76: Reed Hoffmann/AP; Page 92: John Biever; Page 108: Ezra Shaw/Getty Images; Page 124: Heinz Kluetmeier; Page 140: Ted S. Warren/AP; Page 156: Peter Read Miller; Page 172: John Biever; Page 194: John Biever; Page 218: Bob Rosato; Page 242: Damian Strohmeyer; Page 258: David N. Berkwitz; Page 274: John Iacono. ADDITIONAL CREDITS: Page 7: Heinz Kluetmeier; Page 9: Bob Rosato; Page 10: Al Tielemans; Page 277 (from top): Walter Iooss Jr., Robert Beck; Page 278 (from left): Bob Rosato, John Biever; Page 279: Owen C. Shaw/Icon Sportswire; Page 280: The Everett Collection; Page 281 (clockwise from top): Paramount/The Everett Collection, Sony Pictures Entertainment/Photofest, TriStar/Getty Images, Universal/The Everett Collection; Page 282: David Bergman; Page 283 (from top): Al Bello/Getty Images, Leon Halip/Getty Images; Page 284 (from left): Craig Sjodin/ABC/Reuters, Heinz Kluetmeier; Page 285: Walter Iooss Jr.; Page 287: Gene Lower; Page 288: Neil Leifer. ENDPAPERS: Illustrations by BJ Ervick.

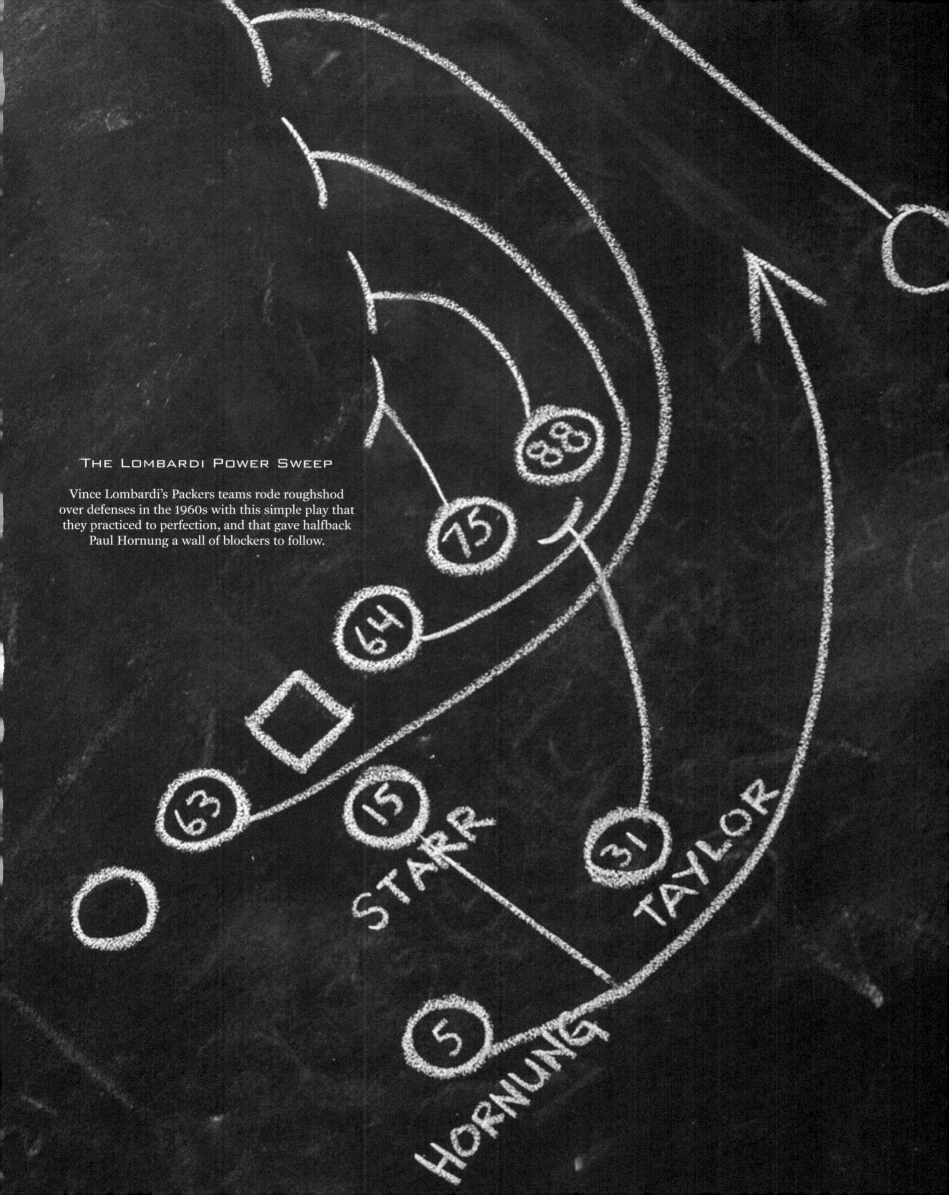

THE LOMBARDI POWER SWEEP

Vince Lombardi's Packers teams rode roughshod over defenses in the 1960s with this simple play that they practiced to perfection, and that gave halfback Paul Hornung a wall of blockers to follow.

Manning-to-Tyree

In the Giants' playbook it was called 62 Y Sail Union. The purpose of David Tyree's route was to take the top off the coverage, but it also gave Eli Manning a deep option, which he went for in the waning moments of Super Bowl XLII.

HARRISON 37

X

21

96 93 97

66 69 60

81

10

RRESS

TOOMER